Assessing the Performance Advantage of Public-Private Partnerships

Assessing the Performance Advantage of Public-Private Partnerships

A Comparative Perspective

Edited by

Stefan Verweij

Assistant Professor of Infrastructure Planning, Governance and Methodology, Department of Spatial Planning and Environment, University of Groningen, the Netherlands

Ingmar van Meerkerk

Associate Professor of Public Administration, Department of Public Administration and Sociology, Erasmus University Rotterdam, the Netherlands

Carter B. Casady

Honorary Senior Research Fellow, The Bartlett School of Sustainable Construction, University College London, UK, and Senior Fellow, Center for Transportation Public-Private Partnership Policy, George Mason University, USA

Edward Elgar PUBLISHING

Cheltenham, UK • Northampton, MA, USA

Published by
Edward Elgar Publishing Limited
The Lypiatts
15 Lansdown Road
Cheltenham
Glos GL50 2JA
UK

Edward Elgar Publishing, Inc.
William Pratt House
9 Dewey Court
Northampton
Massachusetts 01060
USA

A catalogue record for this book
is available from the British Library

Library of Congress Control Number: 2022944520

This book is available electronically in the **Elgar**online
Political Science and Public Policy subject collection
http://dx.doi.org/10.4337/9781800889200

Printed on elemental chlorine free (ECF)
recycled paper containing 30% Post-Consumer Waste

ISBN 978 1 80088 919 4 (cased)
ISBN 978 1 80088 920 0 (eBook)

Printed and bound in the USA

Contents

Figures

Tables

Contributors

Daniel Albalate, Associate Professor of Economics, Universitat de Barcelona, Spain.

Germà Bel, Professor of Economics, Universitat de Barcelona, Spain.

Paula Bel-Piñana, Assistant Professor of Economics, Universitat Abat Oliba CEU, Spain.

Sandro Cabral, Professor of Strategy and Public Management, Insper, Brazil.

Carter B. Casady, Honorary Senior Research Fellow, The Bartlett School of Sustainable Construction, University College London, UK, and Senior Fellow, Center for Transportation Public-Private Partnership Policy, George Mason University, USA.

Akash Deep, Senior Lecturer in Public Policy, John F. Kennedy School of Government, Harvard University, USA.

Mike Duijn, Managing Director of GovernEUR, Erasmus Research and Business Support, Erasmus University Rotterdam, the Netherlands.

Diogo Cunha Ferreira, Professor of Systems and Management, Instituto Superior Técnico, University of Lisbon, Portugal.

Carsten Greve, Professor of Public Management and Governance, Department of Organization, Copenhagen Business School, Denmark.

Graeme Hodge, Adjunct Professor of Law, Faculty of Law, Monash University, Australia.

Erik-Hans Klijn, Professor of Public Administration, Department of Public Administration and Sociology, Erasmus University Rotterdam, the Netherlands.

Joop Koppenjan, Professor of Public Administration, Department of Public Administration and Sociology, Erasmus University Rotterdam, the Netherlands.

Rui Cunha Marques, Professor of Systems and Management, Instituto Superior Técnico, University of Lisbon, Portugal.

Ingmar van Meerkerk, Associate Professor of Public Administration, Department of Public Administration and Sociology, Erasmus University Rotterdam, the Netherlands.

Samantha Metselaar, PhD Researcher, Department of Public Administration and Sociology, Erasmus University Rotterdam, the Netherlands.

Mojahedul Islam Nayyer, PhD Researcher, Department of Management Studies, Indian Institute of Technology Madras, India.

Cian O'Shea, PhD Researcher, Kemmy Business School, University of Limerick, Ireland.

Dónal Palcic, Senior Lecturer in Economics, Kemmy Business School, University of Limerick, Ireland.

Maria Isabel Pedro, Professor of Management Control and Engineering Economics, Instituto Superior Técnico, University of Lisbon, Portugal.

Thillai Rajan A., Professor of Management, Department of Management Studies, Indian Institute of Technology Madras, India.

Eoin Reeves, Associate Professor of Economics, Kemmy Business School, University of Limerick, Ireland.

Claudio José Oliveira dos Reis, Assistant Professor of Management, Universidade Federal do Oeste da Bahia, Brazil.

Gonçalo Santos, Student in Industrial Engineering and Management, Instituto Superior Técnico, University of Lisbon, Portugal.

Stefan Verweij, Assistant Professor of Infrastructure Planning, Governance and Methodology, Department of Spatial Planning and Environment, University of Groningen, The Netherlands.

Rianne Warsen, Assistant Professor of Public Management, Department of Public Administration and Sociology, Erasmus University Rotterdam, the Netherlands.

Preface

From the beginning, the performance of Public-Private Partnerships (PPPs) has been contested. While it is often argued that PPPs outperform traditionally procured projects and/or services, these claims have attracted increasing scrutiny and remain an ongoing topic of interest for both researchers and practitioners. PPPs are expected to, amongst other things, achieve better cost and time performance, drive innovation, and optimize life-cycle asset maintenance. These potential benefits often serve as a core motivation for policymakers to pursue PPP contracts with private-sector actors, especially in the design, construction, financing, operations, and maintenance of economic infrastructure (e.g., transport, energy, or water) and social infrastructure (e.g., schools, prisons, hospitals, or sports infrastructure). However, we are witnessing growing doubts about, and critiques of, this assumed performance advantage from both academics as well as policymakers across the globe.

At the same time, a lack of evidence on this performance advantage question persists. The evidence base for a performance advantage of PPPs over traditional procurement is rather weak. One of the key reasons for this is a paucity of actual comparisons between PPPs and traditional, but relatively similar, types of projects and services. Additionally, existing comparative studies that do assess the performance of PPPs over other types of procurement often involve business case projections or analyses of ex-ante performance. Such studies, however, do not say anything about *materialized* performance or account for the complex and long-term nature of these projects. The extent to which PPPs outperform traditional infrastructure procurement therefore remains a largely unanswered question, as stressed by the recent review study of Petersen (2019) in the *Annals of Public and Cooperative Economics*.

Given this dearth of research on the existence of a PPP performance advantage, it is time to take stock of the evidence, especially now that many countries have considerable experience with PPP projects and more are looking to this model to help bolster their COVID-19 pandemic recovery efforts and sustainable development agendas. With the stakes this high, we argue it is critically important to look at the evidence base and make well-informed decisions about the future of PPPs in the delivery of economic and social infrastructure. Surely, other relevant ideological and political considerations will also play an important role in decisions on PPPs; however, because policymakers continue to appeal to the idea that PPPs add value over other types of procurement, such assumptions and narratives about the performance advantage of PPPs should at least be well informed. Therefore, more evaluations are needed that compare the *actual* performance of PPPs with that of other types of procurement.

The idea for this book originated from a literature review we conducted as part of several other research projects. These research projects investigated the performance of PPPs procured by *Rijkswaterstaat*, the executive agency of the Dutch Ministry of Infrastructure and Water Management. Rijkswaterstaat is responsible for the design, construction, operations, and maintenance of the main infrastructure network in the Netherlands. In our literature review, we looked for studies that analysed the actual performance of PPPs and compared them with similar types of projects or services that were traditionally procured and managed. We observed that these studies are scattered across disciplines, infrastructure (policy) sectors, journals, and regions of the world. This current state of the literature is hampering a systematic accumulation of knowledge on the performance advantage of PPPs. Moreover, it is impeding evidence-based policymaking and decision-making on the procurement of public infrastructure (services) through PPPs.

This book therefore makes an important contribution with its collection of empirical evidence and its synthesis of accumulated knowledge examining the performance advantage of PPPs. With this book, we bring together existing and new research that scrutinizes differences between PPP performance and the performance of traditionally procured projects, as such advancing the evidence base on—and providing explanations and policy recommendations for—the performance advantage of PPPs.

Stefan Verweij, Ingmar van Meerkerk, and Carter B. Casady
The Netherlands and the United States, 2022

Abbreviations

ACSS	Central Administration of the Health System (Portugal)
AMOS	Analysis of Moment Structures
BNB	Northeast Development Bank (Brazil)
BNDES	Brazilian National Development Bank (Brazil)
BoD	Benefit of Doubt
BOM	Build–Own–Maintain
BOO	Build–Own–Operate
BOT	Build–Operate–Transfer
CAG	Comptroller and Auditor General (India)
C&AG	Comptroller and Auditor General (Ireland)
CCM	Configurational Comparative Methods
CV	Coefficient of Variation
D&C	Design and Construct
DB	Design–Build
DBB	Design–Bid–Build
DBFM	Design–Build–Finance–Maintain
DBFMO	Design–Build–Finance–Maintain–Operate
DBFO	Design–Build–Finance–Operate
DBFOM	Design–Build–Finance–Operate–Maintain
DBFOT	Design–Build–Finance–Operate–Transfer
DBM	Design–Build–Maintenance
DBO	Design–Build–Operate
DBOT	Design–Build–Operate–Transfer
DCMF	Design–Construct–Maintain–Finance
DEA	Data Envelopment Analysis
DOE	Department of Education (Ireland)
DoEA	Department of Economic Affairs (India)

DPER	Department of Public Expenditure and Reform (Ireland)
EEC	European Economic Community
EMDE	Emerging Markets and Developing Countries
ENAUSA	Empresa Nacional de Autopistas (Spain)
EOI	Expression of Interest (India)
EPC	Engineering, Procurement, and Construction
EPE	Entidade Pública Empresarial (Portugal)
EPEC	European PPP Expertise Centre
EQS	Equations
ERS	Entidade Reguladora da Saúde (Portugal)
ES	Efficiency Spread
ETB	Educational Training Boards (Ireland)
FGPPP/RN	Guarantor Fund for PPPs in the Rio Grande do Norte (Brazil)
FIFA	Fédération Internationale de Football Association
FM	Facilities Management
FOI	Freedom of Information
FPE	State Participation Fund (Brazil)
FsQCA	Fuzzy-set QCA
GDP	Gross Domestic Product
HAM	Hybrid Annuity Model
IDIP	Integrated Database on Indian Infrastructure Projects (India)
INE	Instituto Nacional de Estatística (Portugal)
InvIT	Infrastructure Investment Trust (India)
IOA	Input–Output Analysis
IRI	International Roughness Index
IRTAD	International Traffic Safety Data and Analysis Group
LIFT	Local Improvement Finance Trust
LISREL	Linear Structural Relationships
LTIC	Long-Term Infrastructure Contract
MCA	Model Concession Agreement (India)
MI	Malmquist Index

MoRTH	Ministry of Road Transport and Highways (India)
MOSPI	Ministry of Statistics and Program Implementation (India)
MTC	Maintenance Company
NDFA	National Development Finance Agency (Ireland)
NHAI	National Highway Authority of India (India)
NHS	National Health Service
NPM	New Public Management
NPV	Net Present Value
O&M	Operate and Maintain
PANE	Programa de Autopistas Nacionales Españolas (Spain)
PBO	Parliamentary Budget Office (Ireland)
PF2	Private Finance 2
PFI	Private Finance Initiative
PG	Productivity Gap
PGC	Plan General de Carreteras (Spain)
PLS	Partial Least Squares
PP	Partido Popular (Spain)
PPC	Public-Private Comparator
PPP	Public-Private Partnership
PSB	Public Sector Benchmark
PSC	Public Sector Comparator
PSOE	Partido Socialista Obrero Español (Spain)
QCA	Qualitative Comparative Analysis
RAM	Regressional Analytic Methods
RFP	Request for Proposal (India)
RFQ	Request for Qualification (India)
RWS	Rijkswaterstaat (Netherlands)
SA	Sociedade Anónima (Portugal)
SAM	Social Accounting Matrix
SLA	Service Level Agreements
SPA	Sector Público Administrativo (Portugal)
SPC	Special Purpose Company

SPV	Special Purpose Vehicle
TOT	Toll–Operate–Transfer
TP	Traditional Procurement
UK	United Kingdom
VfM	Value for Money
VGF	Viability Gap Funding

1. The performance advantage of public-private partnerships: does it exist or not?

Stefan Verweij, Ingmar van Meerkerk, and Carter B. Casady

INTRODUCTION

Research into Public-Private Partnerships (PPPs) has proliferated since the mid-2000s (Cui et al., 2018; De Castro e Silva Neto et al., 2016; Ke et al., 2009; Shi et al., 2020; Tang et al., 2010; Wang et al., 2018), with publications about PPPs originating primarily from the United Kingdom, the United States, Canada, Australia, and, increasingly, China and Europe (Chen et al., 2016; Cui et al., 2018; De Castro e Silva Neto et al., 2016; Ke et al., 2009; Wang et al., 2018). A core theme in this literature on PPPs is their performance (i.e., questions about the extent to which performance is achieved, how it can be achieved, and how it can or should be measured; Chen et al., 2016; Cui et al., 2018; De Castro e Silva Neto et al., 2016; Wang et al., 2018). These are no small questions, and they require our constant attention. The performance question of PPPs is a lingering one (Hodge & Greve, 2007, 2009, 2017; Palcic et al., 2019).

Different conceptions of PPP performance exist and they depend on, among other things,[1] how the PPP phenomenon is defined and understood (Hodge & Greve, 2017; Wang et al., 2018). The definition of PPP as a Long-Term Infrastructure Contract partnership is today the most prominent one (Palcic et al., 2019). These contracts can be found in the development and management of both economic infrastructure (e.g., roads, bridges, ports, railways, airports, telecommunications, and power) and social infrastructure (e.g., schools, hospitals, water supply, housing, sewerage, sports facilities, and care; Grimsey & Lewis, 2004). In this definition, PPPs are commonly understood as a "single project" or as a "specific type of infrastructure delivery mechanism with a specific institutional and financial structure in place to initially fund and deliver construction works as well as operate the long-term facility" (Hodge & Greve,

2017, p. 58). Performance definitions focus on project success and the delivery of projects in terms of on-budget, on-time, and on-quality delivery (Hodge & Greve, 2017). In this "narrow" definition of partnership performance, the focus is on "the achievement of particular service or outcome targets as set out in the partnership agreement (strategy, contract, business plan) and assessed in relation to other factors such as the cost of the partnership's operations" (Jeffares et al., 2013, p. 170).

The present book deals with this narrow definition of partnership performance. Although the label "narrow" here could connote a certain level of simplicity, the evaluation of this performance is not an easy or straightforward task (Jeffares et al., 2013). One important challenge is that project-level data remain hard to come by (Chen et al., 2016; Jeffares et al., 2013). Another challenge relates to evaluation rigor and, in particular, the counterfactual situation of "'traditional procurement' [that] is both horribly vague and also largely unquantified in most assessments" (Hodge, 2010, p. 102). This is an important challenge and one that we posit—as a consequence of the changing motivations of governments to opt for PPPs—has become more important over time.

Core motivations of governments to develop and manage the delivery of infrastructure through PPPs used to focus on increasing the efficiency of public service delivery, the transfer of risks to the private sector, and on reducing the budget and borrowing constraints of governments by using private sector funds (McQuaid & Scherrer, 2010). In many developing countries, these are still core motivations for PPPs (World Bank, 2014, 2017; e.g., Debela, 2019; Kavishe & Chileshe, 2020; Osei-Kyei et al., 2014).[2] However, in general and for developed countries in particular, McQuaid and Scherrer (2010) predicted that "issues concerning the efficiency and effectiveness of PPPs, *compared to their alternatives*, are likely to increase in importance while budget enlarging motivations decrease" (2010, p. 27, emphasis added). For instance, the European PPP Expertise Centre (2015) identified the potential of PPPs to improve Value for Money (VfM) as the most important motivation for using PPPs and defined "improving VfM" as "using PPPs where they can improve the delivery of benefits relative to the associated costs *across a range of alternatives*" (p. 5, emphasis added).

So, it appears the idea that PPPs outperform—or achieve added value over—traditional infrastructure procurement (i.e., the alternative) is nowadays a core motivation of policymakers and infrastructure planners to develop and manage infrastructure through PPPs. This idea is what we call in this book the *performance advantage*. The performance advantage is the idea that when an infrastructure project is developed and managed through a PPP, this results in greater performance compared to the development and management of that project through an alternative type of infrastructure delivery mechanism—the counterfactual situation—that is not a PPP. This idea of a performance advantage of PPPs is also at the basis of the planning of infrastructure projects. When infrastructure projects are planned, the PPP option is benchmarked against a traditional alternative using methods such as the Public Sector Comparator (PSC) or business case projections of PPPs (Petersen, 2019). The PSC is the "benchmark cost of providing the specified service with traditional procurement" (Grimsey & Lewis, 2004, p. 137). It involves the comparison—prior to the implementation of a project—of this benchmark with the costs of implementing the project through a PPP (Grimsey & Lewis, 2005).

In this book, we take issue with this idea of a performance advantage of PPPs and argue that little is known about the extent to which it actually exists (Verweij, 2018). We identify at least three reasons for this. First, the PPP literature tends to be dominated by single case studies (Hueskes et al., 2019; Osei-Kyei & Chan, 2015; Tang et al., 2010; Zhang et al., 2016). The advantages of single case studies notwithstanding, this approach lacks a structured comparison between infrastructure development and management with and without PPPs. Second, the counterfactual situation is often vague and underspecified (Hodge, 2010). Many applications of the PSC are said to be flawed because the parameters and assumptions are set in such a way that the results of the comparison are often biased in favor of PPPs (Boardman & Hellowell, 2017; Boers et al., 2013). Comparing the PPP option to business case projections is then another approach; these projections are often more transparent (Petersen, 2019), which makes it possible to scrutinize the parameters and assumptions. Yet, the problem with comparing the PPP option to the benchmark or a business case projection is that the latter involve ex-ante expectations of performance. This means that it remains unclear whether the prospected performance advantages actually materialized (Boers et al., 2013; Petersen, 2019). This problem is exacerbated, third, by the fact that real project data are often hard to get because the data are not publicly available and are restricted due to confidentiality issues (Chen et al., 2016). The extent to which PPPs outperform traditional infrastructure procurement therefore remains a largely unanswered question (Petersen, 2019). What is needed are evaluations that compare the *actual* performance of PPPs with that of other types of procurement. Because policymakers and infrastructure planners continue to appeal to the idea that PPPs add value over other types of procurement, a critical assessment of this idea is much needed (Hodge & Greve, 2007, 2017; Petersen, 2019). This brings us to the aims of this book.

AIMS OF THE BOOK

This book questions the extent to which the performance advantage of PPPs exists (or not). It has two main objectives. First and most important, this book critically assesses and empirically explores the existence of a performance advantage of PPPs. To that purpose, it presents new comparative empirical studies of the performance advantage in various countries, including Brazil, India, Ireland, the Netherlands, Portugal, and Spain. We also discuss studies that have analyzed the performance advantage of PPPs (see "Current Literature" below). These published studies cover additional countries: Colombia, Costa Rica, Indonesia, Lebanon, Pakistan, Scotland, South Korea, the United Kingdom, and the United States. Second, this book explores explanations for why the performance advantage of PPPs exists (or not). In this respect, it also engages with the questions of why and how the performance advantage may be achieved. PPPs are infrastructure delivery mechanisms and, from the perspective of governments, an important tool for the delivery of public services. How this can be achieved successfully—and better than the traditional alternative against which it was assessed to have added value—therefore matters. By going deeper into these underlying explanations and mechanisms, this book offers important conclusions and recommendations concerning the potential advantages and limitations of PPPs in achieving good performance.

With this book, we want to cater to PPP researchers and students in general, and to scholars and students who work on research examining the performance of PPPs in particular. These scholars and students come from different disciplines. Although PPPs are studied most often by Public Administration, Public Management, and/or Public Policy scholars (Marsilio et al., 2011), we also believe that this book bears relevance to scholars and students from Transport and Infrastructure Planning, Engineering, and Project Management, which are other important disciplines that study PPPs (Shi et al., 2020). Empirically, this book includes contributions from different policy sectors—schools, hospitals, sports, and transport—and PPP researchers and students in these areas may also find this book of value.

This book also caters to policymakers. It engages with the expectations of policymakers that PPPs add value over (i.e., outperform) traditional infrastructure procurement. PPPs are popular with policymakers. In some regions, such as Europe, we see the number of PPP deals and size of investments decreasing and there are increasing discussions about why, when, and in which form to proceed with large-scale Design–Build–Finance–Maintain (DBFM) projects (e.g., European PPP Expertise Centre, 2020). This is, for instance, the case in the Netherlands (Koppenjan et al., 2020; Rijkswaterstaat, 2019; Verweij et al., 2021). In other regions, and especially in Emerging Markets and Developing Economies (EMDEs), PPPs remain very popular (e.g., World Bank, 2020; Casady & Peci, 2021; Casady, 2021). Our book can inform policymakers and planners about whether to opt for PPPs over traditional procurement and, specifically, on which performance indicators PPPs outperform traditional procurement and on which they do not. Because our book also focuses on the reasons why (or not) the performance advantage exists, this can inform policymakers and planners about the ways in which the expected outcomes of PPPs may be achieved. But how should we assess the performance advantage of PPPs?

ASSESSING THE PERFORMANCE ADVANTAGE OF PUBLIC-PRIVATE PARTNERSHIPS

Because governments are often in the position to borrow money at low or risk-free rates, PPPs normally come with higher costs related to private financing; but the expectation is that this is made up for by risk transfer to—and risk management skills of—the private sector partner (Leruth, 2012). Whether the higher costs are justified by the greater performance potential of a PPP compared to traditional procurement is difficult to assess (Petersen, 2019). Yescombe (2013) even stated that:

> Proving the case either way ex-ante for any particular project is virtually impossible since such a proof depends on unprovable assumptions on risks and costs stretching forward for many years (not just construction but also operation, maintenance and lifecycle/renewal costs), and equally ex-post proof is also impossible since a PPP project that did happen cannot be compared with a public procurement that did not. (p. 228)

We agree with this statement. However, this should not discourage us from pursuing a critical assessment of the existence of the performance advantage. It is a core motivation of policymakers to opt for PPPs in the development and management of infrastructure and, as such, requires our critical reflection. It also means that our effort will be important yet necessarily humble.

How the performance advantage can then be assessed thus involves the question of what an appropriate counterfactual situation is. We already ruled out the PSC and business case projections because these concern ex-ante assessments. The next best thing is to compare PPPs "using benchmark data collected for comparable projects of similar type, size, complexity, etc." (Petersen, 2019, p. 230). In this respect, we fully agree with Petersen (2019), who points out that from a "strict evaluation perspective, this approach is in many ways preferable as it represents a more suitable design for constructing control groups and establishing a counterfactual situation" (p. 230).

Using Benchmark Data of Comparable Projects

This book collects studies using benchmark data of comparable projects to assess the performance advantage of PPPs. All studies thus use a similar general design: a quasi-experimental design comparing the performance of

PPP projects with a "control group" of infrastructure projects not procured as PPPs.

This evaluation approach undoubtedly also comes with its limitations and challenges. Most importantly, it is challenging to find a proper control group with comparable benchmark data—in this case: infrastructure projects of similar complexity and size, as well as those developed in comparable eras and within similar institutional frameworks and legal systems. Because project risks, complexity, institutional frameworks, and legal systems may differ considerably across countries and sectors and over time (Casady, 2021; Casady et al., 2020; Hammerschmid & Ysa, 2010; Soecipto et al., 2016), this book presents empirical comparative studies that each focus on a single country, a single infrastructure sector (e.g., roads, schools, or hospitals), and a relatively short timeframe. Hence, we increase the comparability (i.e., improve the suitability of the counterfactual situation) of PPP projects with the traditional alternative. It does not mean that the comparability will be perfect (Petersen, 2019). It does mean, though, that this approach is better able to assess the impact of the specific type of infrastructure delivery mechanism (i.e., PPP or not) on the performance. In that way, we increase the chance that differences in performance can be explained by the type of contract and governance structure rather than other intervening variables. In other words, it allows us to be more certain that the difference in performance (if it exists) between two groups of projects—the PPP versus the traditional alternative—can be interpreted as a performance advantage, or the non-existence thereof. Moreover, it requires that we pay attention to the mechanisms of and possible explanations for any differences.

PERFORMANCE OF PUBLIC-PRIVATE PARTNERSHIPS: DIMENSIONS COVERED IN THIS BOOK

There are many different dimensions and definitions of PPP performance, depending on the specific objectives of the PPPs, the particular meaning of PPPs, the level of analysis one takes, the theoretical and evaluative frameworks applied, and the disciplinary perspective assumed (Hodge & Greve, 2017; Jeffares et al., 2013). This book deals with the narrow definition of partnership performance, focusing on the project level (see the Introduction to this chapter). Hence, it focuses on three dimensions of performance that are commonly used to assess PPP project success: cost performance, time performance, and service quality performance (Hodge, 2010; Hodge & Greve, 2017; Petersen, 2019). Cost performance generally concerns operational costs, capital costs, total (whole-life) project costs including design and construction costs, and on-budget delivery (Hodge, 2010; Petersen, 2019). Time performance focuses on whether projects and services were delivered on time according to the initially planned or agreed upon schedule (Hodge, 2010). Service quality performance relates to VfM, which is achieved when PPPs deliver "improved services for the same amount of money as the public sector would spend to deliver a similar project" (Grimsey & Lewis, 2005, p. 346). It is about optimizing the whole-life project costs and quality (Yaya, 2017). Because many studies focus not necessarily on the relationship between costs and quality, but also on the quality of service delivery in itself, and because the quality of services may refer to different things depending on the policy sector and types of projects, we focus on service quality as one dimension of the performance of PPPs.

CURRENT LITERATURE

Let us first consider what is already available. Studies have been conducted on the materialized performance differences between PPPs and traditional procurement methods by benchmarking PPP projects with data collected for comparable projects (e.g., Liu et al., 2014; Petersen, 2019). A well-known example is the study by Raisbeck and Duffield into the comparative performance of PPPs and traditional procurement in Australia (Allen Consulting Group, 2007; Duffield, 2008; Raisbeck et al., 2010). Their study analyzed 21 PPP projects and 33 traditional projects—social infrastructure, transport infrastructure, water infrastructure, and information technology infrastructure—and found that PPPs outperformed traditional procurement in terms of cost performance (cf. Duffield, 2008). In terms of time performance, they found that PPPs are generally delayed during the period prior to, but only have a very small delay on average after, financial close. In contrast, traditionally procured projects take, on average, less time than anticipated in the period prior to project execution but have frequent delays in the construction phase (Duffield, 2008). Another example is the international study conducted by Gassner et al. (2009) and published by the World Bank. This study found that the PPP projects outperformed—in terms of the quality of the delivery of electricity and water distribution and in terms of productivity—the projects that remained state-owned and state-operated. A third example is a study by Bel et al. (2010) who, based on a meta-analysis of studies from North America, Europe, Asia and the Pacific, and Africa, did not find evidence of lower costs of water distribution and solid waste collection services through private sector participation. Finally, a study by Chasey and colleagues (2012) comparatively analyzed the cost and time performance of North American (i.e., United States and Canada) PPP projects, on the one hand, and Design–Bid–Build (DBB) or Design–Build (DB) projects on the other. They found that the PPPs performed better. However, these examples did not focus on a single country and a single infrastructure sector.

Cost Performance

Petersen (2019) identified just over a handful of studies in which PPP cost and VfM performance were benchmarked with the performance of a counterfactual situation (i.e., traditional procurement of public projects) and that also focused on only one country and one infrastructure sector (Daito & Gifford, 2014; Froud & Shaoul, 2001; Hong, 2016; Pollock et al., 2002; Reeves & Ryan, 2007; Whittington, 2012; Yaya, 2017). In their study of hospitals in the United Kingdom, Shaoul and colleagues found that PPPs are more costly than existing public facilities in capital terms (Froud & Shaoul, 2001; Pollock et al., 2002). Reeves and Ryan (2007) studied schools in Ireland and concluded that PPPs are more costly than traditional procurement and that the VfM (based on costs) was also lower for the PPP projects. Yaya (2017) investigated schools in Scotland and found that "a higher percentage of headteachers of conventionally financed schools (63.64 percent) considered their new schools resulted in good VfM compared to PPP schools (42.86 percent)" (p. 187). Whittington (2012) compared two road projects from the United States—one Design–Build–Finance–Maintain–Operate (DBFMO) project with a focus on the DB phase and one bid–build contract—and found that the projects had no significant differences in cost performance. In another study of road infrastructure projects from the United States, Daito and Gilford (2014) studied 53 Design–Build–Finance–Operate–Maintain (DBFOM) projects and found that they were more costly than DB projects; they also found that there was no significant difference between the VfM of the PPPs and of the traditionally procured projects. Hong (2016), finally, studied two urban rail projects in Seoul, South Korea, and did not find any evidence that the privately financed and operated Build–Transfer–Operate (BTO) project had a cost-efficiency advantage compared to the publicly owned and operated rail system. What these studies reviewed by Petersen (2019) thus indicate is that PPP projects are more costly than traditionally procured projects.

We have identified from the literature some more publications that comparatively analyzed the real cost performance differences between PPP projects and traditionally procured projects. A few studies focused on cost performance in the construction and implementation phases of the projects (Atmo et al., 2017; Dos Reis & Cabral, 2017; Verweij & Van Meerkerk, 2020, 2021). The work by Atmo et al. (2017) on Indonesian power plants analyzed cost performance understood as cost escalations compared to the initially agreed contract price that resulted from contract renegotiations after the contract close. The authors did not find significant differences between the Design–Build–Finance–

Operate (DBFO) projects and the Engineering, Procurement, and Construction (EPC) projects that they compared. Verweij and Van Meerkerk (2020, 2021) studied cost performance in a similar way for Dutch transportation projects (see also Verweij et al., 2020a, 2020b). They collected financial data about the additional work costs occurring in the Design and Construct (D&C) phases of DBFM and D&C projects. They did find that DBFM projects, compared to the D&C projects, had a significantly better cost performance in terms of lower additional work costs. Dos Reis and Cabral (2017) found that sports arenas in Brazil procured via DBFO had a better cost-per-seat ratio than the traditionally procured arenas and that they had better compliance to the initial costs forecast (i.e., cost overrun).

Other studies focused on the cost performance differences in the operation and maintenance phases of projects (Archambeault & Deis, 1997; Cabral & De Azevedo, 2008; Massoud et al., 2003), or on the total project costs (Meduri & Annamalai, 2013). Archambeault and Deis (1997) found that privately operated prisons in the state of Louisiana, United States, were operated more cost effectively than the prison operated through the traditional public model. Cabral and De Azevedo (2008) came to a similar conclusion. In their comparative study into prisons in the state of Bahia, Brazil, they found that the privately operated prison had lower staff costs, utilities costs, and lower maintenance costs compared to the public counterpart. Conversely, Massoud and colleagues (2003) found that the privately operated Design–Build–Operate–Transfer (DBOT) solid waste management facility in Lebanon had higher operating costs per capita and costs per ton than the publicly operated facility. Finally, the study of Meduri and Annamalai (2013) focused on total project costs or cost overrun. Their comparative analysis of 521 Indian transport projects showed that the Build–Operate–Transfer (BOT) projects were significantly more expensive than the projects procured through the traditional public model. When these costs were calculated in terms of costs per lane-kilometer, however, the PPP projects had better performance.

Table 1.1 gives an overview of the existing studies on the cost performance advantage, indicating that the evidence is mixed. Some studies find that PPPs performed better. Others, however, found that the PPPs performed worse or that there were no significant differences.

Time Performance

We identified a number of studies in which the time performance advantage of PPPs, for a single country and a single infrastructure sector, was evaluated. A few of these studies analyzed economic infrastructure projects. The aforementioned study by Atmo et al. (2015, 2017) into Indonesian power plants found that the actual construction time, compared to the planned construction

Table 1.1 Overview of studies on cost performance advantage

Study	Period	Country	Sector	Performance Category	Findings	Performance Advantage
Archambeault and Deis (1997)	1991–96	United States	Prisons	Cost effectiveness	Privately operated prisons were more cost-effective	Positive
Froud and Shaoul (2001); Pollock et al. (2002)	1998–2000	United Kingdom	Hospitals	Costs in capital terms	The PPPs were more costly in capital terms (Petersen, 2019)	Negative
Massoud et al. (2003)	1996–97	Lebanon	Waste Management	Operating cost per capita and cost per ton	Privately operated facility had higher operating costs	Negative
Reeves and Ryan (2007)	2003	Ireland	Schools	VfM	The PPPs were more costly and had lower VfM (Petersen, 2019)	Negative
Cabral and De Azevedo (2008)	2003–2004	Brazil	Prisons	Staff costs, utilities costs, and maintenance costs	Costs were higher in the publicly operated prison	Positive
Whittington (2012)	1998–2005	United States	Roads	Design costs, change order costs, and cost overrun	PPP project had lower costs on all indicators, but no significant difference (Petersen, 2019)	Positive/No

Study	Period	Country	Sector	Performance Category	Findings	Performance Advantage
Meduri and Annamalai (2013)	1996–2010	India	Roads, Bridges	Total project costs and costs per lane-kilometer	PPP projects were more expensive but had significantly lower costs per lane-kilometer	Positive
Daito and Gifford (2014)	1991–2013	United States	Roads	Construction costs and cost efficiency	PPPs had higher construction costs, but no significant difference in cost efficiency (Petersen, 2019)	Negative/No
Hong (2016)	2000–2013	South Korea	Urban Rail	Costs service operation	No evidence that private operation had lower operation costs (see also Petersen, 2019)	No
Atmo et al. (2017)	2000–2014	Indonesia	Power Plants	Project costs compared to contracted price	No significant difference	No
Dos Reis and Cabral (2017)	2010–2014	Brazil	Sports Stadiums	Provision costs: compliance with initial cost forecast and cost per seat	PPPs had better performance on both indicators	Positive

Study	Period	Country	Sector	Performance Category	Findings	Performance Advantage
Yaya (2017)	2000–2012	Scotland	Schools	VfM	The study found that "more headteachers in conventional schools agreed that VfM has been achieved" (Petersen, 2019, p. 237)	Positive
Verweij and Van Meerkerk (2020, 2021)	2008–2017	Netherlands	Roads	Additional work costs during D&C phase	PPPs had significantly better cost performance	Positive

time as detailed in the construction contracts, was lower in PPPs than in traditionally procured projects. In their larger-N analysis of 56 projects, they were also able to conclude that this performance difference was statistically significant (Atmo et al., 2017). Verweij and Van Meerkerk (2021) found that the Dutch DBFM transport infrastructure projects had a better implementation time (i.e., less implementation delay) of the D&C phases than the projects with D&C contracts, although the difference was not statistically significant. In an updated analysis, however, that included additional data points (for the year 2018), they concluded that the difference was significant (Verweij et al., 2020a). Whittington (2012), finally, concluded that the PPP project that he studied was built quicker and earlier than the bid–build contract he compared it with.

Other researchers have focused on the analysis of social infrastructure projects. In their study of Brazilian sports arenas, Dos Reis and Cabral (2017) found that the PPP projects, except one, had better stadium delivery times—defined as delivery on or before the contracted delivery date—than the other projects. The bidding process was also shorter in most PPP projects. O'Shea et al.'s (2019) comparative study of Irish schools indicated that, although the tendering process for the DBFM case was rather long, its construction time was shorter than that of the D&C case. A similar conclusion was reached by Rodrigues and Zucco (2018) for schools in the City of Belo Horizonte in Brazil. They found that the schools with BOT contracts had significantly better time to delivery than the schools with D&C contracts.

Table 1.2 gives an overview of studies on the time performance advantage, indicating that PPPs indeed seem to have an advantage over traditionally procured infrastructure projects.

Service Quality Performance

Lastly, we have identified from the literature multiple studies that focused on the comparison of service delivery quality between PPPs and traditionally procured projects. Depending on the policy sector studied and the data collected, the quality of the service delivery was defined in widely different ways. A few studies focused on economic infrastructure projects (Atmo et al., 2015, 2017; Massoud et al., 2003). Atmo et al. (2015, 2017) looked at the availability of the power plants and their carbon emission levels during the first two years of their operation. Their small-N study suggested that the DBFO projects had better performance than the EPC projects (Atmo et al., 2015). This was later confirmed for plant availability in their larger-N statistical analysis, concluding that the difference between DBFO and EPC was significant in favor of DBFO (Atmo et al., 2017). The study by Massoud et al. (2003) into Lebanese waste management facilities found that, although the PPP case had higher operating

Table 1.2 Overview of studies on time performance advantage

Study	Period	Country	Sector	Performance Category	Findings	Performance Advantage
Whittington (2012)	1998–2005	United States	Roads	Construction time	PPP project was built earlier and took less time	Positive
Atmo et al. (2015, 2017)	2004–2011; 2000–2014	Indonesia	Power Plants	Actual construction time compared to planned time in contract	PPP projects were completed faster and time delay was significantly lower	Positive
Dos Reis and Cabral (2017)	2010–2014	Brazil	Sports Stadiums	Delivery time	PPP projects had better delivery times with one exception	Overall positive
Rodrigues and Zucco (2018)	2009–2015	Brazil	Schools	Construction time: time to delivery from starting construction	PPP projects had significantly better time to delivery	Positive
O'Shea et al. (2019)	2012–2016	Ireland	Schools	Duration of tendering process and construction period	PPP tendering process was longer, but the construction was faster	No/Positive
Verweij and Van Meerkerk (2021); Verweij et al. (2020a)	2008–2017; 2008–2018	Netherlands	Roads	Actual implementation time of D&C phase compared to planned time at contract close	PPP projects had significantly better time performance	Positive

costs than the publicly operated facility (see "Cost Performance," above), this also resulted in "increased performance efficiency and environmental protection improvements" (p. 23).

Most studies to this effect, however, have focused on social infrastructure projects, such as health services (Cercone et al., 2005; Ferreira & Marques, 2021; Gauri et al., 2004; Shet et al., 2011), schools (Barrera-Osorio, 2007; Hafeez et al., 2016; Rodrigues & Zucco, 2018; Yaya, 2017), and prisons (Archambeault & Deis, 1997; Cabral et al., 2010, 2013; Cabral & De Azevedo, 2008). The study by Cercone and colleagues comparatively analyzed seven health care clinics in Costa Rica (Cercone et al., 2005; Gauri et al., 2004). They looked at two sets of service quality performance indicators: target coverage rate (e.g., pap smears, diagnosis and treatment of hypertension and diabetes patients, and prenatal visits) and clinical-level outputs (e.g., clinical visits, mortality rates, and medications). They found that the clinics with contracted private service providers outperformed the public ones on five of seven of the target coverage rate indicators. Regarding the clinical-level outputs, they found that the private ones conducted more general practitioner visits (but fewer specialist visits) and that they provided less-costly healthcare at similar or increased levels of quality. The study offered nuanced conclusions, showing that the PPP model for health care clinics "substituted generalist for specialist services…but did not turn away new patients, refuse emergency cases, or substitute nurses for doctors as care providers" (Gauri et al., 2004, p. 292). Overall, the study suggested that the privately operated clinics were able to "combine advantages of public and private approaches to health care service provision" (p. 292). Shet et al. (2011) analyzed HIV health care facilities in India, comparing three clinics: a public model, a private model, and a public-private model. They looked at a variety of performance indicators, including treatment interruptions, waiting times, adherence barriers, and viral load. Their study showed that the main difference was between the public and public-private clinics on the one hand and the private one on the other, concluding that "adherence and treatment success was significantly higher among patients from public and public-private settings compared with patients from private facilities" (Shet et al., 2011, p. 1). Ferreira and Marques (2021) investigated differences in social performance levels between public hospitals and PPP hospitals with a Design–Build–Finance–Operate–Transfer (DBFOT) contract in Portugal. Having comparatively analyzed a total of 2660 observations, they concluded that differences between the public and PPP hospitals are not considerable.

As previously indicated, a couple of studies focused on schools. Barrera-Osorio (2007) analyzed schools in the City of Bogota, Colombia, comparing PPP schools or private schools providing public education for 15 years with public schools. He looked at indicators such as student dropout rates and educational outcomes in terms of test scores on reading and mathematics. His analysis found that the PPP schools had significantly lower dropout rates, and that students in the PPP schools had significantly better test scores on both school subjects. Hafeez and colleagues (2016) analyzed schools in the city of Karachi, Pakistan. They compared PPP schools to public sector schools, focusing on student test scores for mathematics, English, and the average scores across subjects. Like Barrera-Osoria (2007), they also found that the PPP schools performed significantly better. Rodrigues and Zucco's (2018) analysis of Brazilian schools found that, in addition to better time performance (see "Time Performance," above), the schools also had better quality performance. Specifically, principals of the PPP schools spent significantly more time on pedagogical activities, and they were significantly more satisfied with six out of ten of the operational services, such as response time, quality of maintenance, and quality of operational supplies and materials (e.g., cleaning supplies and toilet paper). Finally, Yaya (2017) compared Private Finance Initiative (PFI) schools with conventionally financed schools in Scotland, looking at the quality and satisfaction with newly built primary school buildings in terms of, inter alia, building quality, service quality, maintenance mechanism, and building condition and suitability. The study found that the results are mixed, but mostly positive in favor of PPP schools (Petersen, 2019), although most differences were not significant.

Some studies also focused on prisons. Archambault and Deis (1997) found that the privately run prisons in Louisiana were not only more cost-effective (see "Cost Performance," above), but also had better service quality performance in terms of public safety, staff safety, and inmate safety. The studies by Cabral and colleagues (2008, 2010, 2013) into Brazilian prisons focused on performance indicators related to security and order—in terms of attempted prison escapes and prison deaths—and service to inmates—in terms of medical care, psychological care, and legal aid. They found that the prisons under private service contracts had significantly lower numbers of attempted escapes and deaths, as well as significantly better legal aid in terms of legal efficiency (Cabral et al., 2010, 2013). The frequency of the services to inmates was also higher in the privately run prison (Cabral et al., 2010; Cabral & De Azevedo, 2008).

Table 1.3 provides an overview of these studies regarding service quality performance. The table makes clear that PPPs have a performance advantage over the traditional alternatives. The results for the cases of health care and education were more mixed, but still generally in favor of the PPP model.

Table 1.3 Overview of studies on service quality performance advantage

Study	Period	Country	Sector	Performance Category	Findings	Performance Advantage
Archambeault and Deis (1997)	1991–96	United States	Prisons	Public safety, staff safety, and inmate safety	Privately operated prisons had generally better safety performance	Positive
Massoud et al. (2003)	1996–97	Lebanon	Waste Management	Performance efficiency and environmental protection improvements	PPPs seemed to have higher performance (but also higher costs; see Table 1.1)	Positive
Cercone et al. (2005); Gauri et al. (2004)	1990–1999; 2000	Costa Rica	Health Care Clinics	Target coverage rate and clinical level outputs	Clinics with contracted private provision outperformed public prisons on five of seven of the target coverage rate indicators; the two models had different profiles in terms of clinical level outputs	Overall positive
Barrera-Osorio (2007)	1999–2003	Colombia	Schools	Student dropout rates and student test scores for reading and English	PPP schools had significantly lower dropout rates and better test scores	Positive

Study	Period	Country	Sector	Performance Category	Findings	Performance Advantage
Cabral et al. (2010, 2013, 2008)	2003–2004; 2001–2006; 2001–2009	Brazil	Prisons	Security and order (prison escapes, assaults, and deaths) and service to inmates (medical care, psychological care, and legal aid)	Privately operated prisons had (significantly) lower escapes, assaults, and deaths, the frequency of services to inmates was higher, and legal efficiency was better	Positive
Shet et al. (2011)	2007–2009	India	Health Care Clinics	Adherence and treatment success	The public and public-private clinics outperformed the private clinic	Overall positive
Atmo et al. (2015; 2017)	2004–2011; 2000–2014	Indonesia	Power Plants	Availability of the power plants and carbon emission levels	PPPs had better operational outcomes and significantly better availability performance	Positive
Hafeez et al. (2016)	2014	Pakistan	Schools	Student test scores for mathematics, English, and average scores	PPP schools had significantly better test scores	Positive
Yaya (2017)	2000–2012	Scotland	Schools	Satisfaction with the quality of the building and services	Results were mixed but mostly positive, although often not significant (Petersen, 2019)	Overall positive

Study	Period	Country	Sector	Performance Category	Findings	Performance Advantage
Rodrigues and Zucco (2018)	2009–2015	Brazil	Schools	Time spent on pedagogical activities and satisfaction with ten operational services	Principals of PPP schools spent more time on pedagogical activities and were significantly more satisfied with six of ten of the operational services	Overall positive
Ferreira and Marques (2021)	2012–2017	Portugal	Hospitals	Process of care in terms of quality of services (care appropriateness, clinical safety) and access to service delivery (timeliness, service availability)	The public hospitals do not perform better than PPP hospitals; in fact, the differences between public and PPP hospitals are not significant	No

STRUCTURE OF THE VOLUME

Although this is an edited volume, the chapters share a common analytical strategy in assessing the performance advantage of PPPs. The analyses are concentrated on identifying any performance differences between groups of projects, one group representing PPPs and the other representing an alternative, non-PPP mode of procurement. Each chapter focuses on a particular country and infrastructure policy sector to increase the comparability of the PPPs with the benchmark data. Chapters also explore possible explanations and mechanisms for the (non-) existence of a PPP performance advantage. The chapter authors of this book were also invited to contribute to this volume because of their previous and/or recent experiences analyzing PPP performance using a comparative approach and benchmarking it against the performance of traditionally procured projects.

In Chapter 2, Graeme Hodge and Carsten Greve reflect on the challenge of evaluating the performance of PPPs. In their *International Handbook on Public-Private Partnerships*, Hodge (2010) identified six evaluation challenges: defining the evaluand, multiple PPP objectives, multiple discourses and disciplines, the evaluator's role, evaluation rigor for individual studies, and accurately reviewing multiple individual studies of PPPs. For the current book, they have developed these challenges and grouped them into four dimensions that should concern today's researchers of PPP performance: evaluation philosophy, performance criteria and measurement, theoretical foundations, and methodology. A range of views on these dimensions is explored and, by reflecting on various examples, the authors illustrate the contested space within which PPP performance evaluation inevitably occurs.

The second chapter is followed by six empirical chapters. The first three of these focus on social infrastructure (schools, hospitals, and sports stadiums) and the latter three focus on economic infrastructure (roads and waterways; for a classification, see Grimsey & Lewis, 2004).

In Chapter 3, Cian O'Shea, Dónal Palcic, and Eoin Reeves compare PPP schools to traditionally procured schools in Ireland, focusing on capital costs, construction costs, operation and management costs, and lifecycle costs, but also on the quality of the assets and services delivered under the PPPs and traditional schools. Using interview data, they go deeper into the different experiences of both public and private managers in running these schools. Chapter 4 by Diogo Cunha Ferreira, Rui Cunha Marques, Maria Isabel Pedro, and Gonçalo Santos compares PPP hospitals to publicy managed hospitals in Portugal. They comparatively analyze the performance differences regarding efficiency, access to health care, care appropriateness, and clinical safety. Chapter 5 takes us across the Atlantic to Brazil. The setting: the 2014 FIFA

World Cup. Claudio José Oliveira dos Reis and Sandro Cabral compare PPP sports stadiums to public and private sports stadiums, focusing inter alia on on-budget delivery, on-time delivery, and the cost per seat. Chapter 6 takes us back to Europe again and to the Netherlands. Based on a recent evaluation study of the performance of DBFM compared to D&C using different sources of data, Ingmar van Meerkerk, Mike Duijn, Rianne Warsen, Stefan Verweij, Erik-Hans Klijn, Joop Koppenjan, and Samantha Metselaar compare and reflect on the cost and time performance of roads and waterways transport infrastructure projects. In Chapter 7, we stick to road transport infrastructure projects and look into the cost, time, and quality performance of projects in India, analyzed by Akash Deep, Mojahedul Islam Nayyer, and Thillai Rajan A. Finally, in Chapter 8, continuing the theme of road transport infrastructure, Daniel Albalate, Germà Bel, and Paula Bel-Piñana use panel data to compare the safety performance of PPP motorways to those of publicly managed motorways in Spain.

Finally, in Chapter 9, we take stock. First, we integrate the literature discussed above with the results from the empirical chapters to answer the main question that drives this book: Does the performance advantage of PPPs exist or not? We also discuss and reflect on the different reasons and mechanisms that explain any performance advantages that exist. Based on this, we develop recommendations for PPP practitioners and propose an agenda for future research.

NOTES

1. The definition of performance also depends on the theoretical or evaluative frameworks used and on the disciplinary perspective assumed (Hodge & Greve, 2017, 2019; Jeffares et al., 2013).
2. The World Bank (2014, 2017), for instance, also identifies that infrastructure is often inadequate due to inefficient and ineffective delivery of the infrastructure, poor planning and project selection, and insufficient public funds; they also indicate that PPPs may alleviate these problems through the transfer of planning and management tasks to the private sector and through private sector funding and financing.

REFERENCES

Allen Consulting Group. (2007). *Performance of PPPs and traditional procurement in Australia*. Infrastructure Partnerships Australia.

Archambeault, W. G., & Deis, D. R. (1997). Cost effectiveness comparisons of private versus public prisons in Louisiana: A comprehensive analysis of Allen, Avoyelles, and Winn correctional centers. *Journal of the Oklahoma Criminal Justice Research Consortium*, *4*, 1–88.

Atmo, G. U., Duffield, C. F., & Wilson, D. I. (2015). Structuring procurement to improve sustainability outcomes of power plant projects. *Energy Technology & Policy, 2*(1), 47–57.

Atmo, G. U., Duffield, C. F., Zhang, L., & Wilson, D. I. (2017). Comparative performance of PPPs and traditional procurement projects in Indonesia. *International Journal of Public Sector Management, 30*(2), 118–36.

Barrera-Osorio, F. (2007). *The impact of private provision of public education: Empirical evidence from Bogota's concession schools*. World Bank.

Bel, G., Fageda, X., & Warner, M. E. (2010). Is private production of public services cheaper than public production? A meta-regression analysis of solid waste and water services. *Journal of Policy Analysis and Management, 29*(3), 553–77.

Boardman, A. E., & Hellowell, M. (2017). A comparative analysis and evaluation of specialist PPP units' methodologies for conducting value for money appraisals. *Journal of Comparative Policy Analysis: Research and Practice, 19*(3), 191–206.

Boers, I., Hoek, F., Van Montfort, C., & Wieles, J. (2013). Public-private partnerships: International audit findings. In P. de Vries, & E. B. Yehoue (Eds.), *The Routledge companion to public-private partnerships* (pp. 451–78). Routledge.

Cabral, S., & De Azevedo, P. F. (2008). The modes of provision of prison services in a comparative perspective. *Brazilian Administration Review, 5*(1), 53–69.

Cabral, S., Lazzarini, S. G., & De Azevedo, P. F. (2010). Private operation with public supervision: Evidence of hybrid modes of governance in prisons. *Public Choice, 145*(1–2), 281–93.

Cabral, S., Lazzarini, S. G., & De Azevedo, P. F. (2013). Private entrepreneurs in public services: A longitudinal examination of outsourcing and statization of prisons. *Strategic Entrepreneurship Journal, 7*(1), 6–25.

Casady, C. B. (2021). Examining the institutional drivers of public-private partnership (PPP) market performance: A fuzzy set qualitative comparative analysis (fsQCA). *Public Management Review, 23*(7), 981–1005.

Casady, C. B., Eriksson, K., Levitt, R. E., & Scott, W. R. (2020). (Re)defining public-private partnerships (PPPs) in the new public governance (NPG) paradigm: An institutional maturity perspective. *Public Management Review, 22*(2), 161–83.

Casady, C. B., & Peci, F. (2021). The institutional challenges of public-private partnerships (PPPs) in transition economies: Lessons from Kosovo. *Economic Research-Ekonomska Istraživanja, 34*(1), 1949–65.

Cercone, J., Briceño, R., & Gauri, V. (2005). Contracting primary health care services—The case of Costa Rica. In G. M. la Forgia (Ed.), *Health system innovations in Central America: Lessons and impact of new approaches* (pp. 109–33). World Bank.

Chasey, A. D., Maddex, W. E., & Bansal, A. (2012). Comparison of public-private partnerships and traditional procurement methods in North American highway construction. *Transportation Research Record: Journal of the Transportation Research Board, 2268*(1), 26–32.

Chen, Z., Daito, N., & Gifford, J. L. (2016). Data review of transportation infrastructure public-private partnership: A meta-analysis. *Transport Reviews, 36*(2), 228–50.

Cui, C., Liu, Y., Hope, A., & Wang, J. (2018). Review of studies on the public-private partnerships (PPP) for infrastructure projects. *International Journal of Project Management, 36*(5), 773–94.

Daito, N., & Gifford, J. L. (2014). U.S. highway public-private partnerships: Are they more expensive or efficient than the traditional model? *Managerial Finance, 40*(11), 1131–51.

Debela, G. Y. (2019). Attractive factors of public-private partnerships (PPP) for road projects in Ethiopia. *Journal of Civil, Construction and Environmental Engineering, 4*(3), 59–68.

De Castro e Silva Neto, D., Oliveira Cruz, C., Rodrigues, F., & Silva, P. (2016). Bibliometric analysis of PPP and PFI literature: Overview of 25 years of research. *Journal of Construction Engineering and Management, 142*(10).

Dos Reis, C. J. O., & Cabral, S. (2017). Public-private partnerships (PPP) in mega-sport events: A comparative study of the provision of sports arenas for the 2014 FIFA World Cup in Brazil. *Brazilian Journal of Public Administration, 51*(4), 551–79.

Duffield, C. F. (2008). *Report on the performance of PPP projects in Australia when compared with a representative sample of traditionally procured infrastructure projects*. University of Melbourne, MERIT.

European PPP Expertise Centre. (2015). *PPP motivations and challenges for the public sector: Why (not) and how*. European Investment Bank.

European PPP Expertise Centre. (2020). *Market update: Review of the European PPP market in 2019*. European Investment Bank.

Ferreira, D. C., & Marques, R. C. (2021). Public-private partnerships in health care services: Do they outperform public hospitals regarding quality and access? Evidence from Portugal. *Socio-Economic Planning Sciences, 73*, 100798.

Froud, J., & Shaoul, J. (2001). Appraising and evaluating PFI for NHS hospitals. *Financial Accountability & Management, 17*(3), 247–70.

Gassner, K., Popov, A., & Pushak, N. (2009). *Does private sector participation improve performance in electricity and water distribution?* World Bank.

Gauri, V., Cercone, J., & Briceño, R. (2004). Separating financing from provision: Evidence from 10 years of partnership with health cooperatives in Costa Rica. *Health Policy and Planning, 19*(5), 292–301.

Grimsey, D., & Lewis, M. K. (2004). *Public-private partnerships: The worldwide revolution in infrastructure provision and project finance*. Edward Elgar.

Grimsey, D., & Lewis, M. K. (2005). Are public-private partnerships value for money? Evaluating alternative approaches and comparing academic and practitioner views. *Accounting Forum, 29*(4), 345–78.

Hafeez, F., Haider, A., & Uz Zafar, N. (2016). Impact of public-private-partnership programmes on students' learning outcomes: Evidence from a quasi-experiment. *Pakistan Development Review, 55*(4), 955–1017.

Hammerschmid, G., & Ysa, T. (2010). Empirical PPP experiences in Europe: National variations of a global concept. In G. A. Hodge, C. Greve, & A. E. Boardman (Eds.), *International handbook on public-private partnerships* (pp. 333–53). Edward Elgar.

Hodge, G. A. (2010). Reviewing public-private partnerships: Some thoughts on evaluation. In G. A. Hodge, C. Greve, & A. E. Boardman (Eds.), *International handbook on public-private partnerships* (pp. 81–112). Edward Elgar.

Hodge, G. A., & Greve, C. (2007). Public-private partnerships: An international performance review. *Public Administration Review, 67*(3), 545–58.

Hodge, G. A., & Greve, C. (2009). PPPs: The passage of time permits a sober reflection. *Economic Affairs, 29*(1), 33–9.

Hodge, G. A., & Greve, C. (2017). On public-private partnership performance: A contemporary review. *Public Works Management & Policy, 22*(1), 55–78.

Hodge, G. A., & Greve, C. (2019). *The logic of public-private partnerships: The enduring interdependency of politics and markets*. Edward Elgar.

Hong, S. (2016). When does a public-private partnership (PPP) lead to inefficient cost management? Evidence from South Korea's urban rail system. *Public Money & Management*, *36*(6), 447–54.

Hueskes, M., Koppenjan, J. F. M., & Verweij, S. (2019). Public-private partnerships for infrastructure: Lessons learned from Dutch and Flemish PhD-theses. *European Journal of Transport and Infrastructure Research*, *19*(3), 160–76.

Jeffares, S., Sullivan, H., & Bovaird, T. (2013). Beyond the contract: The challenge of evaluating the performance(s) of public-private partnerships. In C. Greve, & G. A. Hodge (Eds.), *Rethinking public-private partnerships: Strategies for turbulent times* (pp. 166–87). Routledge.

Kavishe, N., & Chileshe, N. (2020). Driving forces for adopting public-private partnerships in Tanzanian housing projects. *International Journal of Construction Management*, *20*(8), 912–27.

Ke, Y., Wang, S., Chan, A. P. C., & Cheung, E. (2009). Research trend of public-private partnership in construction journals. *Journal of Construction Engineering and Management*, *135*(10), 1076–86.

Koppenjan, J. F. M., Klijn, E. H., Duijn, M., Klaassen, H. L., Van Meerkerk, I. F., Metselaar, S. A., Warsen, R., & Verweij, S. (2020). *Leren van 15 jaar DBFM-projecten bij RWS: Eindrapport*. Rijkswaterstaat en Bouwend Nederland.

Leruth, L. E. (2012). Public-private cooperation in infrastructure development: A principal-agent story of contingent liabilities, fiscal risks, and other (un)pleasant surprises. *Networks and Spatial Economics*, *12*(2), 223–37.

Liu, J., Love, P. E. D., Smith, J., Regan, M., & Sutrisna, M. (2014). Public-private partnerships: A review of theory and practice of performance management. *International Journal of Productivity and Performance Management*, *63*(4), 499–512.

Marsilio, M., Cappellaro, G., & Cuccurullo, C. (2011). The intellectual structure of research into PPPs: A bibliometric analysis. *Public Management Review*, *13*(6), 763–82.

Massoud, M. A., El-Fadel, M., & Abdel Malak, A. (2003). Assessment of public vs private MSW management: A case study. *Journal of Environmental Management*, *69*(1), 15–24.

McQuaid, R. W., & Scherrer, W. (2010). Changing reasons for public-private partnerships (PPPs). *Public Money & Management*, *30*(1), 27–34.

Meduri, S. S., & Annamalai, T. R. (2013). Unit costs of public and PPP road projects: Evidence from India. *Journal of Construction Engineering and Management*, *139*(1), 35–43.

Osei-Kyei, R., & Chan, A. P. C. (2015). Review of studies on the critical success factors for public-private partnership (PPP) projects from 1990 to 2013. *International Journal of Project Management*, *33*(6), 1335–46.

Osei-Kyei, R., Dansoh, A., & Ofori-Kuragu, J. K. (2014). Reasons for adopting public-private partnerships (PPP) for construction projects in Ghana. *International Journal of Construction Management*, *14*(4), 227–38.

O'Shea, C., Palcic, D., & Reeves, E. (2019). Comparing PPP with traditional procurement: The case of schools procurement in Ireland. *Annals of Public and Cooperative Economics*, *90*(2), 245–67.

Palcic, D., Reeves, E., & Siemiatycki, M. (2019). Performance: The missing "P" in PPP research? *Annals of Public and Cooperative Economics*, *90*(2), 221–26.

Petersen, O. H. (2019). Evaluating the costs, quality, and value for money of infrastructure public-private partnerships: A systematic literature review. *Annals of Public and Cooperative Economics*, *90*(2), 227–44.

Pollock, A. M., Shaoul, J., & Vickers, N. (2002). Private finance and "value for money" in NHS hospitals: A policy in search of a rationale? *BMJ, 324*, 1205–09.

Raisbeck, P., Duffield, C. F., & Xu, M. (2010). Comparative performance of PPPs and traditional procurement in Australia. *Construction Management and Economics, 28*(4), 345–59.

Reeves, E., & Ryan, J. (2007). Piloting public-private partnerships: Expensive lessons from Ireland's schools' sector. *Public Money & Management, 27*(5), 331–38.

Rijkswaterstaat. (2019). *Toekomstige opgave Rijkswaterstaat: Perspectief op de uitdagingen en verbetermogelijkheden in de GWW-sector* [Future tasking Rijkswaterstaat: Perspective on the challenges and opportunities for improvement in the civil engineering sector]. Ministerie van Infrastructuur en Waterstaat.

Rodrigues, B., & Zucco, C. (2018). A direct comparison of the performance of public-private partnerships with that of traditional contracting. *Brazilian Journal of Public Administration, 52*(6), 1237–57.

Shet, A., DeCosta, A., Heylen, E., Shastri, S., Chandy, S., & Ekstrand, M. (2011). High rates of adherence and treatment success in a public and public-private HIV clinic in India: Potential benefits of standardized national care delivery systems. *BMC Health Services Research, 11*(277), 1–8.

Shi, J., Duan, K., Wu, G., Zhang, R., & Feng, X. (2020). Comprehensive metrological and content analysis of the public-private partnerships (PPPs) research field: A new bibliometric journey. *Scientometrics, 124*, 2145–84.

Soecipto, R. M., Verhoest, K., Scherrer, W., & Petersen, O. H. (2016). Diverging or converging PPP policies, regulations and supporting arrangements? A comparative analysis of 20 European countries. In A. Roumboutsos (Ed.), *Public-private partnerships in transport: Trends and theory* (pp. 19–43). Routledge.

Tang, L., Shen, Q., & Cheng, E. W. L. (2010). A review of studies on public-private partnership projects in the construction industry. *International Journal of Project Management, 28*(7), 683–94.

Verweij, S. (2018). Meerwaarde door PPS: Welke meerwaarde? [Added value through PPP: What added value?]. *Agora, 34*(3), 34–7.

Verweij, S., Koppenjan, J. F. M., Klijn, E. H., & Van Meerkerk, I. F. (2021). Evaluatie 15 jaar DBFM-projecten: Gooi de expertise niet zomaar overboord. [Evaluation of 15 years of DBFM projects: Don't just throw the expertise overboard]. *Verkeerskunde, 72*(1), 42.

Verweij, S., & Van Meerkerk, I. F. (2020). Do public-private partnerships perform better? A comparative analysis of costs for additional work and reasons for contract changes in Dutch transport infrastructure projects. *Transport Policy, 99*, 430–8.

Verweij, S., & Van Meerkerk, I. F. (2021). Do public-private partnerships achieve better time and cost performance than regular contracts? *Public Money & Management, 41*(4), 286–95.

Verweij, S., Van Meerkerk, I. F., & Klaassen, H. L. (2020a). *De performance van DBFM bij Rijkswaterstaat: Een kwantitatieve analyse van projectendata* [The performance of DBFM at Rijkswaterstaat: A quantitative analysis of project data]. Rijksuniversiteit Groningen en Erasmus Universiteit Rotterdam.

Verweij, S., Van Meerkerk, I. F., & Leendertse, W. (2020b). Het prestatievoordeel van publiek-private samenwerking: Een analyse van transportinfrastructuurprojecten in Nederland. [The performance advantage of public-private partnerships: An analysis of transport infrastructure projects in the Netherlands]. *Beleid en Maatschappij, 47*(3), 269–89.

Wang, H., Xiong, W., Wu, G., & Zhu, D. (2018). Public-private partnership in public administration discipline: A literature review. *Public Management Review*, *20*(2), 293–316.

Whittington, J. (2012). When to partner for public infrastructure? Transaction cost evaluation of design–build delivery. *Journal of the American Planning Association*, *78*(3), 269–85.

World Bank. (2014). Public-private partnerships: Reference guide. World Bank.

World Bank. (2017). Public-private partnerships: Reference guide. World Bank.

World Bank. (2020). Private Participation in Infrastructure (PPI): Annual report 2019. World Bank.

Yaya, R. (2017). Twelve years of Scottish school public private partnership: Are they better Value for Money? *Journal of Public Procurement*, *17*(2), 187–228.

Yescombe, E. R. (2013). PPPs and project finance. In P. de Vries, & E. B. Yehoue (Eds.), *The Routledge companion to public-private partnerships* (pp. 227–46). Routledge.

Zhang, S., Chan, A. P. C., Feng, Y., Duan, H., & Ke, Y. (2016). Critical review on PPP research—A search from the Chinese and international journals. *International Journal of Project Management*, *34*(4), 597–612.

2. The passage of time permits another sober reflection: this time on the performance evaluation challenge

Graeme Hodge and Carsten Greve

INTRODUCTION

Evaluating Public-Private Partnership (PPP) performance requires much care. Many performance assessments of this delivery mechanism have been done, but most have been imperfect and disappointing to date. They have been imperfect in the methodological sense, as Verweij et al. noted in the opening chapter of this volume. But these assessments have been imperfect in other senses, too, and some have portrayed little more than the writer's own biases—personal commentary and opinion, yes, but hardly rigorous assessments of performance. So, what do we mean by 'rigorous', and how might we encourage stronger and more reliable PPP assessments? What does it take to complete a believable assessment we can all trust?

Today's researchers face a daunting challenge to get published. It remains important, though, for evaluators to ask research questions that are relevant and central to decision-making.[1] In this context, the present volume, which encourages greater research rigour in the PPP field, is a welcome addition to the literature. This is particularly so with today's researchers facing increased expectations in terms of approach, structure, theory, and methodology.

This chapter articulates the challenges of measuring and evaluating the performance advantages of PPPs and investigates the extent to which this evaluation space is stable and uncontested.[2] It argues overall that the PPP performance evaluation space is both crowded and contested,[3] and that as a consequence, surprisingly comprehensive and careful detective work is needed before we claim even modestly reliable answers to performance advantage questions. The chapter is structured as follows. First, it summarizes the four dimensions central to a rigorous PPP performance assessment: evaluation philosophy, performance criteria and measurement, theoretical foundations, and methodology. Second, it explores a range of views on these dimensions and observes examples that illustrate the contested space within which PPP performance measurement and evaluation inevitably occur.

THE PPP PERFORMANCE EVALUATION CHALLENGE

Efforts to determine the existence of potential PPP performance advantages did not begin yesterday. As the opening chapter acknowledged, PPP scholars have long wrestled with this. Hodge (2010) contemplated some of the performance evaluation challenges a decade ago, warning that PPP evaluation attempts were 'likely to be subjected to the usual policy evaluation difficulties and language games at the same time as incorporating inherently technical aspects' (p. 81). He emphasized that PPP assessments were not limited to any single discipline and were likely to continue being hotly contested. In this chapter, we build on this foundation and extend these ideas. So, why are evaluations and their conclusions so contested?

For a start, the very notion of evaluation is not as straightforward as one might think. Dictionaries describe evaluation as 'determin[ing] the significance, worth or condition of something by careful appraisal and study' (Merriam-Webster, 2022). Moreover, the meaning of 'value' not only covers 'the worth or return in money', but also 'the relative worth, merit or importance' (Dictionary.com, 2022). So, we are already thinking about evaluation as being broader than economics or finance matters, and covering a wealth of other domains in terms of societal worth as well as relative importance. More formally, too, Weiss (1998) defines evaluation as 'the systematic assessment of the operation and/or the outcomes of a program or policy' (p. 4). Alternatively, Bingham and Felbinger (2002) see evaluation as 'the use of scientific methods to estimate the successful implementation and resultant outcomes of programs or policies for decision-making purposes' (p. 3). These formal definitions emphasize that reliable evaluations are based on using social science research methods which, in the words of Patten and Newhart (2018), 'are designed to be systematic and to minimize biases' (p. 3).

The evaluation discipline's history, which has evolved through a series of personality changes,[4] is also revealing. From a century ago, when 'the role of the evaluator was seen as essentially a technical one', the evaluator's role evolved into more of a descriptive one that discerned patterns, strengths, and weaknesses. Hodge (2010) notes: '[b]y the 1960s and 1970s, the evaluator's role had evolved further to become more that of a judge who would pronounce the degree to which "success" had been achieved' (p. 83). Subsequently, we have viewed the task of evaluation 'in terms of negotiating the claims, concerns and issues present among a multiplicity of constructions'. So, the evaluation role has gradually changed from being a technical and judgemental one, to more of a learning and interpretive task amidst the complex expectations of multiple actors. All this has occurred, too, alongside numerous calls for rigorous and evidence-based assessments of government policies.

Where should we start our current 'sober reflection' journey on PPP performance? One useful place is to return to the series of priority challenges for evaluators highlighted by Hodge (2010). For our present purposes, we have developed these earlier concerns and grouped them into four primary dimensions for today's PPP performance researchers:[5] evaluation philosophy, performance criteria and measurement, theoretical foundations, and methodology.[6] Let us look at each.

Evaluation Philosophy

'Rational' public policy that is 'evidence-based' is deeply appealing. What works best matters, and drawing on stronger scientific research assessments also matters. But whilst 'the appeal of the gold standard for evidence is… admirable…what exactly is evidence? Whose evidence matters most? [And] works best for whom?' (Hodge, 2010, p. 84). Answers to these legitimate questions depend on what we see as the evaluator's role and whose 'rationality' is adopted. And whilst we might see the evaluator's role as simply to assess outcomes or goals, evaluation scholars, such as Dahler-Larson (2005), challenge this. He argues that evaluation 'cannot be reduced to this one role and function' (p. 616). Why? Because the very role of the evaluator is contestable. Hodge (2010) explains the dilemma through three possibilities:

> Are we as evaluators there to undertake a 'scientific approach' and discover knowledge through experimental analysis so that we may determine the degree to which explicit objectives are met, the reason for success or failure and how to improve our success? Alternatively, should we behave more as enlightened consumers or citizens, who may wish to judge the actual goals and objectives set by others without necessarily being constrained by them? As a third option, are we there more as the facilitator, whose role is to present information to others and enable them, not us, to make the judgement? (p. 90)

The philosophical stance we take here matters because each approach emphasizes different priorities and values.

Philosophical matters aside, we certainly need to be crystal clear on what it is we are evaluating—the evaluand. This is again not necessarily as simple as it sounds. We have described PPP as a phenomenon (Hodge & Greve, 2013), and as being many things including a specific project, a project delivery (or organizational) form, a policy, a governance tool, or else having a broader cultural or contextual meaning (see also Casady et al., 2020). So, a choice is required here. Furthermore, even if we agree that an evaluation will assess the performance of one specific type of project delivery form, say a Design–

Build–Finance–Operate–Maintain (DBFOM), this 'evaluand' may easily change its shape in different jurisdictions. The meanings of what appear to be identically structured and similarly worded DBFOM contracts will even differ between projects in different jurisdictions.[7] Also, a DBFOM project in the Netherlands will not be the same as one in China, Russia, or Kuwait, simply because the ways in which governments deal with businesses differ hugely. Even the meaning of what is 'public' and what is 'private' may differ. In other words, even if we specify our evaluand as one particular type of PPP delivery mechanism, our assumption that the evaluand is a 'fixed' factor in our evaluation may well not be true. As well, both the meaning of any research data collected on PPP performance and its veracity is also likely to differ greatly between countries. Having said all this, we have no choice but to define the evaluand and be explicit on its meaning across jurisdictions. It is a necessary starting point for both evaluators and their readers.

We also need to more seriously consider how we learn from existing PPP research studies. To establish the 'truth of the matter' when synthesizing research on a topic, researchers have traditionally undertaken a literature review. It turns out, though, that they are difficult to conduct properly, and reliability cannot be assumed—even when integrating findings from a small number of studies.[8] Different reviewers often see the same empirical results quite differently. There are many reasons for this. Glass (1976) explains that a common method of integrating studies with inconsistent findings is to carp on the design or analysis deficiencies of all but a few studies and then advance the one or two acceptable studies as the truth of the matter (frequently one's own work or the work of one's students or friends!). Taking notice of one or two 'acceptable' studies, though, puts the evaluator in the position of knowledge gatekeeper and judge, and fails to use much of the available information.

One important aspect of the narrative review is therefore the requirement for reviewers to describe to the reader the sampling, measurement, analytical methods, and findings of each of the studies under review. Both Hunter and Schmidt (1990) and Glass et al. (1981) point out that published reviews often violate these reporting precepts.[9] Without information on the degree to which a reviewer uses a systematic approach in their review, the reader cannot sensibly interpret or intelligently assess any conclusions made. A systematic review (or meta-analysis) aims for 'clarity, explicitness, and openness' (Glass et al., 1981), and can employ statistical techniques to summarize many evaluation study findings. The philosophy here is to 'discipline research synthesis by the same methodological standards that apply to primary research' (Cook et al., 1992, p. viii). Systematic reviews have been introduced into almost all areas of research, but are not common.[10] Relevant examples in the context of public-private service provision include Hodge (2000; who summarized enterprise privatization studies and contracting-out studies), Petersen (2019; whose systematic PPP review summarized the extent to which findings favoured one side or other in the debate),[11] Bachellir (2017; who reviewed enterprise sales in developed and developing countries), and both Bel et al. (2010) and Petersen et al. (2018; who reviewed contracting-out public sector services).

Overall, then, if we are aiming for reliable reviews of multiple evaluation studies, then such reviews should be subject to the ethos of strength and veracity that we expect of primary evaluation studies. Hodge (2010) suggests that more trustworthy literature reviews present evidence supporting and disputing claims and counterclaims fairly and accurately, and against a pragmatic rather than a perfect counterfactual. They usually place more weight on those evaluations with stronger methodological research designs—without monopolizing claims to knowledge—and are undertaken by evaluators with wide stakeholder knowledge and a reputation for measured judgements and independence. The open presentation of the data on which it is based is a further desirable trait.

Performance Criteria and Measurement

PPP performance has long been an intellectual heart of much PPP research, and the notion of PPP performance has itself always been contested. Why? Because PPPs have been pursued for many reasons. Some PPP objectives are frequently heard—cost efficiency, Value for Money (VfM), and timeliness, for example—but dozens exist (Hodge & Greve, 2017), covering the implicit as well as explicit, and the political as well as technical. These include goals such as improving business and financial market confidence, increasing government's own financial credentials, enabling the provision of infrastructure without appearing to increase public sector borrowing (the initial rationale for PFI in the UK), and crashing through the speedy delivery of public infrastructure projects through the use of private contract law (Casady & Geddes, 2019).

The point here is not that some of these goals are more or less legitimate than others. They simply reflect the public policy context within which PPPs exist, and the nature of political decision-making. We also know that different disciplines have long emphasized quite different things. And, as Jeffares et al. (2013) said, there are vastly differing performance expectations coming from governments, private stakeholders, political/community groups, and partners, whether expressed as financial, legal, social, or cultural terms. The multiplicity of goals governments expect PPPs to deliver presents a complex challenge for analysts. Disciplines, predictably, still imply which performance goals are most important. Economists prefer economic factors, political scientists and public policy scholars prefer political factors and election mandates, project finance and engineering folk assess risk rewards and project delivery, and sociologists analyse the winners and losers from PPPs. Perhaps this is as it should be.

Just as important as the decision on what to measure is the veracity and accuracy of any empirical measurements or performance estimates made. Measurement integrity in research is just as important as reviewing and citing literature, designing experimental research, and understanding statistical techniques when analysing data (Patten & Newhart, 2018).[12]

Overall, then, choosing performance goal(s), adopting the most appropriate measurement proxies, and then ensuring veracity for what is measured or estimated are all critical and necessary dimensions to our evaluation. And in making these choices, we need to acknowledge the risk that in narrowing the performance domain we have over-simplified 'what matters most' in real-world decision-making and when judging PPP performance.

Theoretical Foundations

The PPP movement has been characterized as enjoying many intellectual foundations, according to Bovaird's (2010) brief intellectual history. We might not initially assume that the choice of underlying theory in our research would affect our measurement of performance, but it does because it reveals our core assumptions about PPPs and how they work.[13] Thinking about core assumptions that inform PPPs is not an easy task, though; as Klijn (2022) says. 'This is because PPP is a hybrid. It contains ideas from various theoretical orientations, and, in practice, arguments are freely used from various different theories to justify PPP use and acclaim its value and effectiveness' (p. 33). Klijn (2022) identifies 'three clusters of ideas: PPP as a monitoring game (an economic perspective), PPP as collaboration (a collaborative and network governance perspective), and PPP as sensemaking (a frame and institutional perspective)'.[14] So what?

Firstly, every theory, as a rationale, points us in a particular direction as to where we should focus our attention. The economic perspective above checks for opportunistic behaviours, the collaborative perspective seeks to facilitate cooperation, and the sensemaking perspective seeks to understand how language and partner activities are framed in working together. This limits our priorities to that arena and implies which domains of performance deserve our attention and which do not. Second, the choice of theoretical underpinning in turn affects our choices for measurement. Each theory emphasizes a limited number of factors and mechanisms of causation, and thus by definition, underplays others. At a minimum, this impacts our choice as to what ought to be measured and what ought not. Third, what is measured under the philosophy of our chosen underlying theory, needs to be intellectually coordinated with our methodology, given that most methods seek to measure causal mechanisms and not simply measure variables in the vague hope of some association being found, even if it is statistically 'significant' and is unlikely to have arisen by chance!

Overall, then, the theoretical lens we adopt in our research usually guides our thinking on what matters most through an evaluation, influences our conception of how PPP performance itself ought to be measured, and implicitly prioritizes measurements to be made. Moreover, the theory adopted requires coordination with the methodology chosen in our analysis.

Methodology

How do we ensure a methodologically sound analysis in our own research, or judge the methodological rigour of others? There are many layers in answering this. We have already tackled some foundations: having an explicit evaluation philosophy (the evaluator's role, defining the evaluand, and accurately synthesizing past research), the care required when selecting performance criteria (from multiple objectives and disciplines), and making reliable measurements. But there is more to think about.

Of course, the formal analytical techniques available to evaluate PPPs are numerous. What makes a rigorous or more scientific assessment, though? We ought to remind ourselves, to start with, that there is no such thing as a perfect evaluation or perfect research technique. All inevitably have strengths and weaknesses. Researchers essentially aim to 'enable conclusions to be made beyond reasonable doubt' (Stufflebeam & Shinkfield, 2007, p. 301). And many research methods do a great job at helping us to make defensible conclusions, including conclusions on cause and effect. Libraries of evaluative methods exist, though, and what is 'defensible' remains a disarmingly open question.

Bingham and Felbinger (2002) take a scientific frame to the issue of defensibility and suggest a continuum of methods for analytical studies of performance. These include experimental designs that feature a time series analysis (where actual observations are compared with a forward projection based on earlier activity), the use of a comparison group (where a comparison group closely resembling programme recipient groups is created and differences between actual observations and such comparison groups are measured), and the use of control groups (where participants are assigned to treatment and control groups randomly—the most powerful experimental design). Simplistically, analyses may be undertaken where the experimental group is separated from the 'control' group in time (i.e., 'before and after' studies) or space (cross-sectional studies), and the double-blind randomized experimental design ranks as the 'gold standard' experimental method. But techniques employing extraordinarily sophisticated mathematical approaches are now available to researchers to employ in their studies. In all cases, the evaluator seeks to measure real-world behaviour and compare these measurements or observations against a counterfactual (or control scenario) that we assume would most likely have occurred had the PPP policy intervention not taken place. Ensuring through statistical methods that any differences in observations could not simply have arisen by chance is part of this assessment, as is maximizing both the internal validity (ensuring that the effects discerned in your data were actually caused by the factors you put forward) and external validity (ensuring the research results you found are also applicable outside one's own study situation/jurisdiction; Bingham & Felbinger, 2002).

Where do PPP research methodologies fit in here? Warsen (2022) provides some answers to this question. Her analysis suggests that whilst PPP research was a growing and diverse international phenomenon, 'little ha[d] been written about the use of various research methods in PPP research'. She noted that case study research and surveys dominated the field, and that literature reviews, policy analysis, and the quantitative analysis of secondary data were also being adopted. All came with strengths and weaknesses. Looking to the future, she saw great potential in several methods not currently widely adopted in PPP research. These included qualitative comparative analysis (QCA), Q-methodology, and experimental research. She also commented that such new methods may have the potential to address new research questions and enhance the methodological diversity within the PPP field. Overall, Warsen (2022) concluded that 'each research method—if properly used—may contribute new knowledge on PPPs'. She also noted that the PPP research community has reached the stage where we should all be 'stepping up our methodological game'. These are strong judgements, with considerable underlying support in our view.

There is clearly much to think about on the matter of research methodology. Perhaps this is not surprising. Research rigour has long been crucial to reliable evaluation. The adoption of systematic approaches in one's research including strong experimental designs with control/comparison groups, statistical analysis of variation, and the adoption of explicit counterfactuals will continue to rank higher than casual observations or loosely based case study commentaries.

THE PPP PERFORMANCE EVALUATION SPACE: CROWDED AND CONTESTED

We have so far in this chapter hinted at a PPP performance evaluation space. It consists of what we think we now know about PPPs, and how it is that we know these things—within the context of public policy. It is rather large. It is also crowded and contested. This is in part because, as Jeffares et al. (2013) rightly said, 'the performance of PPPs is always likely to be contested because of its political context' (p. 171). It is also because researchers are often searching in three directions simultaneously—for better data, for better analytical methods, and for better questions. And each of us will put slightly different priorities on these. Such contestations can become particularly apparent when deciding what proxies we will use for favoured aspects of performance, what we will measure empirically, and then how these measurements ought to be interpreted within the performance evaluation space. Let us illustrate this point through examples in some of the evaluation dimensions.

Evaluation Philosophy

We earlier emphasized the importance of acknowledging the evaluator's role, having a clear and jurisdictionally unique evaluand, and the need for care when learning from past studies. Much of the work undertaken to date falls at this first set of hurdles. For a start, many analysts are unaware of the alternative roles that evaluators can take, and simply present their own analysis as either a reliable 'scientific analysis' or that of an enlightened citizen—without acknowledging their role as self-appointed judge.

Even the simple matter of specifying a clear evaluand is not met. Much of the authors' own work could be subject to this criticism! And looking at the first chapter of this book, the initial review of 'what is already available' refers to dozens of different PPP evaluands. These range from Design–Build–Finance–Maintain–Operate (DBFMO) contracts and alliance contracts in Australia (Duffield, 2008; Allen Consulting, 2007; Raisbeck et al., 2010), through arrangements adopted by 'all the electricity distribution and water and sanitation companies that experienced [private sector participation] between the beginning of the 1990s and 2002' (Gassner et al., 2009, p. 2), to both contracted-out garbage services and public or privately owned water utilities (Bel et al., 2010).[15]

Our desire to learn reliably from past studies has likewise often fallen short methodologically. Most of the authors' own work when reviewing PPP performance has again not adopted a systematic search of the literature as the basis for our reviews.[16] The literature review presented in the first chapter of this book likewise does not inform the reader how the review literature was gathered, leaving the reader unable to interpret the review conclusions presented.

These comments should be framed as observations rather than criticisms, though. As Patten and Newhart (2018) remind us, 'flaws are widespread in research' (p. 57). These comments simply illustrate the high standards we set ourselves once we set out to understand and reliably learn from past research and claim to improve the veracity of these research findings through our own work.

Performance Criteria and Measurement

Our guidance above when conceptualizing performance and adopting appropriate measurement proxies noted longstanding contestation. This is unsurprising, given PPP goal multiplicity, the shortfalls of any proxy chosen, and disciplinary habits narrowing performance interpretations.

Real-world PPP evaluations are again nowhere near a gold standard level of integrity on this evaluation dimension. Whilst some authors (e.g., Hodge & Greve, 2013) have long acknowledged goal multiplicity and the need to see performance as a broad notion, many evaluators still deny the existence of ideas from other disciplines and reject findings they do not support or understand. Close examination of performance proxies and the way in which performance can be framed is therefore always warranted. We know that rigorous research requires the adoption of 'valid' measures for performance, and that, as Patten and Newhart (2018) said, 'researchers call a measure valid to the extent that it measures what it is designed to measure and accurately performs the function(s) it is purported to perform' (p. 123). So, let us make some casual observations of the 'cost' and 'time' aspects of performance at the heart of this book.

There have been many ways to measure PPP costs. Vining and Boardman (2008) argue that from an economics perspective, the most relevant cost criteria for evaluation is 'the sum of total social costs' or 'the sum of the production costs' incurred by governments 'plus their transaction costs, plus (net) negative externalities' (p. 150). They warn that these costs can occur 'over an extensive time period' and that such relevant costs are not limited to those appearing in the project's budget. This is, perhaps understandably, a challenge bigger than most analysts are willing to take on, and most evaluators prefer narrower 'cost' interpretations. The meta-analysis of Petersen (2019) presented four examples of proxies: capital costs, the cost to users through tolls, operational costs, and contractual commitment. He saw the evidence as 'point[ing] to PPPs being more expensive than conventional procurement'. This contrasts the positive performance advantage concluded by studies such as Verweij and Van Meerkerk (2020) who found 'less additional work costs' (p. 289). Chapter 1 of this book added other measures to this list of cost proxies, including cost-effectiveness, VfM estimations, and client perceptions. The most common proxy for PPP cost, though, appears to have not been measuring cost directly at all, but monitoring the extent to which 'on-budget delivery' has been achieved. Numerous evaluations have repeated claims of performance advantage using this measure, but few have explicitly acknowledged that 'on-budget' criteria are simply a proxy for cost. They may well measure cost 'predictability' or 'certainty' quite well, but be a poor proxy for absolute cost or, more accurately, unit cost, which is the superior cost measure for taxpayers.[17] The number of studies of PPPs focussing on the unit cost performance measure is still staggeringly small. The text by Blanc-Brude, Goldsmith, and Välilä (2006) remains one high-quality exception. Their careful regression analyses across EU countries 'found P3s were 24 per cent more expensive than our expectations from traditional procurement—ironically, at about the same magnitude of traditional project cost-over-runs' (Hodge & Greve, 2017, p. 65). Another example, from Chapter 1 in this book, was the ambiguous result of Meduri and Annamalai (2013).[18] More important here is to acknowledge the difference between the many glowing 'on-budget' performance advantage claims and the few less flattering and more mixed results from unit cost studies. To be fair, analysing unit costs for a whole-of-life PPP project is not for the feint hearted because it is simply very difficult and involves numerous assumptions. But studies such as Leviakangis (2007) have tried, with findings opposite to the 'on-budget' cost advantage claims.[19]

We also ought to make two points on measurement accuracy. From an experimental perspective, all measurements or cost estimates have a degree of uncertainty associated with them, 'no matter how good the experimenter and the experimental design' (Kirkup, 1994, p. 15). Experimental data are therefore formally specified with their associated estimates of uncertainty; for example, a temperature measurement of 15.5°C is actually 15.5°C ± 0.5 (i.e., somewhere between 15.0°C and 16.0°C). So what? To begin with, PPP analysts need to be aware of the uncertainties with which they are dealing. Such uncertainties also need to be formally considered when calculations are made using these measurements. The second point to be made here is on the matter of significant figures—an often-overlooked topic. If, for example, a present value calculation for a project and its performance advantage over the 'Public Sector Comparator' is nominated as $123.6 million, then this implies that the performance advantage sits somewhere between $123.5 million and $123.7 million. Such figures are usually rubbish, scientifically speaking. This accuracy is simply not there to claim, for many reasons. There is inherent inaccuracy in the initial estimates (or measurements) for a start. If these uncertain figures are then put into a calculation, perhaps even including broad assumptions which themselves may have only had one or two significant figures, the whole calculated result is far less certain than its publication implied and should probably have only been quoted to one or two significant figures. So, simply recalling our high school physics lessons on experimental data should lead us to agree with Jeremy Colman, the British Deputy Auditor General, when he commented that 'many appraisals were guilty of spurious precision'.[20] Added to this uncertainty is the further serious issue of model contestability. Calculations such as Net Present Value usually include the adoption of particular models which are themselves contested, and yet are presented by analysts without any acknowledgement of the uncertainty associated with the model adopted. The adoption of the private finance school (and its Capital Asset Pricing Model) as against the welfare economics school (or vice versa) is a classic example here (Hodge & Greve, 2021).

Overall, this means that a more reliable picture of the range of the expected performance advantage is possible, but only if analysts are more sanguine when presenting their calculation results. Of course, the estimated performance advantage range (after accounting for all of the above uncertainties) may not meet our societal expectation for ever-increasing precision and indeed may not look brilliant in the theatre of politics. If in a $2.2 billion projected PPP a performance advantage (i.e., benefit over traditional project delivery method) of say, $10 million (+/– $220 million) was published, we would be forced to repeat the Socratic paradox with significant humility. All we know is that we know (almost) nothing! No doubt it would be political suicide, as well, but it would be more honest from a strict experimental and scientific perspective.

What about the 'time' performance dimension? We know that 'on-time delivery' is a common proxy adopted to measure this aspect of performance. And it certainly has practical veracity because it is immediately understandable by citizens (and ministers who cut the ribbon). But it is equally a self-referencing and pliable criterion which fits neatly into the urgency of the project delivery narrative. The above-mentioned comments on measurement uncertainties also hold here, and politics inevitably comes into this performance measurement space. For example, Melbourne's EastLink Road project was delivered in 2008 on-budget and 'five months ahead of schedule', according to proponents.[21] But this 'project procurement' frame neglects the messier historical project delivery story of a dozen or more governments over a four-decade period after the 1960s. After all, the state initially established road- and land-use strategies, operated various planning and transport institutions, ensured suitable land was put aside for the facility, maintained the land, and then handed over this facility (at the last minute, in historical terms) to enable construction. The point here is that the time proxy we choose is only one of many possibilities, and the project management frame is quite different to a broader governance frame.[22] Again, the real question here is not any claim of absolute validity for the time measure chosen, but one of defensibility. Or as Patten and Newhart (2018) rightly said, 'validity is a matter of degree' because no measure is perfectly valid (p. 123).[23]

Lastly, we ought to note that when we collect data for multiple projects, analysts cannot necessarily assume that sampling statistical procedures will always take care of the inherent data uncertainty. This depends on the analytical technique adopted.

Theoretical Foundations and Methodology

Theory influences what we look for and seek to measure in our evaluation. It is for many researchers a central searchlight in scientific discovery.[24] We earlier noted that our theoretical frames might broadly take a monitoring perspective, a collaboration perspective, or a perspective of sensemaking. We commented that the choice made therefore prioritizes those performance domains deserving our attention and sets the path for what will be measured. We also commented that we need to coordinate what is measured to our methodology, given the usual interest in establishing causal mechanisms.

The methodological evaluation space has always been full of contests, as we said earlier. The iconic debates between qualitative and quantitative research methods are legendary. These need to be well understood because they continue today. Interestingly though, whilst statistical and numerical research is becoming the dominant approach in many journals, medical researchers are simultaneously being reminded that 'qualitative research can answer specific research questions that cannot to be adequately answered using (only) quantitative designs', and that these two approaches should be seen as 'equal' (Busetto et al., 2020, p. 8).[25] Likewise, the journal *Nature* recently implored researchers 'not to ignore the power of qualitative methods' because they 'were still essential to understand how climate social policies are designed or implemented'. They recommended a mixed-method approach when answering 'the complex questions related to climate and society' (Nature Climate Change, 2021, p. 717). So, this debate continues: quantitative researchers continue to value and strive for objectivity, whilst qualitative researchers 'question whether objectivity is obtainable', or even feasible and desirable (Patten & Newhart, 2018, p. 278).

Numerous books guide researchers on methodologies available today, and skimming through any of these shows a multitude of options as to quantitative and qualitative research techniques. Topics covered for quantitative research include statistical testing techniques, such as regression analysis, time series analysis (including autoregressive integrated moving average models), structural equation modelling—including LISREL (Linear Structural Relationships), AMOS (Analysis of Moment Structures), EQS (Equations), Mplus, and PLS (Partial Least Squares)—experimental design, panel data analysis (also known as longitudinal data or cross-sectional time series data), factor analysis, cluster analysis, Input–Output Analysis (IOA) and Social Accounting Matrix (SAM) models, and cost–benefit analysis (Dwyer et al., 2012). Guidance on qualitative methods covers topics such as grounded theory, ethnographic methods, focus groups, interview techniques, participant observation, cross-cultural approaches, archival research, and community case study research.

Perhaps the PPP measurement rubber hits the road, though, with new PPP research methods with which we may be less familiar. We noted the work of Warsen (2022) earlier. She saw potential in methodologies such as QCA, Q-methodology, experimental research, and mixed methods as we expand our research approaches beyond PPP case studies and surveys. And we agree. But there is a caveat here. Most researchers are probably generally aware of the lengthy evolution of traditional research techniques, such as case studies, surveys, or regression analysis, but they may also remain unaware of the serious contestations concerning their methodological rigour. This is even more so with newer research techniques. Indeed, such debates may even be invisible to researchers. Let us take an example: PPP research using fuzzy-set QCA (fsQCA).

Example: Examining fsQCA

FsQCA has become a high-profile analytical research method for PPPs (Verweij, 2015; Kort et al., 2016; Warsen et al., 2019; Casady, 2021). It has been billed as a superior approach to social inquiry (Krogslund et al., 2015). We, too, have been excited by its promise of marrying quantitative and qualitative data, and its appealing logic. But putting aside enthusiasm and fanfare, how reliable is it? Warsen (2022) explicitly noted its strengths and weaknesses, but this appears to be a rare exception in PPP research. We have not observed any fsQCA-based PPP article over the past five years giving any serious acknowledgement or discussion of the published methodological debates now existing on fsQCA. The impressive work of Gerrits and Verweij (2018), for instance, acknowledges such debates, but avoids 'partak[ing] in the very technical, methodological QCA debate that is currently taking place' (p. 13), before arguing that QCA provides 'a more thorough understanding of the complex causality that has led to certain outcomes in infrastructure projects' (p. 116).

Does this matter? Well, yes. More defensible PPP evaluation and PPP research is fully aware of weaknesses as well as its claimed strengths. So, PPP scholars need to read widely. Warsen (2022) noted four criticisms:[26] (1) type-one errors; (2) the excessive sensitivity of results to parameter values and choices; (3) neglect of measurement errors; and (4) aggregation bias. Each deserves more serious consideration than offered to date, as follows.

Type-one errors

Here, the concern is that fsQCA confirms relationships (i.e., pathways to outcomes), when in fact there are none in the data, so that 'even very strong QCA results may plausibly be the result of chance' (Braumoeller, 2015, p. 471).

Excessive sensitivity

'FsQCA is an extraordinarily sensitive method whose results are worryingly susceptible to minor parametric and model specification changes', according to Krogslund et al. (2015, p. 21). It finds complex connections between variables, even for so-called causal combinations containing randomly generated variables, and thus 'produces tenuous results'.

Measurement errors

'Measurement error affects conclusions from QCA quite dramatically', according to Hug (2013, p. 257). He comments that many studies 'gloss over possible measurement errors', and that Boolean algebra then leads to 'dramatically misleading inferences' (p. 252).

Aggregation bias

Braumoeller (2017) argues that 'fsQCA analyses of the complex causes of necessary and sufficient conditions (Ragin, 2000, pp. 234–8) incorporate two definitional assumptions that are individually innocuous but jointly worrisome': the cumulation assumption and the triangular data assumption. To him, these two assumptions can 'produce a form of aggregation bias', a 'heretofore-unappreciated danger in fsQCA' (p. 243). Of course, such methodological critiques are usually followed by a response—typically charging that such criticisms are based on misconceptions of set-theoretical thinking and misinformed, or the result of the poor application of the method.

Reading more widely and skimming the debates between Configurational Comparative Methods (CCMs), such as QCA, and Regressional Analytic Methods (RAMs), is instructive. Thiem et al. (2016) observe that even after a quarter-century of debate in political science and sociology, these two schools of scholars 'continue talking at cross purposes' (p. 742). They comment that the misunderstandings dominating the debates concern algebraic systems, hypotheses classes, and the concept of causal complexity, and are central, rather than peripheral, to the issue of research veracity. Importantly, they also argue that such misunderstandings exist as much within as between these two research communities.[27]

To us, some of these misunderstandings appear to be wholly understandable. For a start, the work by Thiem et al. (2016), for instance, observes that CCMs are based on the logic of Boolean algebra, 'whereas RAMs work according to the laws of linear algebra', and this 'give(s) rise to semantically incommensurable languages despite occasional resemblances in syntax' (p. 765). Moreover, the propositional logic of Boolean algebra which underpins CCMs, is nowhere near as commonly taught or understood as the linear algebra which is the foundation of RAMs. Less understandable and somewhat worrying, though, is the fact that long-term proponents of QCA, such as Ragin, Schneider, and

Wagemann, have been accused of inconsistently interpreting fundamental concepts, such as 'necessity', in accordance with a Boolean definition (Thiem & Baumgarter, 2016). In a similar vein, Thiem and Baumgarter (2016) comment that Ragin's fs/QCA software 'relies on an algorithmic routine—minimal disjunctivity—which is very useful in logic synthesis yet totally unsuitable for the purpose of causal data analysis' (p. 805).

Thankfully, more recent debates between methodological scholars appear to have reinforced an attitude of increased care and cautiousness. On the one side, Thomann and Maggetti (2020), for example, seek to assist QCA scholars in carefully designing better studies, and outline multiple approaches to QCA studies and the various analytical choices to be made by researchers. On the other hand, Baumgartner and Thiem (2020) evaluate QCA by conducting a battery of simulation tests and caution QCA users. They qualify their support for its veracity, finding that 'QCA perform[ed] faultlessly in a series of methodologically appropriate tests, but only in conjunction with the parsimonious solution type' (p. 281). Importantly, they found 'the QCA method to be untrustworthy' (p. 281) when generating the conservative and intermediate solution types, despite these having been long been recommended by methodologists such as Ragin, Schneider, and Wagemann. To their minds, these evaluation results have serious implications, and they call for 'a radical rethink on some hitherto central tenets of QCA methodology' (p. 302).

Where to with Methodology?

So, where does this leave PPP scholars? We are not here suggesting that researchers necessarily abandon fsQCA as a method for social scientific inquiry, and we continue to greatly admire the work of our good colleagues. There is simply a need to reconcile such critiques on fsQCA against traditional methods, with care and humility as to the superiority of one research technique over others. Our point is that limitations in new statistical approaches are not always clear (Skaaning, 2011). As Cooper and Glaesser (2011) put it, all analytic techniques need to be used with an understanding of the main likely threats to validity. It 'is especially important to report these threats explicitly when, as with fsQCA, mathematics such as fuzzy sets and logic, whose properties are new to most social scientists, are embedded in easily available and easy-to-use software' (p. 11).

Overall, then, we ought to remind ourselves that debates over qualitative versus quantitative research have a long history and will not be resolved in the short term. Secondly, this CCMs versus RAMs debate is also only one of the ongoing methodological debates occurring between scholars. We could add debates over Bayesian versus frequentist statistics, or between data versus algorithmic modellers to this (Thiem et al., 2016). Third, perhaps it is time for us to take more seriously their warning to us that 'methodologists should thus stop arguing about the superiority of one set of methods in dealing with causal complexity, and instead begin to appreciate their distinct capabilities, leveraging respective strengths wherever apposite' (Thiem et al., 2016, p. 765). At a minimum, and fourthly, users of techniques such as QCA (and fsQCA) should tread more cautiously in the future, employing the improvements suggested by QCA critics, as well as testing the robustness of their findings. After all, if the criticisms of scholars such as those mentioned above hold water, fsQCA results may be just as unreliable as the results from poor case studies, despite any initial appearance of a dazzling mathematical rationale. In the end, we are aiming for defensibility in our performance assessments, and being aware of these methodological contests helps ensure that we pursue a path of scholarship rather than academic marketing.

Before moving to some conclusions, we ought to be a little clearer on the intellectual approach taken in this book as well. To the credit of the three editors, many of the principles put forward in this chapter have already been carefully considered in terms of the book's structure. As a consequence, the approach taken by this current book already reflects a far more careful approach to PPP research than is usual. For example, the request that a consistent evaluand be adopted in each chapter, the requirement to compare actual PPPs with actual traditionally procured projects, the transparency of proxy performance measures coming from different project data sets, and the limited number of specified performance measures to be considered, are all admirable. These constraints potentially strengthen both individual chapter analyses and synthesizing lessons from all of the empirical work. Overall, this book has sought to adopt a quasi-experimental design approach and thereby establish a strong foundation for new knowledge.

But will we succeed in our quest to more reliably articulate the existence of claimed performance advantages of PPPs? This is a crucially important question—yet one also best left to readers to decide. Seasoned scholars have long recognized that there can be a frustratingly long distance between one's data analysis aims on the one hand, and the interpretation of one's findings and our final conclusions on the other. Chapter authors, though, have certainly been given a flying start in the journey.

CONCLUSION

There is much for PPP researchers to get right if we seek more reliable and trustworthy evaluations to assist public policy decision-making. In the context of public policy research, it is necessary to be disciplined across four dimensions: evaluation philosophy, performance criteria and measurement, theoretical foundations, and research methodology. This chapter has articulated challenges in both measuring and evaluating the performance advantages of PPPs and has probed the extent to which this evaluation space is stable and uncontested. We have found that the PPP performance evaluation space is both crowded and highly contested. As a consequence, careful detective work is needed before we claim even modest answers to performance advantage questions. So, we should by all means shoot for the gold research standard. But we equally need to understand that analysts will inevitably continue to learn from a multitude of sources and across studies, all with strengths and weaknesses. And so be it. As Patten and Newhart (2018) remind us, accumulating knowledge is a collective endeavour where ‘each well-designed study provides evidence that may support, amend, refute, or deepen the understanding of existing knowledge’. And ‘much like language, scientific knowledge is a living conversation in which new studies and new inquiries allow what we know to grow and change over time’ (p. 4).

NOTES

1. Renowned statistician John Tukey famously said that ‘an approximate answer to the right question is worth a great deal more than a precise answer to the wrong question’ (see https://en.wikiquote.org/wiki/John_Tukey). We might contrast ‘the right question’ with questions posed as a result of a database becoming available or because a new analytical technique can be employed to answer this ‘new’ (but not particularly relevant) question with the aim of publication.
2. This chapter, by design, does not analyze what we now know about PPP performance, but focuses on how we think we know these things and the delicate, sometimes tenuous, nature of this knowledge.
3. This phrase is inspired by the research of Kells (2012).
4. See Parsons (1995), who drew on the work of Guba and Lincoln (1987).
5. Hodge (2010) nominated six challenges: the evaluator’s role, defining the ‘evaluand’, accurately reviewing multiple individual studies of PPPs, multiple PPP objectives, multiple discourses and disciplines, and evaluative rigour for individual studies. This chapter also treats the notions of *evaluation* and *research*, both of which can assess causal linkages, as similar.
6. Whilst these four dimensions for research rigour appear here to be explicit and neat, they are often presented in different guises in our own research writing, and we connect them in different ways of our own making.
7. Indeed, lawyers continually aim to distinguish between what might appear to be similarly worded contracts in the *same* jurisdiction and argue that small changes to contracts can mean very different things in law.
8. Glass et al. (1981) cite classic work analysing the findings of five reviews of the efficacy of psychotherapy and drug therapy. These five reviews integrated the findings from 14 studies and covered largely the same body of literature. The reviews came to conflicting resolutions, with some concluding that the combination of both psychotherapy and drug therapy together were clearly superior to drug therapy alone, while others determined that no firm conclusions could be reached.

9. Jackson (1978) analysed a random sample of 36 integrative reviews from leading journals in education, psychology, and sociology. Hunter and Schmidt (1990) reported Jackson's analysis of these 36 review articles: only four reported major aspects of the search for relevant studies; only seven indicated whether or not the full set of located studies on the topic was analysed; just over half of the 36 reported the direction and magnitude of the findings of any of the primary studies; and only three cited the mean, range, or another summary of the magnitude of the primary study's findings.
10. Not all studies titled 'meta-analyses' are systematic reviews. The review of enterprise sales by Garaca (2017) is one such example; it simply presents 'dizzying lists' (as Hunter & Schmidt, 1990, p. 468, observed) of studies collected from undefined sources using an unknown method and attempting to qualitatively synthesize these.
11. It is probably more straightforward to summarize quantitatively the 'before-and-after' performance findings when entities are privatised in that they are one month public and the next month private. PPP projects, however, are usually compared against a theoretical counterfactual, the performance calculations for which are complex and almost intractable.
12. These four matters constitute Parts 5, 2, 7, and 8, respectively, of the Patten and Newhart (2018) research methods text.
13. The interesting work of Warsen et al. (2020) is instructive here. They analysed the PPP assumptions of the Netherlands, Canada, and Denmark using Q-methodology. As Klijn (2022) noted, professionals, particularly those from Canada and the Netherlands, had quite different ideas about how to govern PPPs. Canadian professionals tended to favour a New Public Management (NPM) orientation dominated by performance criteria and monitoring (including rewards and punishment), whereas those in the Netherlands emphasized a governance approach focusing on collaboration and adapting the contract to the situation. Given this, PPP performance evaluations in these two countries may well preference different dimensions of performance and different measurement proxies for priority.
14. We should also note the multiple theoretical performance domains nominated by Jeffares et al. (2013), Huxman and Hubbert (2009), and Skelcher (2010).
15. This matter of PPP definition is not merely an academic issue of semantics and continues to plague researchers. Hodge and Greve (2019) showed some of the major differences among definitions of PPPs from a range of economists and highlighted that the 'Design and Construct' (or 'Design–Bid–Build') specifications were usually taken as 'traditional' approaches to infrastructure delivery. Jurisdictions such as the United States, however, define these mechanisms as PPPs. This group may even be the majority (54 per cent) of projects claimed to be PPPs in the US, according to Martin (2017, 2018). If this is so, the failure of researchers, such as Levitt et al. (2019), to define PPPs in their work (see Verweij, 2020) is curious.
16. Fortunately for the authors, the meta-analytic findings on PPP VfM of Petersen (2019) pointed to 'mixed performance of PPP compared to conventional procurement' and were 'broadly in line' with our international assessments over the years (p. 239).
17. One chapter author was fond of saying during conference discussions on the matter of 'unit costs' that he sent his children through independent (private) schools and that, as a parent, he paid his bills 'on-time' and 'on-budget'. He

pointed out, though, that his education cost per child was far higher through the private education system than through the public education system.

18. Meduri and Annamalai (2013) analysed 521 road projects in India. Their raw data description suggested that PPP projects were 11 per cent less expensive per lane-kilometer than traditionally procured projects. It also documented PPP projects as, on average, almost twice as long as public road projects. Interestingly, their analysis then 'demonstrated the strong effects of economies of scale in the road sector' and they further concluded that Indian 'private sector road projects derive substantial benefits from economies of scale', which more than offset the increase in costs resulting from the private sector bearing the risks of the project (p.41).
19. Interestingly, the financial analysis of Leviakangas (2007) concluded that 'the State's and project investor's interests do not coincide easily' and that 'private finance does not seem to be economical for the state' (p.216).
20. Hellowell and Pollock (2010, p.S26) note about Colman's additional criticism that these analyses were often based on 'pseudo-scientific mumbo-jumbo'.
21. See https://www.dtf.vic.gov.au/partnerships-victoria-ppp-projects/eastlink (accessed 2 October 2021).
22. This story can of course be spun to suit one's own political persuasions. The opposing story might go something like this: governments did little for four decades and did not turn one sod of earth—until a privately financed PPP initiative delivered the road with speed and efficiency, enabling early benefits to be realised by all users.
23. On the service quality criterion, we could fill a book with commentary. Hundreds of potential quality proxies for public sector services have been discussed going back decades: Waller et al. (1976), Hatry et al. (1977), and Jowett and Rothwell (1988). We may also ask what quality perceptions people hold, with suitable caution.
24. Note that if the idea of 'grounded theory' is adopted, then the empirical data discovery phase is the searchlight; ideas and concepts emerge from this, and hypotheses and theory may follow. Under this approach, theoretical issues emerge from the data rather than precede it. Thus, the very idea of theory guiding the collection of data is contested here.
25. We might also view quantitative and qualitative approaches as complimentary, with their usefulness somewhat dependent on the research questions being asked.
26. Other criticisms include Tanner (2014), who concluded that 'QCA adds little value to current methods of policy scholarship, and its contribution in fact falls far short, compared with present-day standard practices' because it does not 'deliver useful, credible insights for the policy research community' (pp.287–90).
27. Interestingly, one reviewer of the present chapter pointed out that 'the jury is still out on whether QCA is more qualitative or quantitative'. To their mind, QCA is both: 'It is quantitative in the sense that is uses numerical data or that it quantifies qualitative data; and it is qualitative in the sense that it assumes a causes-of-effects approach'. Furthermore, they referred to Verweij and Trell (2019), who noted that QCA focuses on identifying the 'causes of effects' and that this contrasts the usual variable-oriented research strategies that typically focus on 'identifying the effects of causes'.

REFERENCES

Allen Consulting. (2007). *Performance of PPPs and traditional procurement in Australia*. Infrastructure Partnerships Australia.

Bachellir, P. (2017). A meta-analysis of the impact of privatization on firm performance. *Management Decision*, *55*(1), 178–202.

Baumgartner, M., & Thiem, A. (2020). Often trusted but never (properly) tested: Evaluating qualitative comparative analysis. *Sociological Methods & Research*, *49*(2), 279–311.

Bel, G., Fageda, X., & Warner, M. E. (2010). Is private production of public services cheaper than public production? A meta-regression analysis of solid waste and water services. *Journal of Policy Analysis and Management*, *29*(3), 553–77.

Bingham, R. D., & Felbinger, C. L. (2002). *Evaluation in practice: A methodological approach*. Chatham House.

Blanc-Brude, F., Goldsmith, H., & Välilä, T. (2006). *Ex ante construction costs in the European road sector: A comparison of public-private partnerships and traditional public procurement*. European Investment Bank.

Bovaird, T. (2010). A brief intellectual history of the public-private partnership movement. In G. A. Hodge, C. Greve, & A. E. Boardman (Eds.), *International handbook on public-private partnerships* (pp. 43–67). Edward Elgar.

Braumoeller, B. F. (2015). Guarding against false positives in qualitative comparative analysis. *Political Analysis*, *23*, 471–87.

Braumoeller, B. F. (2017). Aggregation bias and the analysis of necessary and sufficient conditions in fsQCA. *Sociological Methods & Research*, *46*(2), 242–51.

Busetto, L., Wick, W., & Gumbinger, C. (2020). How to use and assess qualitative research methods. *Neurological Research and Practice*, *2*(14), 1–10.

Casady, C. B. (2021). Examining the institutional drivers of public-private partnership (PPP) market performance: A fuzzy set qualitative comparative analysis (fsQCA). *Public Management Review*, *23*(7), 981–1005.

Casady, C. B., Eriksson, K., Levitt, R. E., & Scott, W. R. (2020). (Re)defining public-private partnerships (PPPs) in the new public governance (NPG) paradigm: An institutional maturity perspective. *Public Management Review*, *22*(2), 161–83.

Casady, C. B., & Geddes, R. R. (2019). Private participation in US infrastructure: The role of regional PPP units. In R. E. Levitt, W. R. Scott, & M. J. Garvin (Eds.), *Public-private partnerships for infrastructure development: Finance, stakeholder alignment, governance* (pp. 224–45). Edward Elgar.

Dictionary.com. (2022). *Value*. https://www.dictionary.com/browse/value (retrieved 14 July 2022).

Cook, T. D., Cooper, H., Cordray, D. S., Hartmann, H., Hedges, L. V., Light, R. J., Louis, T. A., & Mosteller, F. (1992). *Meta-analysis for explanation: A case book*. The Russell Sage Foundation.

Cooper, B., & Glaesser, J. (2011). Paradoxes and pitfalls in using fuzzy set QCA: Illustrations from a critical review of a study of educational inequality. *Sociological Research Online*, *16*(3) 106–119.

Dahler-Larson, P. (2005). Evaluation and public management. In E. Ferlie, L. E. Lynn, & C. Pollitt (Eds.), *The Oxford handbook of public management* (pp. 615–39). Oxford University Press.

Duffield, C. F. (2008). *Report on the performance of PPP projects in Australia when compared with a representative sample of traditionally procured infrastructure projects*. University of Melbourne.

Dwyer, L., Gill, A., & Seetaram, N. (2012). *Handbook of research methods in tourism: Quantitative and qualitative approaches*. Edward Elgar.

Garaca, I. (2017). *Effects of privatization on SOE performance – A meta-analysis* [Paper presentation]. International OFEL Conference on Governance, Management and Entrepreneurship, Zagreb, Croatia.

Gassner, K., Popov, A., & Pushak, N. (2009). *Does private sector participation improve performance in electricity and water distribution?* World Bank.

Gerrits, L. M., & Verweij, S. (2018). *The evaluation of complex infrastructure projects: A guide to qualitative comparative analysis*. Edward Elgar.

Glass, G. V. (1976). Integrating findings: The meta-analysis of research. *Educational Researcher*, *5*(10), 3–8.

Glass, G. V., McGaw, B., & Smith, M. L. (1981). *Meta-analysis in social research*. SAGE.

Guba, E. G., & Lincoln, Y. S. (1987). The countenances of fourth-generation evaluation: Description, judgement, and negotiation. In D. J. Palumbo (Ed.), *The politics of program evaluation* (p. 127). SAGE.

Hatry, H. P., Blair, L. H., Fisk, D. M., Greiner, J. M., Hall, J. R., & Schaenman, P. S. (1977). *How effective are your community services? Procedures for monitoring the effectiveness of municipal services*. The Urban Institute and the International City Management Association.

Hellowell, M., & Pollock, A. M. (2010). Do PPPs in social infrastructure enhance the public interest? Evidence from England's national health service. *Australian Journal of Public Administration*, *69*(1), S23–S34.

Hodge, G. A. (2000). *Privatisation: An international review of performance*. Westview Press.

Hodge, G. A. (2010). Reviewing public-private partnerships: Some thoughts on evaluation. In G. A. Hodge, C. Greve, & A. E. Boardman (Eds.), *International handbook on public-private partnerships* (pp. 81–112). Edward Elgar.

Hodge, G. A., & Greve, C. (2013). Introduction: Public-private partnership in turbulent times. In G. A. Hodge & C. Greve (Eds.), *Rethinking public-private partnerships: Strategies for turbulent times* (pp. 1–32). Routledge.

Hodge, G. A., & Greve, C. (2017). On public-private partnership performance: A contemporary review. *Public Works Management & Policy*, *22*(1), 55–78.

Hodge, G. A., &, Greve, C. (2019). *The logic of public-private partnerships: The enduring interdependency of politics and markets*. Edward Elgar.

Hodge, G. A., & Greve, C. (2021). What can public administration scholars learn from the economics controversies in public-private partnerships? *Asia Pacific Journal of Public Administration*, *43*(4), 219–35.

Hug, S. (2013). Qualitative comparative analysis: How inductive use and measurement error lead to problematic inference. *Political Analysis*, *21*(2), 252–65.

Hunter, J. E., & Schmidt, F. L. (1990). *Methods of meta-analysis: Correcting error and bias in research findings*. SAGE.

Huxman, C., & Hubbert, P. (2009). Hit or myth? Stories of collaborative success. In J. O'Flynn & J. Wanna (Eds.), *Collaborative governance* (pp. 45–50). Australian National University Press.

Jackson, G. B. (1978). *Methods for reviewing and integrating research in the social sciences*. George Washington University.

Jeffares, S., Sullivan, H., & Bovaird, T. (2013). Beyond the contract: The challenge of evaluating the performance(s) of public-private partnerships. In G. A. Hodge & C. Greve (Eds.), *Rethinking public-private partnerships: Strategies for turbulent times* (pp. 166–87). Routledge.

Jowett, P., & Rothwell, M. (1988). *Performance indicators in the public sector*. Macmillan Press.

Kells, S. (2012). *Performance auditing in the public sector: Crowded, contested and at a crossroads*. Monash University.

Kirkup, L. (1994). *Experimental methods: An introduction to the analysis and presentation of data*. John Wiley & Sons.

Klijn, E. H. (2022). Theories of public-private partnerships. In G. A. Hodge & C. Greve (Eds.), *Research agenda for public-private partnerships and the governance of infrastructure*. Edward Elgar.

Kort, M., Verweij, S., & Klijn, E. H. (2016). In search for effective public-private partnerships: An assessment of the impact of organizational form and managerial strategies in urban regeneration partnerships using fsQCA. *Environment and Planning C: Government and Policy*, *34*(5), 777–94.

Krogslund, C., Choi, D. D., & Poertner, M. (2015). Fuzzy sets on shaky ground: Parameter sensitivity and confirmation bias in fsQCA. *Political Analysis*, *23*(1), 21–41.

Leviakangas, P. (2007). *Private finance of transport infrastructure projects: Value and risk analysis of a Finnish shadow toll road project*. University of Oulu.

Levitt, R. E., Scott, W. R., & Garvin, M. J. (2019). *Public-private partnerships for infrastructure development: Finance, stakeholder alignment, governance*. Edward Elgar.

Martin, L. L. (2017). *Evaluating the performance of public-private partnerships (PPPs) in the United States: Issues of definition & classification* [Paper presentation]. 6th Conference of the International Public-Private Partnerships Scholars Network, Limerick, Ireland.

Martin, L. L. (2018). *Public-private partnerships (P3s): What local government managers need to know*. International City/County Management Association.

Meduri, S. S., & Annamalai, T. R. (2013). Unit costs of public and PPP road projects: Evidence from India. *Journal of Construction Engineering and Management*, *139*(1), 35–43.

Merriam-Webster. (2022). *Evaluate*. Merriam-Webster.com. https://www.merriam-webster.com/dictionary/evaluate (retrieved 14 July 2022).

Nature Climate Change. (2021). Powers of qualitative research. *Nature Climate Change*, *11*, 717.

Parsons, W. (1995). *Public policy: An introduction to the theory and practice of policy analysis*. Edward Elgar.

Patten, M. L., & Newhart, M. (2018). *Understanding research methods: An overview of the essentials*. Routledge.

Petersen, O. H. (2019). Evaluating the costs, quality, and value for money of infrastructure public-private partnerships: A systematic literature review. *Annals of Public and Cooperative Economics*, *90*(2), 227–44.

Petersen, O. H., Hjelmar, U., & Vrangbæk, K. (2018). Is contracting out of public services still the great panacea? A systematic review of studies on economic and quality effects from 2000 to 2014. *Social Policy & Administration*, *52*(1), 130–57.

Ragin, C. C. (2000). *Fuzzy set social science*. University of Chicago Press.

Raisbeck, P., Duffield, C. F., & Xu, M. (2010). Comparative performance of PPPs and traditional procurement in Australia. *Construction Management and Economics*, *28*(4), 345–59.

Skaaning, S. E. (2011). Assessing the robustness of crisp-set and fuzzy-set QCA results. *Sociological Methods & Research*, *40*(2), 391–408.

Skelcher, C. (2010). Governing partnerships. In G. A. Hodge, C. Greve, & A. E. Boardman (Eds.), *International handbook on public-private partnerships* (pp. 292–304). Edward Elgar.

Stufflebeam, D. L., & Shinkfield, A. J. (2007). *Evaluation theory, models, and applications*. John Wiley & Sons.

Tanner, S. (2014). QCA is of questionable value for policy research. *Policy and Society*, *33*(3), 287–98.

Thiem, A., & Baumgarter, M. (2016). Back to square one: A reply to Munck, Paine, and Schneider. *Comparative Political Studies*, *49*(6), 801–806.

Thiem, A., Baumgartner, M., & Bol, D. (2016). Still lost in translation! A correction of three misunderstandings between configurational comparativists and regressional analysts. *Comparative Political Studies*, *49*(6), 742–74.

Thomann, E., & Maggetti, M. (2020). Designing research with qualitative comparative analysis (QCA): Approaches, challenges, and tools. *Sociological Methods & Research*, *49*(2), 356–86.

Verweij, S. (2015). Producing satisfactory outcomes in the implementation phase of PPP infrastructure projects: A fuzzy set qualitative comparative analysis of 27 road constructions in the Netherlands. *International Journal of Project Management*, *33*(8), 1877–87.

Verweij, S. (2020). Public-private partnerships for infrastructure development: Finance, stakeholder alignment, governance. *Public Works Management & Policy*, *25*(3), 333–6.

Verweij, S., & Trell, E. M. (2019). Qualitative comparative analysis (QCA) in spatial planning research and related disciplines: A systematic literature review of applications. *Journal of Planning Literature*, *34*(3), 300–317.

Verweij, S., & Van Meerkerk, I. F. (2020). Do public-private partnerships perform better? A comparative analysis of costs for additional work and reasons for contract changes in Dutch transport infrastructure projects. *Transport Policy*, *99*, 430–8.

Vining, A. R., & Boardman, A. E. (2008). Public-private partnerships: Eight rules for governments. *Public Works Management & Policy*, *13*(2), 149–61.

Waller, J. D., Kemp, D. M., Scanlon, J. W., Tolson, F., & Wholey, J. S. (1976). *Monitoring for government agencies*. The Urban Institute.

Warsen, R. (2022). The use of research methods in public-private partnership research. In G. A. Hodge & C. Greve (Eds.), *Research agenda for public-private partnerships and the governance of infrastructure*. Edward Elgar.

Warsen, R., Greve, C., Klijn, E. H., Koppenjan, J. F. M., & Siemiatycki, M. (2020). How do professionals perceive the governance of public-private partnerships? Evidence from Canada, the Netherlands and Denmark. *Public Administration*, *98*(1), 124–39.

Warsen, R., Klijn, E. H., & Koppenjan, J. F. M. (2019). Mix and match: How contractual and relational conditions are combined in successful public-private partnerships. *Journal of Public Administration Research and Theory*, *29*(3), 375–93.

Weiss, C. H. (1998). *Evaluation: Methods for studying programs and policies*. Prentice Hall.

3. From the hypothetical to reality: an analysis of ex-ante and ex-post VfM in Irish PPP schools

Cian O'Shea, Dónal Palcic, and Eoin Reeves

INTRODUCTION

Since the early 1990s, many governments around the world have followed the lead of the UK and adopted Public-Private Partnerships (PPPs) as a mechanism for addressing several infrastructure-related challenges. Advocates propose that PPPs in the form of long-term infrastructure contracts offer a more efficient model for delivering public infrastructure and services compared to traditional public procurement. This is attributable to features of PPPs, such as the private sector's long-term life-cycle approach and the potential for better sharing of project risks. Crucially, as PPPs are often privately financed, governments are attracted by the possibility of delivering infrastructure without adding to public deficits and debt.

PPPs have attracted significant academic interest, with studies from different disciplines examining many of the arguments for and against the PPP approach. Whereas economic theory has provided some clear conceptual insights into the choice between a PPP and traditional procurement, as outlined in Chapter 1 of this book, there is a lack of clarity regarding how PPP projects have actually performed compared to traditionally procured counterparts. Välilä (2020) attributes this paucity of comparative performance studies to several factors. For example, there is a lack of life-cycle data on PPP projects in the public domain, with information on PPPs often deemed commercially sensitive and not easily accessible. Also, as infrastructure projects are frequently stand-alone and unique, there are obstacles to finding comparable samples of PPP and Traditionally Procured (TP) projects. Finding comparable data is also hindered by differences in reporting requirements for traditional and PPP projects.

This chapter addresses this gap in the literature by comparing the performance of PPPs and TPs in the Irish schools sector. Our analysis applies ex-ante data used in the Value for Money (VfM) assessments that provided much of the original justification for adopting PPPs. In addition, the fact that our sample PPP and TP schools were procured 20 years ago permits an analysis of ex-post performance over an extended period, which makes an original contribution to the literature on PPP performance. The chapter commences with a short description of PPP procurement in Ireland, followed by a review of the relevant literature on performance. We then describe our sample schools and data collection methods before presenting the results of our comparative analysis. The chapter concludes with a summary and discussion of our findings.

BACKGROUND: PUBLIC-PRIVATE PARTNERSHIPS IN IRELAND

PPPs have been an important tool of public investment policy in Ireland since the announcement of a number of pilot projects in 1999. Initially, the use of PPPs was justified by the need to address Ireland's severe deficit of public infrastructure during the period of rapid economic growth that commenced in the early 1990s. Prior to the global and domestic economic crisis that began in 2008, PPPs were used extensively to procure infrastructure, such as motorways, schools, courthouses, and water treatment facilities. By the late 2000s, Ireland was one of the small but growing number of countries in which PPPs accounted for a significant percentage (5 percent–15 percent) of overall public investment (Burger & Hawkesworth, 2011).

The pace of PPP investment slowed considerably when the Irish economy entered a recession during the global financial crisis, and several planned projects were either postponed or abandoned. Nevertheless, a second phase of PPP investment commenced in July 2012, when the government launched an economic stimulus plan that relied mainly on a programme of non-Exchequer financed PPPs to deliver investment in public infrastructure. The overall extent of PPP investment to date in Ireland is summarised in Table 3.1, which shows that 31 privately financed PPP projects with a combined capital value of over €5.4 billion have been procured to date. DBFM (Design–Build–Finance–Maintain) and DBFOM (Design–Build–Finance–Operate–Maintain) contracts have been the dominant forms of PPPs procured in Ireland, with the exception of nine concession-type contracts employed in the transport and waste management sectors. There are also new PPP projects in the pipeline, which are planned to deliver infrastructure in sectors including social housing and nursing homes.

Several studies have examined different aspects of PPP usage in Ireland. For example, Reeves (2003, 2015) has analysed the evolution of overall PPP policy at the national level. Sector-specific studies have explored the use of PPPs for the procurement of schools (O'Shea et al., 2019), water and waste-

Table 3.1 Infrastructure PPPs in Ireland as of December 2020

Sector	No. of projects	Project classification	Capital value (€, in millions)	Projected total cost of payments (€, in millions)
Housing	2	DBFM	248.0	629.0
Health	1	DBFM	140.0	435.9
Leisure	1	DBFOM	189.8	764.7
Justice	2	DBFOM	292.2	991.7
Education	9	DBFM	778.8	2722.9
Transport	15	DBFOM and concession	3456.7	5413.5
Waste management	1	Concession	346.0	
Total	31		5451.5	10957.7

Notes: DBFM = Design–Build–Finance–Maintain; DBFOM = Design–Build–Finance–Operate–Maintain.
Source: Department of Public Expenditure and Reform (2021).

water facilities (Reeves, 2011), waste management (O'Nolan & Reeves, 2018), motorways (Palcic et al., 2018), and housing (Bisset, 2009; Hearne, 2012). To date, most of the Irish empirical research has assessed different aspects of PPP performance. For example, the question of VfM in the schools sector has been analysed in a number of studies (Hurst & Reeves, 2004; Reeves & Ryan, 2007). Burke and Demirag (2015) and Palcic et al. (2018) examined risk transfer and financial aspects on a number of motorway PPPs. The majority of these studies covered the ex-ante PPP procurement period and the early stages of the project life-cycle after the operational stage of contracts had commenced. There are no studies that we are aware of examining the longer-term performance of PPP contracts in Ireland. This chapter addresses this gap and builds upon our previous comparative research (O'Shea et al., 2019). In our earlier study, we found that construction was faster under PPPs compared with traditional procurement; however, the combined procurement and delivery times for both procurement methods were similar. We also found there was little evidence that the widely recognised drivers of VfM (risk transfer and competition for contracts) were features of PPP procurement in this case. In addition, the need for further examination as such projects mature over their life-cycle was identified.

VALUE FOR MONEY AND THE PERFORMANCE OF PUBLIC-PRIVATE PARTNERSHIPS

In Europe, the use of PPPs is primarily justified in terms of an objective to achieve superior VfM relative to traditional infrastructure procurement

(European PPP Expertise Centre, 2015). Ireland largely follows the definition of VfM adopted in the UK, which HM Treasury (2006) defined as:

> The optimum combination of whole-of-life costs and quality (or fitness for purpose) of the good or service to meet the user's requirement. The term whole-of-life is used to refer to the life-cycle of the good or service. VfM is not the choice of goods and service based on the lowest cost bid. (p. 7)

In broad conceptual terms, VfM corresponds with economic concepts of efficiency. A substantial economic literature proposes PPPs as a more efficient alternative to various forms of TPs. This literature highlights several key drivers of economic efficiency under PPPs, particularly in relation to bundling and risk transfer. DBFM-style PPPs, such as those adopted in Ireland, combine multiple contractual elements into a single long-term contract, creating greater scope for efficiency gains when compared to TP (usually Design and Construct [D&C]) approaches (De Bettignies & Ross, 2010; Hart, 2003; Martimort & Pouyet, 2008; Bennett & Iossa, 2006). Moreover, the inclusion of private finance can help ensure superior risk management and due diligence, as equity and debt providers risk losing their investments (Culp, 2011; Demirag et al., 2011). PPPs can also transfer significantly more responsibility and risk to the private sector, which creates incentives that do not normally apply under traditional procurement.

In theory, transferring risks can create superior economic incentives to motivate the contractor to complete the project on time, on budget, and to the required quality standard (Grimsey & Lewis, 2004). The potential for superior risk transfer and management has been central to the proposed performance advantage of PPPs (Froud, 2003). Of course, such risk transfer comes at a premium, and there will be a point where transferring further risk may cease to represent VfM (Hearne, 2012). Indeed, governments may be unwilling to truly transfer the risk of a closed public service and may be inclined to intervene (Froud, 2003). For risk transfer to be considered effective, it must be actively monitored and enforced (Connolly et al., 2009), which can be difficult and expensive for the public sector (Lonsdale, 2005; Reeves, 2008).

The bundling of elements within a long-term contract may also incentivise greater innovation at the design, construction, and operational phases. By combining D&C with the operational stages, the private sector can be incentivised to produce more efficient designs with greater scope for innovation to meet required operational service levels (Engel et al., 2014; Yescombe, 2007). This gives the contractor greater freedom to innovate and compete on reducing life-cycle costs (Roumboutsos & Saussier, 2014). However, empirical evidence of superior innovation under PPPs is mixed given the challenges in measuring and demonstrating innovation, with both case-study and quantitative approaches in the literature failing to produce a clear consensus (Eaton et al., 2006; Leiringer, 2006; Van den Hurk, 2016).

The empirical literature on the performance of PPP focuses overwhelmingly on VfM; however, the empirical evidence to date fails to provide definitive conclusions on the relative performance of PPPs (Hodge & Greve, 2017). Moreover, the extant empirical literature is dominated by ex-ante analyses that focus on whether PPPs lead to better performance in terms of time and cost efficiency (see Chapter 1 for more details). This focus on the ex-ante and construction stages means little attention has been given to the most significant period of a PPP project's life-cycle, namely, the operational phase (Verweij & Van Meerkerk, 2021). Therefore, this chapter addresses this gap in the PPP literature by assessing the long-term VfM performance of PPP versus TP procurement of schools in Ireland.

DATA AND METHODS

We adopt a broad definition of VfM as the metric of performance for our study. In this regard, VfM is considered in terms of financial cost and the quality of asset-based services over an extended 20-year period. We utilise information gathered from official ex-ante VfM analyses conducted for the first schools PPP bundle procured in Ireland. This ex-ante analysis provides a reference point for assessing performance over the project life-cycle to date. A detailed overview of the PPP and TP schools included in our comparative analysis is provided in Table 3.2, followed by a description of our data collection methods and the performance metrics we utilise.

Our case study includes the first PPP project signed in Ireland in 2001, which consisted of a pilot bundle of five schools procured using a DBFM model. The construction of the schools commenced in 2001 and was completed in 2002, with the Operate and Maintain (O&M) phase of the 25-year contract due to end in 2027. The successful bidder for the pilot schools PPP project was UK-based Jarvis Projects Ltd., which subsequently encountered financial difficulties, resulting in the contract being taken over by a German firm, Hochtief AG, in 2005. To conduct our comparative analysis, an appropriate group of TP schools was required. Large-scale new-builds of second-level schools in Ireland are rare; therefore, we chose five TP schools of similar size to the pilot schools that were constructed around the same time. Another criterion for the choice of TP schools was the fact that four of these schools were also selected as comparators in a government-sponsored midterm review of the pilot PPP schools. The D&C of these schools were all procured separately by the DOE, with the responsibility for maintenance transferred to school management once completed.

Table 3.2 *Sample of Public-Private Partnership (PPP) and Traditionally Procured (TP) schools*

School name and location	Procurement method	Capacity (no. of students)	Gross floor area (m^2)	Year completed
Ballincollig CS, Co. Cork	PPP (DBFM)	1000	8277	2002
Maria Immaculata CC, Co. Cork	PPP (DBFM)	700	6208	2002
St. Caimin's CS, Co. Clare	PPP (DBFM)	600	6531	2002
St Attracta's CS, Co. Sligo	PPP (DBFM)	675	7046	2002
Largy College, Co. Monaghan	PPP (DBFM)	500	5451	2002
St. Mary's Secondary School, Co. Cork	TP (D&C)	700	4397	2003
Hazelwood College, Co. Limerick	TP (D&C)	600	3220	2002
Colaiste Chraobh Abhainn, Co. Wicklow	TP (D&C)	750	5250	2004
Blackwater CS, Co. Waterford	TP (D&C)	775	4930	2002
Castletroy College, Co. Limerick	TP (D&C)	1200		2001

Notes: (1) The gross floor area for Castletroy College was unavailable; (2) DBFM = Design–Build–Finance–Maintain; (3) D&C = Design and Construct.
Source: Department of Education (DOE; 2021).

Both stages of our analysis use secondary data sourced from a mix of publicly available reports and documents from the Irish Comptroller and Auditor General (C&AG), the National Development Finance Agency (NDFA), the DOE, the Department of Public Expenditure and Reform, Parliamentary Budget Office, and the Oireachtas (Irish Parliament). In Ireland, commercial sensitivity concerns surrounding contracts and fears that such information could be exploited by future bidders have limited the project information available in the public domain. As the publicly available information was insufficient to conduct our analysis, we acquired previously unavailable secondary data through Freedom of Information (FOI) requests. In addition, to further enhance the validity of our case-study approach, we identified 14 key project stakeholders with whom we performed semi-structured interviews to triangulate with our secondary data.

The first stage of our analysis examined how VfM was estimated and compared at the ex-ante stage, focusing on capital and operational costs. We then compared this ex-ante data with the available ex-post data on capital costs and funding for operations and maintenance over the 20-year timeframe of our analysis. Commercial sensitivity concerns resulted in heavily redacted project documentation, which was further compounded by a lack of record-keeping by government departments. As such, it was necessary to work through the constraints on available information and perform an extensive documentary analysis to build a clear picture of how PPP was judged to have the potential to deliver VfM over its life-cycle.

In the second stage of our analysis, which examines ex-post performance, we conducted semi-structured interviews with 14 key stakeholders, including school principals (PPP and TP), Special Purpose Vehicle (SPV) managers, facilities management (FM) staff, and public sector staff. Interviews were conducted between September 2020 and May 2021 and lasted between 45 and 120 minutes. Each interview was adapted slightly to the expertise and knowledge of the respondents; for example, more technical questions could be directed at facilities managers, while questions regarding quality and contractual governance could be directed at school principals and public sector staff. By employing this flexible approach, we ensured respondents could speak freely and elaborate on their personal experiences (Robson, 2007). Each interview asked respondents to describe their experiences with the projects, using a questionnaire that focused on operational performance, quality, risk transfer, and contractual governance, with themes identified from the literature. Once completed, the interview data were transcribed and thematically analysed across respondents, along with our secondary data, using NVivo 12.

COMPARATIVE ANALYSIS OF PPP AND TP PERFORMANCE

Our comparative analysis covers three main areas: (1) we compare the official ex-ante estimates of the capital costs for the PPP bid to the Public Sector Benchmark (PSB; a proxy for traditional procurement) to understand how the project was expected to deliver VfM, and we then compare these to the actual costs incurred ex-post; (2) we conduct the same comparative analysis for the ex-ante estimates for operational costs under PPP versus the PSB and compare these to actual operational costs in PPP schools and our comparator sample of TP schools; and (3) we compare the quality of buildings, services, and governance in the post-construction phase for PPP schools versus our comparator TP schools.

Before presenting our analysis, it is important to provide some background information on the ownership and governance of schools in Ireland. Educational PPPs represent the largest sector of social infrastructure PPPs in Ireland, with nine projects worth a combined capital value of €778.8 million procured in the sector since the first pilot schools project in 2001 (see Table 3.1). The majority of educational PPP projects have comprised schools bundles, which is the focus of the analysis provided in this chapter. Primary- and secondary-level educational institutions in Ireland are primarily funded by the state and privately managed. The DOE is responsible for setting educational policy, and educational services are provided on behalf of the state using a school patronage system. Patrons are comprised of religious denominations, non-profit companies, voluntary organisations, or state-run local Educational Training Boards (ETBs). In effect, the state devolves the responsibility of managing and operating schools to the patrons and the respective boards of management of individual schools. Alongside this complex system of governance exists a variety of funding models. Different models apply to different school types, and schools are ultimately responsible for their own management, operation, and procurement of services.

PPPs must work within this system of devolved patronage. In Ireland, multiple schools have been bundled to create PPP projects, which differ from the traditional approach of single one-off school procurements. This means PPP projects involve transferring several functions that are typically the responsibility of schools to the DOE and to the NDFA, which is the state's PPP procurement and contract management agency. PPP contracts for schools in Ireland are designed in the context of patrons and boards of management retaining their responsibility for teaching activities, while PPP companies are responsible for the maintenance of school facilities during the contractual period.

We recognise that the ex-ante nature of the VfM appraisals and the methodological issues highlighted in Chapter 1 mean that this approach provides limited insights into the question of actual, materialised performance. Nevertheless, the VfM appraisal provides a valuable starting point for our analysis of PPP performance by serving as a benchmark for the subsequent examination of ex-post performance. In relation to the VfM analysis conducted for the pilot schools project, there were significant flaws in the process that have previously been highlighted by the C&AG (2004) and Reeves and Ryan (2007). In short, the VfM analysis conducted prior to contract close estimated that the procurement of the schools via PPP would be 6 percent cheaper than conventional procurement. However, once errors in relation to the overestimation of residual values and the timing and discounting of payments were corrected, the PPP approach was found to be approximately 13 percent–19 percent more expensive than conventional procurement (C&AG, 2004). Of course, it must be noted that the PSB is hypothetical and represents a hypothetical scenario for traditional procurement projects, which often experience significant cost and time overruns themselves (Flyvbjerg et al., 2003).

A much-delayed government-commissioned midterm review of the pilot schools project was published in July 2021. Part of the review's remit was to test whether VfM was being achieved given that the schools have been operational for a sufficiently long period of time (the 25-year operational period will expire in 2027). However, the midterm review did not compare the actual costs incurred in the ex-post period to the ex-ante PSB estimates. Instead, the review compared the ex-ante PPP costs included in the financial model at contract close in 2001 to the costs of four comparator schools procured by conventional means (the same four schools are included in the present analysis). Moreover, the capital costs under the PPP and conventional approach were also presented in a misleading way in the review, with the capital costs of PPP schools spread out over the 25-year contract period and presented in Net Present Value (NPV) terms, whereas capital costs for the TP schools were presented in NPV terms but spread out over the construction period only. Despite the data limitations that we face, in the next section, we compare ex-ante and ex-post capital and operational costs for the pilot PPP schools versus the PSB and a comparator sample of TP schools and, in doing so, address some of the shortcomings of the financial analysis included in the official midterm review of the pilot PPP schools bundle.

Comparing Ex-Ante and Ex-Post Capital and Construction Costs

Table 3.3 presents a comparison of the capital costs estimated for the PSB and the PPP bid, sourced from a post-project review completed in November 2002 that corrected for some of the errors made in the original VfM analysis produced in September 2001. It shows that capital costs under the PPP model were 21 percent higher than those estimated for the PSB, with much of this difference attributable to higher construction-related costs. Higher capital costs under PPP are in line with expectations where a greater focus on reducing future life-cycle and O&M costs over a 25-year contract period can lead to higher initial D&C costs. Acquiring information on the actual cost of construction ex-post is highly problematic since detailed cost figures are not available for PPP projects due to commercial sensitivity concerns. From the limited information available in the public domain, the total capital cost for the five schools recorded in the PPP company accounts is €84.5 million, which is very close to the €85.8 million cost estimate included in the post-project review of VfM from November 2002.

A separate report sourced under FOI that was published in December 2002 (Gardiner & Theobald, 2002) compared the construction, capital, and life-cycle costs for one of the PPP schools (Ballincollig) versus a school procured by conventional means (Kilcoole), which is one of the TP schools included in our analysis. Table 3.4 provides a breakdown of the capital costs incurred for both schools included in this report and shows that total capital costs for the PPP school were 24 percent higher than the TP school, which is very much in line with the ex-ante estimates included in the VfM appraisal. The midterm review of the pilot PPP schools bundle, published in July 2021, also provided information on the actual construction costs for four of the five TP schools included in our case study. The report found that the average construction cost per m^2 for the four TP schools was €1133.1 on an NPV basis. Given that the TP schools

Table 3.3 *Comparison of ex-ante total capital costs for PSBs and PPPs (2002)*

Capital costs	PSB (€ per m²)	PPP (€ per m²)	Percentage difference (PPP vs. PSB)
Construction costs	€48 840 006	€60 661 368	+24%
	(€1 413)	(€1 755)	
Fixtures and equipment	€9 326 315	€7 130 796	−24%
	(€270)	(€206)	
Professional fees, inc. VAT	€6 984 651	€4 686 599	−33%
	(€202)	(€136)	
Construction inflation buyout	€5 816 632	N/A	N/A
	(€168)	N/A	
ICT costs	N/A	€4 042 827	N/A
		(€117)	
Developer's margin	N/A	€3 018 838	N/A
		(€87)	
Legal and financing fees	N/A	€6 304 738	N/A
		(€182)	
Total	€70 967 604	€85 845 168	+21%
	(€2 053)	(€2 484)	

Note: ICT = Information and Communications Technology.
Source: Farrell Grant Sparks (2001, 2002) VfM Reports for DOE, September 2001 and November 2002.

Table 3.4 *Comparison of ex-post capital costs (€ per m²)*

Cost	TP	PPP	Percentage difference (PPP vs. TP)
Basic building costs	952.48	1153.56	21%
External works	118.22	198.21	68%
Abnormal costs	39.63	59.98	51%
Furniture and fittings	67.55	23.35	−65%
Total works cost	1177.88	1435.1	22%
Fixed price buyouts	66.79	101.67	52%
Professional fees	157.84	208.62	32%
Total capital costs	1402.51	1745.39	24%

Notes: (1) The report compares the capital costs of constructing Ballincollig Community School (PPP) and Colaiste Chraobh Abhainn Kilcoole (TP). To facilitate the comparison, site-specific abnormal costs (relating to ground conditions, planning contingent works, etc.) and facilities management-related capital costs were omitted. (2) TP = Traditional Procurement.
Source: Gardiner & Theobald Report for the DOE, December 2002.

were constructed over a one- to two-year period, this NPV figure is likely to be very close to the actual construction cost figure in nominal terms and is in line with the €1177.88 construction cost per m^2 for the TP school shown in Table 3.4. Overall, it is clear that construction and capital costs incurred on the PPP schools were significantly higher on an ex-ante basis when compared to the PSB estimate, and also on an ex-post basis when compared to the actual construction and capital costs incurred for a comparator sample of TP schools constructed during the same period.

Comparing Ex-Ante and Ex-Post O&M and Life-Cycle Costs

Table 3.5 presents a comparison of the ex-ante estimates for O&M costs for the PPP bid versus the PSB. Lower FM costs are the principal driver of the greater estimated operational cost efficiencies estimated for the PPP approach. Hard-FM building maintenance and life-cycle costs account for most of the substantial difference between the two models, while soft-FM costs, such as cleaning and grounds maintenance, account for the remaining difference. While estimated O&M costs are notably lower under PPP, the addition of PPP-specific costs significantly reduces this differential. Financing costs, such as the sinking fund deposit and the project-specific SPV overheads, erode the overall difference in estimated O&M costs between the two cases.

There appear to be several factors influencing the estimated difference at the operational phase. Hard-FM services, such as building maintenance, involve a significant level of risk transfer to the private sector under PPP, which remains the responsibility of the individual school under the PSB estimate. In the absence of specialised FM skills, TP schools may pay significantly more to maintain buildings over the 25-year period. Project bundling under PPP is also likely to result in significant economies of scale for the private contractor under PPP. The life-cycle replacement was priced into the estimated capital costs under the PPP model, with a fund drawn from over the contract's life. In the PSB case, life-cycle replacement costs remain the state's responsibility once the design and build of the school is complete and handed over. Soft-FM services, such as cleaning, do not require the same level of risk transfer, with estimated cost performance likely driven by economies of scale for the FM company over five schools rather than the single schools under the PSB.

Conducting a comparative analysis of the actual O&M costs of PPP versus TP schools is complicated by the fact that detailed annual data on the actual operational costs incurred for both PPP and TP schools are not publicly available. To work around this constraint and shed light on ex-post O&M costs under both procurement approaches, we compare the funding allocated to schools by the DOE for operational purposes as a proxy, as it represents the cost to the state of providing both types of schools. In the case of both TP

Table 3.5 Comparison of ex-ante annual operational cost estimates (2002)

Recurring cost	PSB	PPP bid	Percentage difference (PPP vs. PSB)
Building maintenance	€654 360	€283 195	−57%
Life-cycle replacement and FF&E	€452 928	€12 697	−97%
Utilities	€213 722	€123 668	−42%
Cleaning	€426 607	€430 341	1%
Grounds maintenance	€132 116	€52 059	−61%
Caretaking	€153 854	€107 382	−30%
Maintenance of telecoms	€2 539	€1 905	−25%
Services overheads	€99 586	€145 130	46%
Total annual FM costs	€2 610 099	€1 561 964	−40%
ICT maintenance costs (Years 1–3)	€474 387	€405 587	−15%
SPV overheads	€0	€410 710	
Sinking fund deposit	€0	€557 496	
Total recurrent costs	€2 610 099	€2 530 170	−3%

Note: FF&E = Furniture, Fixtures and Equipment; FM = Facilities Management; SPV = Special Purpose Vehicle.
Source: Farrell Grant Sparks (2001, 2002) VfM Reports for DOE, September 2001 and November 2002.

and PPP schools, the DOE provides grants based on school type and pupil numbers to cover O&M costs. Schools must apply for additional funding on an ad-hoc basis if, for example, emergency work or expansion is required. For TP schools, there is no distinction between funding (non-pay grants) provided for educational activities and maintenance activities, with individual schools having discretion over how they allocate this funding. Capital and emergency grants are not a consistent annual source of funding for schools and require a lengthy application process. The DOE provides a reduced grant to PPP schools in lieu of the contractually agreed unitary payment to the PPP company.

In examining the funding allocated to both school models in Table 3.6, we observe clear differences. Over the 13-year period examined, the cost of funding O&M activities in PPP schools was 29 percent–42 percent higher than TP schools on a per-pupil basis (adjusting for individual school characteristics).[1] The lower grant payment received by PPP schools from the DOE is more than made up for by the significant unitary payment made on their behalf to the PPP Co. This portion of the unitary payment is dedicated to FM and maintenance services and includes a risk premium. As such, PPP schools have two distinctive sources of funding provided for O&M. In contrast, TP schools have a single source of funding provided for all O&M tasks. Ad-hoc emer-

Table 3.6 *Comparison of average annual ex-post operational funding per pupil (2008–2020)*

Source of school funding	PPP	TP	Percentage difference (PPP vs. TP)
Operational grants	€238.78	€334.38	40%
Maintenance/caretaker grants	€–	€78.75	
Unitary payments toward FM	€425.23	€–	
Average annual O&M funding	€664.01	€413.13	−38%
Average ad-hoc capital and emergency grants	€9.37	€65.10	595%
PPP SPV overhead	€150.22	€–	
Total	€823.60	€478.23	−42%

Notes: (1) The above grant figures are the averages for four of our PPP schools and four of our TP schools, as it was not possible to source grant data for one PPP and one TP school. Average capital and emergency grants are for the 2008–2019 period, as 2020 grants were omitted due to exceptional COVID-19 payments made, which distorted the averages. (2) O&M = Operate and Maintain.
Source: Authors' analysis using information acquired via FOI requests from NDFA, DOE, and ETBs.

gency and capital grants vary significantly by school and year and are used to cover emergency remediations and improvements. While a true like-for-like comparison of O&M costs requires complete information on the allocation and pricing of risks, it is clear that the annual cost of running PPP schools was significantly higher.

Notwithstanding the limited scope for making like-for-like comparisons of O&M costs, our analysis highlights significant differences between PPP and TP schools. First, PPP schools benefit from certainty regarding funding (allocated to the PPP contractor) for school maintenance. In contrast, the funds available for TP schools that apply for capital grants for maintenance are subject to budget availability. Second, while total annual funding allocated to both models is similar, there is a clear disparity in how much of this funding is allocated towards maintenance. The availability (unitary) payment for PPP schools is specifically earmarked for maintenance (i.e., FM). As a result, the separate annual DOE grant allocated to PPP schools is fully available to cover operational costs related to educational activities. This is supported by the findings of the midterm review (DOE, 2021), which highlighted significantly higher deferred maintenance in TP schools, indicating that maintenance and life-cycle replacement works were not being undertaken when required. The review estimated that the cost of deferred maintenance was 85 percent–99 percent lower in PPP schools when directly compared with their TP counterparts. Interviewees drew specific attention to this difference and indicated that TP schools are at a significant disadvantage in relation to maintenance as they are required to fund all O&M costs from a single source. Our interviews indicated that TP schools often allocate funds to school operations, thereby reducing the resources available for maintenance.

> We've been highlighting the need for a dedicated budget for facilities maintenance for a number of years, but right now, there's no money set aside for that purpose. We are told we must do everything with the money provided when really what we're given is only going to keep the lights on and to keep classes running. (TP Principal B)

In contrast, PPP school principals indicated that the availability payments made on their behalf for FM freed up their budget and that they would be unable to provide the level of FM provided under the contract in a traditional school.

> I know my budget well, and I know how much I'd receive if this was a traditional school, and I know for certain that the grants available would not allow me to maintain the school to its current standard. We wouldn't have nearly enough grant funding to provide the level of service we get being a PPP. (PPP Principal A)

Overall, it is clear from the funding data and interview responses that PPP schools cost significantly more on an annual basis per pupil relative to TP schools. Our results are also supported by the recent findings of the midterm review (DOE, 2021), which shows that the level of funding provided for FM was 137 percent higher under PPP compared to conventional schools. However, an important point needs to be highlighted here. While PPPs may cost significantly more annually, their costs may be more representative of the true maintenance requirements of a school building, as specific funds are allocated for school FM and school operations (non-maintenance). In comparison, while funding allocated to TP schools is lower, it is not adequate to meet their O&M requirements, as highlighted by the midterm review (DOE, 2021).

Comparing Quality and Governance under PPP and TP

The quality of assets and services provided under PPP is an important dimension of VfM (Ball et al., 2007). However, quality is not easily measured and is seldom considered when these procurement methods are compared. Most extant studies have relied on stakeholder perceptions of the quality and services provided in PPP projects (Petersen, 2019; Yaya, 2017). These studies are open to the criticism that perceptions are subjective and dependent on an individual's expectations and assumptions. We seek to avoid the pitfalls of relying entirely on stakeholder perceptions of quality by using multiple sources to assess the comparative performance of both procurement models. We find that service quality depends on the governance structures used to coordinate stakeholders and the risk-management approaches employed in both procurement models. Therefore, we examine the processes involved in governing schools' infrastructure under both models of procurement, in addition to project inputs (e.g., building materials) and outputs (building design and service-level quality).

School buildings quality

Interview respondents and documentary evidence indicate that although PPP schools were more expensive to construct, they were built to a high quality that often exceeded the minimum standards set by the DOE. For example, whereas TP schools were generally built using load-bearing concrete walls, PPP schools were constructed using more expensive concrete-frame walls, and interviewees indicated that this led to faster construction of buildings that were easier to maintain. In addition, higher specification fixtures and fittings and better-quality materials (e.g., paints that are more likely to withstand everyday wear and tear) were used in PPP schools: 'Take the classroom fixtures, they were really good quality and still in great condition, you'd feel bad throwing them out, but once their time was up on the life-cycle replacement plan, we put brand new ones in, and you could hardly tell the difference' (PPP Co. Employee C).

Higher construction costs were also associated with innovations in the design of PPP school buildings. The most frequently cited example was the larger circulation space (wider corridors) in PPP schools. Although unintended, this design feature helped PPP schools better adapt to social distancing requirements that arose as a result of COVID-19.

The evidence highlights how PPP schools were designed with a view to a 25-year life-cycle. Hence, higher construction costs were linked to lower operation costs over the PPP project life-cycle.

> There was no point being cheap or cutting corners when the schools were built. I mean, ultimately ourselves and our investors are responsible for the buildings two-and-a-half times longer than we would be under a normal construction contract, so you don't want to be hitting year 20 and having some large defect or structural issue wiping out the returns. (PPP Co. Employee A)

In contrast with PPP, all respondents connected with TP schools drew attention to some level of construction defects, and there were mixed levels of satisfaction with the results of remedial work. In addition, latent defects and structural issues, such as dampness, cracks in external and internal walls, and roof leaks, were also identified: 'Honestly, as long as it has four walls and a roof on it, and it hasn't fallen down yet, we'll be happy enough. But you'd always be afraid that some expensive issue is hiding around the corner for you' (TP Principal C).

These observed differences reflect contrasting approaches to risk management. Although D&C risks are transferred to the private sector under PPP and TP, there are substantial differences in how these risks are managed once schools are in operation. In PPP schools, D&C risks are tied to the project's operational phase, with the SPV retaining responsibility for construction-related risks until the 25-year contract ends.

> Ultimately, we are bearing all design and construction risks until the very last day. Latent issues are likely to occur towards the end of the project, so if something goes wrong a day, a month, a year before we hand back the school, we are responsible for it, which is much longer than a traditional construction guarantee. (PPP Co. Employee A)

In contrast, the allocation of D&C risks to private contractors in TP schools is based on ten-year post-construction guarantees.

> We obviously have and had issues with cracks in the building's façade, but ultimately we're responsible for it. We considered looking to the private builders and consulted with legal experts, but the company was long gone bust, so we'll have to deal with it now. We have our fingers crossed it's not too serious. (TP Principal B)

Schools maintenance (FM)

The PPP contractor is contractually obliged to provide schools with a specified level of maintenance over 25 years. Maintenance is broken down into four categories: reactive, preventative, life-cycle, and cleaning/groundskeeping. Reactive maintenance involves responding to issues flagged by school management. Facilities managers are contractually obliged to resolve reactive issues within set periods or face a penalty. Preventative maintenance covers on-site inspections and remedial works that prevent the future need for time-sensitive reactive maintenance. In addition, PPP schools have strict annual schedules for life-cycle maintenance, for example, painting and the replacement of fixtures and fittings mandated at specific intervals.

Respondents reported a high level of satisfaction with the performance of maintenance tasks under PPP. All PPP-related respondents spoke of the high standards of maintenance delivered under the contract, with preventative maintenance and life-cycle upgrades leading to a perception that the facilities still felt modern: 'I've had principals and teachers who would come in from other more recently built schools asking us how old the building is, and shocked when we tell them it's nearly 20 years old, and the response is always "I thought it was new!"' (PPP Principal B).

These observed differences reflect the allocation of availability risk to PPP contractors. Responses from interviewees indicate that the adoption of availability risk incentivises PPP contractors to ensure school facilities are fit for purpose. Moreover, the monitoring of availability risk was found to be actively managed by the NDFA, with penalties applied if single classrooms or other parts of facilities are not available for use. In contrast, the TP model provides no scope for transferring availability risk, and this is not a feature of contractual governance in TP schools. In the event that TP school facilities are unavailable, this problem is managed by school principals who may be required to source alternative accommodation, which can be costly in terms of time and scarce budgetary resources. This difference lends to the strong consensus among principals and teaching staff that the PPP model allowed them to focus more on their core educational roles: 'I don't have to rush off and get a groundsman to fix something or an electrician to come and sort something when it goes wrong; that definitely takes stuff off my desk and gives me more time to focus on running the school itself' (PPP Principal A).

This experience contrasted sharply with TP schools, where most maintenance, which was the responsibility of TP school principals, was reactive in nature. Although the facility management responsibilities could be devolved to caretakers and assistant principals in larger schools, school principals continued to hold responsibility for budget management and procurement. Trade-offs were common under TP, with temporary fixes required when schools faced strict budgetary constraints: 'If two things break at once, well, we'll prioritise whatever would stop the school running safely and wait until the next grant cycle to fix whatever else is broken. You're putting plasters on the rest and hoping it holds' (TP Principal B).

All TP respondents expressed a desire to engage more in preventative and life-cycle maintenance but felt they were constrained by inadequate funding from the DOE. This resulted in making difficult choices and prioritising certain items for maintenance. School principals commonly sought to raise additional resources through fundraising initiatives involving parents and the wider community: 'I'd love to keep the place looking fresh, and I could spend money refreshing everything with a lick of paint, but then I couldn't buy new microscopes or maths sets for the labs' (TP Principal C).

Compared to the PPP model, principals in TP schools spent significantly more time dealing with FM issues as well as procurement in cases where schools required extensions to existing buildings.[2]

> Building and procurement is the only area we get some support in, but if we have to build a new facility or expand, my whole life becomes that project's management. I'm dealing with builders, architects, quantity surveyors, planners, engineers; and

> I'd say I have very little of my time to spend on the educational portion of my job. (TP Principal A)

Overall, the observed differences in the quality of school buildings and FM are associated with different incentives and risk-management approaches that apply under both procurement models. These are elements of the wider governance systems to which we turn our attention in the next subsection.

Quality of governance

Under both PPP and TP models, the DOE devolves responsibility for the operation and maintenance of school infrastructure to a partner organisation. The operation of PPP schools is governed by a long-term contractual agreement between the DOE and a project-specific SPV. In contrast, TP schools involve the non-contractual devolution of responsibility to a school's board of management. While both partners manage the facilities on behalf of the state, the governance of contractual relations under PPP is characterised by a much higher degree of formality.

The relationship between the PPP contractor and the public authority managing the contract (NDFA) is governed by a system of Service Level Agreements (SLAs). Responsibility for monitoring performance is assigned to the NDFA, which conducts in-person audits and flags any breaches of the contract and remedies required. Our examination of audit reports revealed a strict approach to contract management that sometimes created tensions between public- and private-sector partners.

> At the end of the day, we are paying for the service that is specified, and we have a duty to ensure the taxpayer receives good value for the money spent, so we're just making sure the expected standards are reached, and that's just good contract management. You know deductions are there in case, and we'd rarely have to use them, but they're there. (Public Sector Official A)

> We have no problem with the oversight, but it is rigorous; for example, on our last audit, the grass had not grown after the poor weather, and that was cited, which is obviously a difficult fix. …But as I see it, if they are detailing the small things and nit-picking, I'd say we're probably doing something right. (PPP Co. Employee B)

The evidence indicates that the system of audits and penalties has encouraged effective performance in PPP schools. Penalties are rarely applied, and the consensus view is that the FM company has effectively and promptly remedied issues reported through the audit and helpdesk system: 'Penalties obviously apply if PPP Co. fails to meet the standards set out in the SLAs, but most issues will be resolved within the agreed timeframe. They would never be a large part of the relationship, but it's always in our back pocket' (Public Sector Official B).

As a formal contract does not govern relationships between key players in TP schools, the nature of governance contrasts significantly with that in PPP schools. In TP schools, governance is heavily devolved to school management and patrons. School principals have complete responsibility for the operation and maintenance of school buildings, and interviewees indicated that the level of guidance and training from the DOE is minimal. DOE audits focus on pedagogic activities, and little attention is paid to O&M in schools. Over the last 20 years, a total of eight inspections were conducted in the five TP schools covered in our study, with just four inspection reports containing references to the perceived standard of the school building. The approach to monitoring maintenance activities in TP schools is entirely unsystematic.[3] There are no systems in place to enable schools or the DOE to track the age, condition, or life-cycle of fixtures and fittings.

> A lot of the time when we're talking about replacing something or fixing it, often, when it breaks will be the first sign that something needs to be done. We'd then have to rely on memory to determine when it was installed, or serviced last, maybe see if we've kept physical records. It is something we definitely need to improve on, and it's certainly marked as a future project for us, but it's still a low enough priority in all our activities. (TP Principal A)

These findings are consistent with a recent report on school estate management by the Irish C&AG (2020). The report found that repairs and upgrades to facilities in TP schools are not systematically recorded by the DOE even though the department provides direct funding for emergency remediation. This absence of monitoring and reporting means the DOE can be unaware of the requirements for repairs, upgrades, or even replacement of individual schools.

DISCUSSION AND CONCLUSION

The performance of PPPs is an elusive concept, and its assessment is complicated by the different levels at which PPPs are viewed. Hodge and Greve (2017) argue that in conceptual terms, PPP performance can be judged from a narrow perspective (the project level), a broader organisational or project delivery perspective, right through to the policy and governance perspectives and broadest levels of societal change and benefit. While recognising that PPPs are a phenomenon that can be examined at different levels, our main objective of assessing the performance of PPP schools procurement in Ireland requires that we make choices about the level at which we view PPPs and the criteria we use to undertake our analysis. In that regard, we decided to assess PPPs in terms of what is arguably their most frequently articulated technical rationale, namely VfM. Notwithstanding criticisms of the use and practice of VfM assessment in the PPP literature, its use is justified for a number of reasons. First, policymakers commonly identify VfM as a principal objective of PPP. Second, as ex-ante VfM assessments explicitly compare PPP with a hypothetical public ownership approach, these assessments align with the main motivation of our comparative study of schools procurement in Ireland. Also, as the commonly accepted definition of VfM includes both asset and service quality, this facilitates assessing PPP performance over the project life-cycle.

Two of the principal challenges associated with this VfM-based line of inquiry are: (1) the difficulty in accessing project-level information, and (2) the identification and analysis of a suitable counterfactual situation of 'traditional procurement' that is said to often be "both horribly vague and also largely unquantified in most assessments" (Hodge, 2010, p. 102). We worked around the first challenge in accessing information by making several requests under the Freedom of Information Act. Further information was sourced from project-related documents in the public domain and interviews with several key stakeholders. This permitted the collection of data for a group of five PPP schools and a comparable group of similarly sized TP schools constructed at the same time.

The original official ex-ante VfM assessment for the group of five schools anticipated that the PPP approach would achieve the principal objective of delivering VfM. In the absence of full information, it cannot be accurately determined if these financial savings materialised over the contract's life. However, our analysis indicates that the total capital cost (ex-ante and ex-post) of the schools built using the PPP model was significantly higher than both the PSB and TP comparator schools.

In relation to O&M and life-cycle costs, the original VfM assessment estimated appreciably lower costs under PPP, which would drive overall VfM over the duration of the contract. It is not possible to determine if the original estimates materialised ex-post, as the initial VfM assessment was based on a hypothetical PSB. To examine ex-post costs for O&M under PPP, we sourced data on a comparable group of TP schools and compared the funding allocated by government to cover O&M costs under both procurement approaches. Our analysis shows that PPP schools are allocated significantly higher funding to cover O&M and life-cycle costs. This leads us to an interesting conclusion. Our evidence shows significant differences between the original ex-ante analysis (based on a hypothetical PSB) and what the ex-post data reveal when funding for PPP is compared to that allocated to TP schools in reality. As the *de facto* cost to the state of PPP schools is significantly higher compared to TP schools, it remains unclear as to whether VfM (in purely financial terms) is being achieved in line with the forecast of the original VfM assessment.

Moving beyond a strictly financial analysis, our study provides new and important evidence on VfM, broadly defined. It is important to consider that the objective of PPPs is not simply to procure capital assets but also to improve the quality of public-service delivery. The evidence strongly suggests that the higher levels of funding allocated to PPPs result in higher-quality buildings and superior operation and maintenance of schools. Significantly, school principals devote less time to FM and have greater budget certainty. These features represent the most significant performance advantage of PPPs in our case study. While the annual cost of funding PPPs is higher than funding TPs, the contractual agreements ensure that a consistent level of quality is delivered across PPP schools. Whether these advantages could be accrued under TP requires future exploration. However, it appears realistic to expect that adopting a project life-cycle approach and implementing a more systematic approach to managing school facilities is possible under TP. In that regard, the use of PPP has served important lessons for the future procurement and management of school projects. Another important difference between PPP and TP procurement relates to the allocation of project risks. The financial data we present indicate that this risk transfer comes at a price. The question for policymakers is whether superior quality assets and services justify the costs incurred in transferring these project risks.

Whereas our findings concerning VfM mainly relate to Hodge and Greve's (2017) conceptualisation of PPP performance at a project level, our study highlights additional issues that are relevant in considering how PPP performs as a tool for public-service delivery. Specifically, our study identifies inequality outcomes of importance to wider education and infrastructure policy in Ireland. The evidence shows that the PPP approach delivers bigger schools that are more expensive to construct in relative terms. Moreover, PPP schools are allocated higher annual public funding per pupil. They have certainty about the resources available for operation and maintenance that are specified in the contractual agreement between the DOE and its private partner. This results in a significant degree of inequity between PPP and TP schools, which was raised by the Irish C&AG (2004) in an early review of the Grouped Schools PPP. Our study finds that this funding inequity between the pilot PPP and TP schools has continued since the construction of the schools in the early 2000s. Whether there have been similar inequities in the funding allocated to new schools subsequently procured under TP and PPP is an important question that deserves attention in future research on the comparative performance of procurement methods and wider infrastructure policy in the Irish education sector.

To conclude, our study highlights the challenging nature of comparing different types of infrastructure and service procurement over an extended period of time. Whereas our study finds that PPP offers advantages compared to the traditional approach, the evidence highlights trade-offs at the project and policy levels. It appears that better-quality infrastructure and governance is more expensive, and the use of PPP schools confers advantages to a small number of schools that raises important equity issues. Policymakers should be aware of these trade-offs when deciding on how important social infrastructure will be procured in the future.

NOTES

1. For example, some schools received additional supports due to socio-economic disadvantage or providing for pupils with additional needs.
2. The July 2021 midterm review identified that PPP principals spent on average less than 5 percent of their time on FM tasks, compared to traditional principals who spent between 10 percent and 50 percent depending on the level of works required at their school.
3. The July 2021 midterm review highlights that the average regulatory compliance among PPP schools was over 95 percent while it was 35 percent among traditional schools.

REFERENCES

Ball, R., Heafey, M., & King, D. (2007). The Private Finance Initiative in the UK. *Public Management Review*, *9*(2), 289–310.

Bennett, J., & Iossa, E. (2006). Building and managing facilities for public services. *Journal of Public Economics*, *90*(10–11), 2143–60.

Bisset, J. (2009). *Regeneration: Public good or private profit?* TASC/New Island.

Burger, P., & Hawkesworth, I. (2011). How to attain value for money: Comparing PPP and traditional infrastructure public procurement. *OECD Journal on Budgeting*, *2011*(1), 1–56.

Burke, R., & Demirag, I. (2015). Changing perceptions on PPP games: Demand risk in Irish roads. *Critical Perspectives on Accounting*, *27*, 189–208.

Comptroller and Auditor General (C&AG). (2004). *Report on value for money examination: The grouped schools pilot partnership project.*

C&AG. (2020). *Management of the schools estate: Report on the accounts of the public services 2019.*

Connolly, C., Reeves, E., & Wall, A. (2009). Isomorphism: An explanation for the popularity of public-private partnerships? *The Irish Accounting Review*, *16*(1), 1–19.

Culp, G. (2011). Alternative project delivery methods for water and wastewater projects: Do they save time and money? *Leadership and Management in Engineering*, *11*(3), 231–40.

De Bettignies, J. E., & Ross, T. W. (2010). The economics of public-private partnerships: Some theoretical contributions. In G. A. Hodge, C. Greve, & A. E. Boardman (Eds.), *International handbook on public-private partnerships* (pp. 132–58). Edward Elgar.

Demirag, I., Khadaroo, I., Stapleton, P., & Stevenson, C. (2011). Risks and the financing of PPP: Perspectives from the financiers. *British Accounting Review*, *43*(4), 294–310.

Department of Education (DOE). (2021). *Review of the PILOT PPP schools bundle AA projects*.

Department of Public Expenditure and Reform. (2021). *PPP projects contract value and financial commitment to end 2020*. Dublin: Department of Public Expenditure.

http://ppp.gov.ie/wp-content/uploads/2021/05/Contract-value-and-financial-commitment-to-end-2020.xlsx

Eaton, D., Akbiyikli, R., & Dickinson, M. (2006). An evaluation of the stimulants and impediments to innovation within PFI/PPP projects. *Construction Innovation: Information, Process, Management*, *6*(2), 63–7.

Engel, E., Fischer, R., & Galetovic, A. (2014). *The economics of public-private partnerships: A basic guide*. Cambridge University Press.

European PPP Expertise Centre. (2015). *PPP motivations and challenges for the public sector: Why (not) and how*. European Investment Bank.

Farrell Grant Sparks. (2001). *Pilot PPP schools: Value for money comparison*.

Farrell Grant Sparks. (2002). *PPP pilot bundle: Post-project VfM report*.

Flyvbjerg, B., Bruzelius, N., & Rothengatter, W. (2003). *Megaprojects and risk: An anatomy of ambition*. Cambridge University Press.

Froud, J. (2003). The private finance initiative. *Accounting, Organizations and Society*, *28*(6), 567–89.

Gardiner & Theobald. (2002). *Comparison of costs at Ballincollig/Kilcoole*.

Grimsey, D., & Lewis, M. K. (2004). *Public-private partnerships: The worldwide revolution in infrastructure provision and public finance*. Edward Elgar.

Hart, O. (2003). Incomplete contracts and public ownership: Remarks, and an application to public-private partnerships. *The Economic Journal*, *113*, 69–76.

Hearne, R. (2012). *Public-private partnerships in Ireland – Failed experiment or way forward for the state*. Manchester University Press.

HM Treasury. (2006). *Value for money assessment guidance*.

Hodge, G. A. (2010). Reviewing public-private partnerships: Some thoughts on evaluation. In G. A. Hodge, C. Greve, & A. E. Boardman (Eds.), *International handbook on public-private partnerships* (pp. 81–112). Edward Elgar.

Hodge, G. A., & Greve, C. (2017). On public-private partnership performance: A contemporary review. *Public Works Management and Policy*, *22*(1), 55–78.

Hurst, C., & Reeves, E. (2004). An economic analysis of Ireland's first public-private partnership. *International Journal of Public Sector Management*, *17*(5), 379–88.

Leiringer, R. (2006). Technological innovation in PPPs: Incentives, opportunities and actions. *Construction Management and Economics*, *24*(3), 301–308.

Lonsdale, C. (2005). Post-contractual lock-in and the UK Private Finance Initiative (PFI): The cases of national savings and investments and the Lord Chancellor's Department. *Public Administration*, *83*(1), 67–88.

Martimort, D., & Pouyet, J. (2008). To build or not to build: Normative and positive theories of public-private partnerships. *International Journal of Industrial Organization*, *26*(2), 393–411.

O'Nolan, G., & Reeves, E. (2018). The nature of contracting hazards in public-private partnerships—Evidence from Ireland. *International Journal of Public Administration*, *41*(15), 1205–1216.

O'Shea, C., Palcic, D., & Reeves, E. (2019). Comparing PPP with traditional procurement: The case of schools procurement in Ireland. *Annals of Public and Cooperative Economics*, *90*(2), 245–67.

Palcic, D., Reeves, E., & Stafford, A. (2018). Lifting the lid: The private financing of motorway PPPs in Ireland. *The Economic and Social Review*, *49*(2), 217–39.

Petersen, O. H. (2019). Evaluating the costs, quality, and value for money of infrastructure public-private partnerships: A systematic literature review. *Annals of Public and Cooperative Economics*, *90*(2), 227–44.

Reeves, E. (2003). Public-private partnerships in Ireland: Policy and practice. *Public Money and Management*, *23*(3), 163–70.

Reeves, E. (2008). The practice of contracting in public-private partnerships: Transaction costs and relational contracting in the Irish schools sector. *Public Administration*, *86*(4), 969–86.

Reeves, E. (2011). The only game in town: Public-private partnerships in the Irish water services sector. *Economic and Social Review*, *42*(1), 95–111.

Reeves, E. (2015). A review of the PPP experience in Ireland: Lessons for comparative policy analysis. *Journal of Comparative Policy Analysis: Research and Practice*, *17*(5), 467–80.

Reeves, E., & Ryan, J. (2007). Piloting public-private partnerships: Expensive lessons from Ireland's schools' sector. *Public Money and Management*, *27*(5), 331–8.

Robson, C. (2007). *How to do a research project: A guide for undergraduate students*. John Wiley and Sons.

Roumboutsos, A., & Saussier, S. (2014). Public-private partnerships and investments in innovation: The influence of the contractual arrangement. *Construction Management and Economics*, *32*(4), 349–61.

Välilä, T. (2020). An overview of economic theory and evidence of public-private partnerships in the procurement of (transport) infrastructure. *Utilities Policy*, *62*.

Van den Hurk, M. (2016). Bundling the procurement of sports infrastructure projects: How neither public nor private actors really benefit. *Environment and Planning C: Government and Policy*, *34*(8), 1369–86.

Verweij, S., & Van Meerkerk, I. F. (2021). Do public-private partnerships achieve better time and cost performance than regular contracts? *Public Money and Management*, *41*(4), 286–95.

Yaya, R. (2017). Twelve years of Scottish school public-private partnerships: Are they better value for money? *Journal of Public Procurement*, *17*(2), 187–228.

Yescombe, E. R. (2007). *Public-private partnerships: Principles of policy and finance*. Butterworth-Heinemann/Elsevier.

4. PPP hospitals in Portugal: what does benchmarking tell us about their relative performance?

Diogo Cunha Ferreira, Rui Cunha Marques, Maria Isabel Pedro, and Gonçalo Santos

INTRODUCTION

The Portuguese National Health Service (NHS) was created in 1979, bringing universal and accessible health care services to all citizens. This NHS follows the principles of a Beveridge system; that is, the government (on behalf of the state) provides and finances health care through tax payments (Barros et al., 2011). It is safe to say that the health budget suffers much scrutiny, as tax-payers fund it, and it represents a substantial proportion of the gross domestic product (Ferreira & Marques, 2018).

Throughout the years, traces of inefficiency and inadequate management have been constant in the NHS. Since the 1980s, the Portuguese NHS went through several reforms, mainly focusing on improving hospital performance and introducing incentives to enhance service quality and customer satisfaction (Nunes & Ferreira, 2019). The most significant reform period started in 2002, transforming hospitals belonging to the Administrative Public Sector into hospital enterprises (Nunes & Ferreira, 2019). The latter, although publicly owned, were governed privately. Three years later, those hospitals were transformed into corporate public entities (Barros et al., 2011). These transformations were driven by the New Public Management (NPM) paradigm, which constituted an effort to improve efficiency in the public sector by applying tools and ideas from private management (Ferreira & Marques, 2015). The concept of the Public-Private Partnership (PPP) project in Portugal was born from the introduction of the NPM ideas into the public sector; its popularity has been rising worldwide ever since (Roehrich et al., 2014). PPP is a public procurement model in which a contract between a public entity and a private one is signed; the latter provides a service and is rewarded by the former, imposed by a set of conditions specified in the contract (Barros

& Martinez-Giralt, 2009). The utilization of this type of contract in the health sector led to the creation of PPP hospitals.

In recent years, PPP arrangements in the health care sector have experienced considerable growth (Torchia et al., 2015). Since the introduction of the PPP hospitals concept in Portugal, four PPP projects were developed: Hospital de Cascais, Hospital de Braga, Hospital de Vila Franca de Xira, and Hospital Beatriz Ângelo. This was the so-called first health care PPP wave characterized by including infrastructure and clinical services. A second wave based only on infrastructure services was later deployed. PPP hospitals of the first wave faced or are facing the end of their contracts. In addition, there are growing concerns about the impact of these arrangements within the health care system. Some notorious policymakers, mostly from left-wing parties, have argued against PPP hospitals. Still, their arguments are frequently biased and unsupported by empirical evidence. Discussion about renewing (or not) the contracts or creating new ones is thus in the spotlight.

Empirical evidence of the benefits of using PPP projects in health care is mixed (Marques & Silva, 2008; Roehrich et al., 2014). This raises concerns about private companies operating and managing hospitals—structures with enormous social responsibility. Little attention has been paid to the literature discussing differences between public hospitals and PPP hospitals, especially regarding the performance gap between them (Kruse et al., 2018). The coexistence of PPP and publicly managed hospitals demands in-depth analysis of their performance. Our study evaluates performance in terms of four main dimensions: technical efficiency (or simply efficiency, which is linked to cost performance—see Chapter 1), access to health care, appropriateness of care, and clinical safety (which are linked to service quality performance—see Chapter 1; Barros et al., 2011). Indeed, these are the main dimensions monitored by the Portuguese Ministry of Health, meaning that they are probably the most relevant for this entity (the main stakeholder). Therefore, this study goes beyond the social performance assessed by Ferreira and Marques (2021) by inserting the efficiency dimension when comparing the two groups of hospitals. This is because it is often claimed that when PPPs are managed by private companies, they should be more cost-efficient than their public counterparts. Such a scenario may constitute a problem for patients because of potential trade-offs between efficiency, quality, and access. Past research suggests that Portuguese PPP hospitals are as good as publicly managed hospitals regarding quality performance (Ferreira & Marques, 2021). Those studies, however, are limited to a specific category of performance and do not address all type of performance simultaneously. Therefore, the main question is: Does considering a broader range of dimensions result in a group of hospitals with poorer overall performance than their counterparts? Suppose there is no compensation between those dimensions because of possible trade-offs. In that case, we may expect that PPP arrangements exhibit an overall performance higher than the corporatized entities' for the reasons above.

Only after these performance dimensions have been estimated and compared can sustainable and empirically based policies governing PPPs be developed (Ferreira et al., 2018a). It is necessary to have unbiased information available and to compare the performance of both models. Currently, very few studies provide a comparative analysis of the performance levels of both public and PPP hospitals (Cruz & Marques, 2013; Ferreira & Marques, 2016; Entidade Reguladora da Saúde [ERS], 2016; Nunes & Matos, 2017; Ferreira & Marques, 2021). To the best of our knowledge, no study has analyzed the performance of those groups of hospitals based on the four performance categories. Hence, given the gap in the literature and the importance and contemporary nature of the theme, it was considered relevant to evaluate whether PPP hospitals can outperform corporatized ones. Therefore, this study focuses on that aspect, providing a complete analysis of hospital performance for both models, considering the Portuguese experience. We also merge a method typically used to construct composite indicators with the Malmquist Index for group comparison, which is innovative in both fields: health economics and operational research.

A simple way to define our main objective is to answer the question: Do PPP hospitals outperform corporatized ones? This study uses suitable benchmarking models applied to a detailed data set to compare the two groups of hospitals and draw lessons from them. Notably, we use a specific Data Envelopment Analysis (DEA) model—the Benefit of Doubt (BoD)—to measure hospital performance. BoD is suitable when data are expressed in ratios or as any other key performance indicator. Additionally, we use the Malmquist Index for group comparison to measure group performance. The sample comprises data about Portuguese hospitals from 2015 to 2019. Consequently, we can obtain objective conclusions from comparing both models to understand whether one group provides better levels of care than the other. Furthermore, the results of this research can affect policymakers' decisions and, most importantly, should impact citizens' opinions.

THE PORTUGUESE NATIONAL HEALTH SERVICE

In 1974, a democratic revolution occurred in Portugal, ending a dictatorship that had lasted over 40 years. The Portuguese Constitution was approved two years later, recognizing the citizens' right to health care by "creating a universal, free-of-charge NHS" (Barros et al., 2011).[1] On July 28, 1978, an order was published, known as *Despacho Arnaut*, which anticipated the NHS. It allowed all citizens access to medical-social services, regardless of their ability to pay. Following the constitution and *Despacho Arnaut*, the law that enabled the right to health care was approved in 1979, and, accordingly, the NHS was implemented.[2] The NHS guarantees universal, general, and accessible health care services to all citizens. Universal access means access by all citizens regardless of their economic or social status (i.e., ability or willingness to pay). "General" includes all areas and needs (Nunes & Ferreira, 2019). Although these constitutional principles have prevailed, the "free-of-charge" concept did not. A revision of the constitution, made in 1989,[3] changed the access to "tendentiously free"; that is, users of the NHS now have to pay moderate fees besides taxes (Ferreira & Nunes, 2019).

Secondary Health Care in Portugal: Hospitals

Hospitals in Portugal mainly provide secondary care. The report *Estatísticas da Saúde 2017* defines the hospital as a health facility providing medical and surgical treatment and nursing care for sick or injured people and which may contribute to disease prevention, scientific research, and teaching (Instituto Nacional de Estatística [INE], 2019).

One can differentiate hospitals into two types: public and private. The state is the owner and prominent supporter of public hospitals. A private hospital has a private entity as its owner and leading supporter, either for-profit or not, and can offer universal or restricted access (Ferreira et al., 2018b).

In 2017, there were 225 hospitals in Portugal, representing an increase of 27 hospitals (about 14 percent) compared to 2007. In 2017, there were 114 private hospitals (15 more than in 2007) and 111 public hospitals in Portugal, of which four were PPP hospitals. Given that all PPP hospitals also offered universal access, the number of granted universal access hospitals was roughly 1 per 100 000 inhabitants in 2017.

Hospital Management Models

Between 1979 and 2002, all public hospitals were under the management of the Administrative Public Sector (in Portuguese, the *Sector Público Administrativo* [SPA]; Ferreira & Marques, 2015). SPA hospitals were subjected to public/administrative law, as they were publicly managed and owned. After that period, several reforms occurred following the NPM paradigm, which consists of adopting management and organization principles from the private sector to the health system and reinforcing the agreements with the private and social sectors (Nunes & Ferreira, 2019). At the end of 2002, most traditional SPA hospitals had already been transformed into public limited companies or hospital enterprises (in Portuguese, *Sociedade Anónima* [SA]).[4] SA hospitals had limited liabilities obeying commercial/private law (Ferreira & Marques, 2016).

In 2005, the government transformed all SA hospitals and other SPA hospitals into corporate public entities (Public Enterprise; in Portuguese, *Entidade Pública Empresarial* [EPE]).[5] The main goal was to maintain the hospitals' unequivocal public nature and enhance the supervision and intervention of the Ministries of Health and Finance. SA and EPE management models differ from public management because they have more autonomy in certain aspects. They do not follow a private management model because their autonomy is supervised. Concerning administration, this is an intermediate situation between the SPA hospital and the private hospital.

Meanwhile, some PPP hospital projects were launched.[6] PPP arrangements have private investment, public funding, private management, and public ownership. Nonetheless, PPP hospitals do not stop providing public services (as they are inserted within the NHS), although under a legal framework different from the corporatized hospitals (EPE). The next section details this type of arrangement. Four PPP hospitals have emerged in Portugal since then. Some more were also announced, but their creation was dismissed (Tribunal de Contas, 2009). Table 4.1 provides a summary of the four types of hospitals.

Table 4.1 Comparison of types of public hospitals in Portugal

	SPA hospital	SA/EPE hospital	PPP hospital
Capital Structure	Public	State as the only shareholder	Private
Governance	Board of Directors	Board of Directors; general meeting; supervisory bodies	Board of Directors; general meeting; supervisory bodies
Funding	Public and private	Public and private	Public
Internal control	Under the responsibility of the Ministry of Health	Like private companies, uses tools such as performance assessment and accountability	Private management
Indebtedness	No authorization for financial debt	Financial debt cannot exceed 30% of share capital	No restrictions
Investment decisions	Limited autonomy	Extended autonomy	Total autonomy
Human resources	Civil service regime (needs approval from authority); no incentives policy	Individual contracts; outsourcing; incentives policy	Outsourcing; incentives policy

Notes: Equipment reverts to the state at the end of the concession.
Sector Público Administrativo (SPA); *Sociedade Anónima* (SA); *Entidade Pública Empresarial* (EPE); Public-Private Partnership (PPP).

PUBLIC-PRIVATE PARTNERSHIPS

An Overview

PPP projects were developed and used for the first time in the United Kingdom in the 1970s. They appeared to undertake major public projects without the prerequisite of exclusive public funding, while also sharing the risk with the private sector (Roehrich et al., 2014). There is not a textbook definition of the PPP arrangement. Sometimes it is only referred to as a traditional project carried out by the public sector or as a simple contract between the private and public sectors. In fact, a PPP is a public procurement model. However, as Reich (2000) explains, a good PPP project definition has three points. First, the existence of at least one private, for-profit organization and one not-for-profit or public organization. Second, both entities want to create social value. Third, both entities share efforts and gains. Here lies one of the main aspects of the PPP arrangement: the risk sharing between both partners. The capacity of absorbing risk is higher in the public sector, thus the PPP makes sense if and only if the private partner is more efficient, as efficiency gains should compensate the payments to the risk-bearing private partner. Such risk sharing is mandatory to avoid a scenario in which all the risk is handled by a single partner. In health care, this can be associated with the constant technological development, a reason often noted for leaving clinical management out of the PPP (Barros, 2019).

Another important aspect of PPPs is their long-term nature (typically decades) that may imply unstable contract management (e.g., because of political and legal shifts). These periods often feature renegotiations and payment of indemnities to the private partner(s) (Pereira et al., 2021).

In Portugal, decree-law no. 86/2003 of April 26 defines the PPP as:[7] "Contract or the union of arrangements whereby private entities, designated as private partners, undertake, on a long-term basis, toward a public partner, to ensure an activity aimed at the satisfaction of a collective need, and assume responsibility, in whole or in part, for the financing and operation thereof."

PPP models can be classified according to their goals. The following models are worth mentioning: Build–Own–Maintain (BOM), Build–Own–Operate (BOO), Design–Build–Operate (DBO), Design–Build–Finance–Operate (DBFO), Design–Build–Finance–Operate–Transfer (DBFOT), and Local Improvement Finance Trust (LIFT). The DBFOT model, notable for its worldwide popularity and well-known adherence (Cruz & Marques, 2013), is the existing PPP arrangement in Portugal (Ferreira & Marques, 2021). It is a contract between the state and a private entity in which the latter is responsible for the construction, financing, operation and maintenance of infrastructure, and provision of health services.

Generically, the PPP model has several advantages compared with other public hospital management models, such as using the private-sector investment capability to fulfill the public needs. Also, including private operators from the beginning of the programming and construction process positively affects costs and execution time of the work. Operating expenses also become more predictable and controllable. Another advantage is that most of the responsibilities and risks rest on the private entity, especially the financing risk, which lasts until the end of the agreement (Ferreira & Marques, 2016). On the other hand, there may be a loss of public control over the quality of the services provided due to inadequate accountability mechanisms of the private partner (Simões, 2004). This seems to be one of the most widespread arguments against PPP arrangements (Marques & Berg, 2011).

PPPs in Health Care

PPP arrangements in health care have been extensively used in the hospital sector across the world. One reason is that hospitals consume a meaningful share of the health sector budget (Barros, 2019). The PPP projects in this sector are differentiated based on the activities included in the contract. Arrangements can go from only considering a private entity's hospital infrastructure management to offering full service provision at all levels of care (Ferreira & Marques, 2021). In the health sector, there are mainly three models: the United Kingdom (UK) model, the Portuguese model, and the Alzira model (Cruz & Marques, 2013).

The UK model

PPP arrangements under this model aim to create/restructure and operate hospital infrastructure. Two main PPP contract models coexist in the UK health care system—DBFOT and LIFT; deciding on one instead of the other depends on the Value for Money analysis. Hospital and clinical management are not a part of this model. It can build or restructure the hospital depending on the option chosen. Based on this, there are two classifications: greenfield, if the created structure is new, or brownfield, for infrastructure restructuring, rehabilitation, or expansion. At the end of the contract period, usually 25 to 30 years, the assets are returned to the state. The state finances the partnership during the contract according to the availability of the contracted services and performance. Adopting this model has been common in many European countries and Canada, Japan, South Africa, and Australia. The wide acceptance of this particular model may result from the fact that clinical management is not the private sector's responsibility, leaving the hospital's core business to the public sector (Simões, 2004).

The Alzira model

The Alzira model follows the DBOFT contract and is characterized by having full service provision at all levels of care. It is not limited to the hospital perimeter, extending to primary care centers (Ferreira & Marques, 2021). The concessionaire manages the hospital resources, ensuring that only pre-determined cases are seen in the hospital, while less urgent ones go to health centers. By doing this, there is an expected increase in efficiency through using specialized facilities. The most relevant example of this model is the Hospital de La Ribera, located in Alzira (hence the name of the PPP model), Valencia, Spain (Caballer-Tarazona et al., 2016). However, Valencia's Health Authority terminated Alzira's public-private administrative concession in March, 2018 (Comendeiro-Maaløe et al., 2019).

The Portuguese model

The Portuguese model featuring PPP arrangements follows the DBFOT contract model and is a hybrid between the other two models. According to this model, the contract dictates the infrastructure and soft facilities services management as in the UK model. However, different from the latter, the Portuguese model includes the clinical and medical activities in the contract. Therefore, it is the responsibility of the private contractor to recruit, train, and manage clinical staff and to maintain, operate, and purchase medical supplies. The Portuguese model was applied in the four hospitals of the first health care PPP wave.[8]

PPP hospitals in Portugal

The first experience of implementing a private management model in a public hospital began in 1995 with signing a contract for the private management of a general hospital, Hospital Fernando Fonseca (Cruz & Marques, 2012), a regional hospital with 670 beds that was integrated into the NHS. By government decision, this partnership ended by 2008, turning it into an EPE hospital. Since 2001, this kind of contract in health care became more frequent and announced the first wave of hospitals in a PPP regime.

This first wave consists of a management contract with two managing operators: one for building management and another for the clinical services component. The entity responsible for the construction and management of the building has a contract for 30 years. Meanwhile, the entity responsible for managing clinical staff and delivering health care to citizens has a contract for just ten years. This means that the private sector cannot disengage during the contract period benefiting from competition, since poor performers will be

Table 4.2 Main features of the Portuguese first wave of hospital PPPs

	Private partner responsible for infrastructure management	Private partner accountable for clinical management
Model	DBFOT, including clinical services	
Contract issues	To design, build, and preserve (manage) the infrastructure and hard facilities (ancillary services)	To manage clinical staff and deliver health care to all citizens
Duration	30 years	10 years
Responsible	Hospital building management company	Hospital facility management company
Activity	Design, construction, and maintenance of hospital facilities, hard facilities management, and heavy fixed equipment	Hospital management, clinical service management, soft facilities management, and mobile equipment
Payment	Based on services availability (penalties for service failures)	Based on contracted production (penalties for low quality)

Note: Design–Build–Finance–Operate–Transfer (DBFOT).
Source: Adapted from Tribunal de Contas (2009) and Cruz and Marques (2012, 2013).

replaced (Barros & Martinez-Giralt, 2009; Cruz & Marques, 2013). Table 4.2 briefly summarizes the main features of the first wave of hospital PPPs.

Past Research on the Performance of PPP Hospitals Worldwide

Research and evaluation of performance in PPP arrangements have been a constant concern for health researchers, resulting in several studies regarding this topic. At the international level, some outstanding work was done, including by Torchia et al. (2015). This global study addressed governance issues in health PPPs; the authors conducted a systematic review of 46 articles published in peer-reviewed journals from 1990 to 2011. They suggested that although PPPs are addressing emerging public health issues worldwide, several questions about their effectiveness, efficiency, and convenience remain unanswered.

Drawing on the experience of countries such as Australia, Spain, and the UK, McKee et al. (2006) reviewed the experience with variants of the PPP model in health care. The authors could not reach a consensus on whether the model was flawed or whether the difficulties that appeared resulted from mistakes made during the execution of the model. The authors stated that such uncertainty surrounding the value of the PPP model in health care needs urgent resolution. In contrast, Barbetta et al. (2008) used the DEA technique to identify differences in efficiency between public and private Italian hospitals. The authors concluded that differences between models resulted more from institutional settings in which they operate than the incentive structures embedded in the different proprietary forms. Roehrich et al. (2014) analyzed over 1400 publications about PPP arrangements in health care covering 20 years. This study illustrates that further empirical research needs to explore evidence on the limitations of PPP arrangements in delivering public sector infrastructure and services.

Caballer-Tarazona et al. (2016) evaluated the efficiency of the PPP experience in five Spanish hospitals to identify the influence of private management over hospital outcomes. The authors concluded that the PPP group obtained good results but was not always better than publicly managed institutions. Alonso et al. (2016) also studied the Spanish health care PPP option. Their work concluded that clinical staff employment levels seem substantially lower in PPP hospitals than in publicly managed hospitals. Finally, Kruse et al. (2018) compared the performance of public hospitals with their private counterparts regarding efficiency, accessibility, and quality of care in the European Union. According to the authors, public hospitals were at least as efficient as private hospitals. However, the evidence concerning differences in quality of care does not allow us to conclude which is the best group.

From this review, one may infer that there is extensive literature regarding PPP hospitals. Nonetheless, only a few works assess and compare the performance of PPP hospitals against other secondary health providers. There is a trend in the conclusions from those studies: either there are no relevant differences in performance between publicly managed and PPP hospitals, or PPPs show better results than the former group. It seems that there is a trend pointing out that publicly managed hospitals do not provide better health care than PPP ones, and the latter appear to be either equal or even better than publicly managed hospitals.

Past Research on PPP Hospitals in Portugal

There are some notable works studying the reality of hospital PPPs in Portugal. In a study requested by the Ministry of Health, the health regulatory authority—ERS (2016)—evaluated four aspects to compare PPP hospitals with the EPE hospitals: technical efficiency, effectiveness, clinical quality, and regulatory costs. The regulator found that PPP hospitals are generically more efficient than publicly managed hospitals regarding technical efficiency, estimated through DEA, although the authors found no statistically significant differences. In terms of effectiveness, PPP hospitals presented better relative performance on some indicators when compared to the non-PPP group average, but also showed the worst performance in others. Regarding quality, the study found that PPP hospitals have favorable results, on average, compared to corporatized hospitals. In the end, we drew no overall conclusion on the advantages or disadvantages of PPP hospitals.

Nunes and Matos (2017) studied hospitals' performance in a PPP regime, designing a benchmarking exercise with DEA for 2013–15. Three of the four analyzed hospitals were efficient in the three studied years and one was considered inefficient. According to the results of this study, improvements in hospital efficiency and productivity resulting from implementing PPPs were achieved in part. Most of the PPP hospitals were efficient when compared with themselves and with other hospitals of the NHS.

Ferreira and Marques (2021) used BoD alongside recent data about Portuguese hospitals (2012–17). They evaluated whether PPP hospitals can deliver health care services with social performance (i.e., quality and access) levels at least as good as corporatized EPE hospitals. The authors concluded that PPP arrangements do not tend to have lower performance levels when compared to EPE hospitals. From this review, one can draw similar lessons to the ones obtained in the previous section. In Portugal, a few scholars are studying and comparing the performance of PPP hospitals against the EPE ones. In general, they conclude that most PPP hospitals are characterized by good performance levels and do not tend to display lower performance levels compared to public hospitals. The issue, however, is that most of them consider one specific performance dimension in their analysis—for example, only quality or efficiency—but not both simultaneously. Therefore, a study evaluating a broader range of variables to obtain more complete performance measurements of hospitals is needed.

METHODOLOGY

One can compare homogeneous decision-making units exhibiting similar production technologies through a frontier. This frontier characterizes the most efficient production profiles in the industry, being thus composed of organizations producing an optimal output level using an optimal quantity of inputs. These organizations (or benchmarks) are dominant entities (i.e., they outperform the others in the sample).

To this day, the DEA technique is the predominant method of the non-parametric model adopted and has been extensively used in the health sector to analyze providers' performance (Hollingsworth & Peacock, 2008). DEA is a data-driven linear programming model that easily constructs the best-performer frontier based only on data, not requiring assumptions about the frontier shape or of the efficiency's statistical distribution. These are often considered the most important advantages of DEA compared to the parametric alternatives such as Stochastic Frontier Analysis.

Most studies evaluating and comparing different types of hospitals in Portugal use the DEA technique or some version of it (Ferreira & Marques, 2015; Nunes & Ferreira, 2018; Ferreira & Nunes, 2019). One can acquire knowledge on the optimal weighting scheme for hospital performance benchmarking from the hospital data. This stems from one conceptual point of the DEA approach. Behind this lies the idea that when a hospital performs well on a particular indicator, that policy dimension is crucial to the hospital. In contrast, the hospital gives less importance to dimensions on which it performs worse compared to the other hospitals in the group. Thus, by placing higher importance on relative strengths, hospitals set their own "optimal" weighting schemes (Cherchye et al., 2007b, 2011). Consequently, we use the DEA model to evaluate hospitals' performance. However, since this study monitors hospitals' performance through key performance indicators, a particular DEA model version is used: the BoD.

Unlike the traditional DEA technique, the BoD approach treats the key performance indicators as outputs within the original output-oriented DEA model (Van Puyenbroeck, 2018). The main advantage of applying the BoD is its flexibility in weight choice (optimization). Any other weighting approach would worsen the position of the evaluated hospital relative to the other hospitals (Cherchye et al., 2011). Using it, hospitals cannot argue that their poor relative performance on one indicator is due to a harmful or unfair weighting approach. BoD has already been applied in a broad range of fields, including economic evaluation (Zaim et al., 2001; Cherchye et al., 2007a), health care (Matos et al., 2021), and human development (Despotis, 2005).

This study also adds the Malmquist Index (Caves et al., 1982) to its methodology. Ultimately, this index compares two frontiers computed through DEA, each associated with a specific group (e.g., PPPs vs. publicly managed hospitals). By projecting hospitals in each frontier, we can compare those groups (also called clusters), which offers insights about their relative performance, allowing us to disclose whether a group outperforms the others. Based on this, Camanho and Dyson (2006) developed the Malmquist Index for group comparison. It can be multiplicatively decomposed into two indexes: one reflecting the performance spread of hospitals within the same group and another demonstrating the difference in productivity between the best-practice frontiers of the different groups.

DATA AND ANALYTICAL METHODS

An appropriate, extensive, and reliable database is needed to evaluate hospitals' performance successfully. As such, one must carefully select the variables and the sources to be used. In general, the choice of variables follows criteria such as data availability and quality and a comprehensive literature review. The official database of the Portuguese Ministry of Health, the Central Administration of the Health System (ACSS),[9] and the online platform Transparência[10] provided the data used in this study.

Variables

This study considers four clusters of key performance indicators: 1) efficiency, 2) access, 3) care appropriateness, and 4) clinical safety. The variables chosen are as follows:

1. Efficiency: the existence of resources to be used when needed and not wasted. It can be expressed in terms of service availability, productivity, and finance.
   Services availability: inpatient per hospital beds (↑)
   Productivity: inpatient per full-time-equivalent (FTE) doctor (↑); inpatient per FTE nurse (↑); hospital occupancy rate (↑)
   Finance: operational costs per inpatient (↓)
2. Access: the ability of citizens to use a specific service whenever necessary and at their will.
   Inpatient per hospital beds (↓)
   Inpatient per FTE doctor (↓)
   Inpatient per FTE nurse (↓)
   Rate of first non-urgent medical appointments within the maximum legislated guaranteed time (↑)
   Rate of surgeries with waiting time less than or equal to the maximum response guaranteed time (↑)
   Average delay before surgery (↓)
   Rate of hip surgeries in the first 48 hours after fracture, patients older than 65 (↑)
3. Care appropriateness: ability to provide patient-centered care services backed by evidence-based guidelines.
   Rate of ambulatory surgeries for outpatient procedures (↑)
   Rate of readmissions within five days after discharge (↓)
   Rate of readmissions within 30 days after discharge (↓)
   Rate of readmissions within 180 days after discharge (↓)
   Rate of admissions with delay over 30 days (↓)
   Rate of cesarean deliveries (↓)
4. Clinical safety: ability to prevent complications or even prevent deaths from happening during care.
   Pressure ulcer rate (↓)
   Rate of hemorrhagic stroke mortality (↓)
   Rate of ischemic stroke mortality (↓)
   Catheter-related bloodstream infection rate (↓)
   Postoperative pulmonary embolism/deep vein thrombosis per 100 inpatients (↓)
   Postoperative septicemia per 100 inpatients (↓)

Rate of vaginal births with third- and fourth-degree lacerations (↓)

Some of these key performance indicators are desirable (↑), contributing positively to performance, while others are not (↓). The performance indicator *ambulatory surgery rate* for outpatient procedures is an excellent example of a desirable variable. For example, minor surgeries should always occur in ambulatory services. There is an increase in total costs of the surgery and the risks of a severe infection when minor surgery patients stay in the hospital. Performing minor surgeries in ambulatory services, besides providing better care appropriateness, also enhances the efficiency of the hospital. Hence, higher values of this indicator correlate with better levels of quality.

There are three cases in which the performance indicator can be either desirable or undesirable, depending upon the point of view. The indicators inpatient per hospital beds, inpatient per FTE doctor, and inpatient per FTE nurse present two possible interpretations from an access or efficiency/productivity perspective. In terms of access, it is better to have fewer patients per doctor and nurse. When considered as an efficiency/productivity approach, it is better to have more patients treated per doctor and nurse. Therefore, these indicators should be either maximized or minimized, forcing us to develop two distinct strategies. This issue demands two different model designs: one maximizing those variables (considering them in the set of efficiency variables) and another minimizing them (placing them in the group of access variables). These variables are not considered twice in the same model (i.e., maximized and minimized simultaneously). Instead, we considered two models—*M* and *m*—in which the variables are maximized under the efficiency criteria (discarded from the access group of variables) and minimized under the access criteria (discarded from the efficiency group).

Statistical Analysis

The statistical analysis of the sample made per indicator includes the two-sample t-test and the Kruskal–Wallis test. Both tests help compare the two groups of hospitals (EPE and PPP hospitals). The rejection of the null hypothesis in the t-test implies no evidence that the two groups have different averages. Likewise, the rejection of the null hypothesis by the Kruskal–Wallis test suggests the absence of statistical evidence that the two groups have different medians. According to our statistics, it is also possible that only in three indicators (inpatient per hospital beds; readmission rate within 180 days after discharge; and catheter-related bloodstream infections rate) is the null hypothesis rejected. In these cases, both EPE and PPP hospitals exhibit similar performance.

Excluding some exceptions, both tests provide similar conclusions on the best-performer group, resulting from the considerable size of the sample. Based on the results obtained, some extracted findings regarding the types of indicators are:

- PPP hospitals outperform EPE hospitals regarding health care appropriateness.
- EPE hospitals outperform PPP hospitals concerning clinical safety, although not in all key performance indicators.
- In terms of access, there is a generalized superior performance of PPP hospitals.
- There is no clear evidence supporting the hypothesis that one group outperforms the other concerning efficiency.

These findings do not provide any consistent conclusion on the best type of hospital management, thus justifying the use of a benchmarking tool to optimize the weights (multipliers) given to each dimension, as explained before.

The Pearson's correlation coefficients for the key performance indicators used in this work clarify whether the variables provide the same information (i.e., are highly correlated). The coefficients are small or even non-statistically significant ($p < 0.05$), except for five coefficients, which exhibit a considerable correlation among them. However, only two pairs of coefficients are correlated at more than 0.70: inpatient per hospital beds and inpatient per FTE nurse ($r = 0.84$); and readmission rate within five days after discharge and readmission rate within 30 days after discharge ($r = 0.81$). These high correlations may introduce redundant information into the model. By removing one variable of each pair, the amount of redundant data is likely reduced. The dataset going forward comprises 21 variables characterizing the key performance indicators. The variables removed are inpatient per FTE nurse and readmission rate within 30 days after discharge. All remaining key performance indicators were rescaled into the range 0–100, such that higher values represent better outcomes. Through this procedure, we followed the transformation proposed by Kung and Wen (2007) and Ferreira et al. (2019).

Sample

Data sources provide information about more than 40 Portuguese public hospitals. However, units with a considerable amount of missing data are not included in the final sample. Specialized hospitals (e.g., oncology centers, maternity facilities, and psychiatric hospitals) were also removed from the sample because their production technology differs from general hospitals. Local health units were also erased from the sample since they arise from the vertical integration of a general hospital and primary health care centers. The sample comprises 28 general hospitals (24 corporatized EPE hospitals and four PPP hospitals). The last PPP hospital to start its operations was Hospital Vila Franca de Xira, in March 2013. Because of substantial missing data in 2014, the analysis period began in January 2015, and lasts until September 2019 (4 years and 9 months). In this month, the Hospital de Braga lost its PPP status, becoming an EPE hospital. We considered all monthly data for the considered key performance indicators. We constructed the best-performer frontier associated with hospitals in Portugal, allowing benchmarks for a specific month to be found in a distinct period. This implies that our frontier comprises 1596 observations, distributed as follows: 1368 EPE hospitals (Cluster A) and 228 PPP hospitals (Cluster B).

Models

This study considers two models (Models I and II) to analyze hospital performance. These models are intended to improve the robustness of the findings and the conclusions of this research. The creation of these two models results from having key variables with data missing where their exclusion was not an option. Two PPP hospitals (Cascais and Loures) do not provide any information on productivity (inpatient per FTE doctor) and economic (operational costs per inpatient) indicators. Model *I* contemplates all the hospitals (four PPPs), excluding those two variables in question, thus considering all inputs. Model *II* excludes Cascais and Loures hospitals from the sample, considering the two variables instead:

- Model *I*: variables with missing data are removed from the database, resulting in a sample of 1596 units.
- Model *II*: removes hospitals with missing data from the database (this model uses all indicators), resulting in a sample of 1482 observations, of which 114 regard PPP hospitals.

As discussed above, each model unfolds into two versions, *m* and *M*. Their difference lies in maximizing or minimizing the different indicators.

RESULTS AND DISCUSSION

After implementing both models, BoD and the Malmquist Index for group comparison, and using the database described above, a comprehensive range of results is discussed in this section.

BoD Results

The BoD model estimates performance scores per hospital, resulting in 1596 performance scores for each version of Model *I* and 1482 scores for each version of Model *II*. A statistical analysis, similar to the one conducted for the key performance indicators, was completed for these results. We added the confidence intervals, the coefficient of variation (CV), and the frequency of good performers to the analysis. The frequency of good performers provides the probability of getting hospitals whose performance is at least equal to τ = 90%.

Model *I m*

Table 4.3 provides the basic statistics for all the performance scores between 2015 and 2019 concerning Model *I m*. The first impressions from Table 4.3 are as follows:

- Only the cluster of EPE hospitals contains efficient observations (performance level = 1.00).
- The best PPP performer has a performance level of 0.977, so we can consider it a benchmark because the score is close to 1.
- The worst performer belongs to the EPE hospital group, with a performance score of 0.749.
- The lowest performance level of a PPP hospital was 0.798, not much different from the worst performer in the EPE group.
- PPP hospitals have a higher average performance consistency (average performance score = 0.891, 90 percent confidence interval [0.888; 0.895]) than EPE hospitals (average performance score = 0.855, 90 percent confidence interval [0.856; 0.859]).
- The standard deviation in both groups is considerably low, and the same is true for the CV: both groups have a coefficient of 0.04, meaning that the performance results have low dispersion (or heterogeneity).
- The probability of finding good social performers (performance score larger than 0.90) is three times higher for PPP hospitals (39 percent) than the EPE hospitals (12 percent).

Although the best hospital performance belongs to the EPE hospital group, it is possible to say that PPP hospitals are not expected to be worse performers than EPE hospitals. PPPs have a considerably higher average score and a much higher percentage of good performers, these being two quite essential characteristics when comparing both types of hospitals. The results suggest that to become efficient, both EPE and PPP hospitals need to increase their average performance levels by 14 percent and 11 percent, respectively.

Table 4.3 *Global performance basic statistics (Model I m), 2015–19*

	Hospital overall	EPE hospitals	PPP hospitals
Entries	1596	1368	228
Maximum value	1.000	1.000	0.977
Maximum {CI}	0.864	0.859	0.895
75th percentile	0.885	0.879	0.916
Mean	0.863	0.858	0.891
Median	0.860	0.855	0.887
25th percentile	0.834	0.831	0.868
Minimum {CI}	0.861	0.856	0.888
Minimum value	0.749	0.749	0.798
F(τ = 0.90)	15.60	11.700	39.040
Standard deviation (s)	0.039	0.037	0.035
Coefficient of variation (CV)	0.050	0.040	0.040

Note: CV measures heterogeneity among observations; it is calculated by dividing s by the mean. CI = confidence interval.

Figure 4.1A portrays the average performance of each regime per year of the study (2015–19). By studying this figure, it is possible to understand how hospital performance has developed throughout the years. Despite having a small decline of less than 0.5 percent in 2016, EPE hospitals increased their performance every analysis year. PPP hospitals experienced an overall increase in performance of 1.5 percent. PPP hospitals also improved their performance levels each year, except for 2016. In that year, they experienced a performance decline of more than 1 percent. The net improvement of the PPP hospitals' performance during the studied period was 0.5 percent.

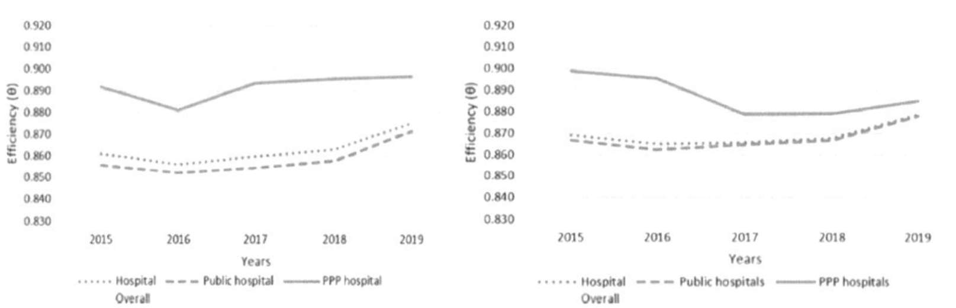

Note: Graph A: Model *I m*; graph B: Model *II m*.

Figure 4.1 *Hospitals' yearly average performance variation between 2015 and 2019*

It is also visible that PPP hospitals had better performance every year than their publicly managed (corporatized) counterparts. The difference between both models was around 3 percent–4 percent. Nevertheless, in the past three years, they appeared to be converging. In 2019, the difference between the two management models reached its lowest point: 2.6 percent.

This study used two statistical techniques consistent with the BoD methodology to assess the statistical significance of the differences in performance between both models: the Student's t-test for means and the Kruskal–Wallis non-parametric test for distributions. These tests determine if there are statistically significant differences between the two groups of hospitals. Table 4.4 provides the BoD results for both tests per year and for all the years together (2015–19).

Similar outputs were obtained for both tests: p-values were always well below the significance level of 5 percent, except for the Student's t-test for 2019. Both tests reject the null hypothesis of similar performance of the hospital groups, which means that one group outperforms the other. In this case, this group is composed of the PPP hospitals (Cluster B). For instance, PPP hospitals exhibit a higher average performance level in 2.85 percent–3.90 percent compared with EPE hospitals regarding the pooled sample. In conclusion, for this model (Model *I m*), both tests declare PPP hospitals as the best group for every year.

Model *II m*

Model *II m* uses all key performance indicators, removing the PPP hospitals with missing data (Hospital de Cascais and Hospital de Loures). Starting by analyzing the yearly average performance levels of the hospital models, we observe that PPP hospitals are always above EPE hospitals in terms of average performance (see Figure 4.1B). Analyzing the individual evolution of EPE hospitals reveals that they increase their performance every year, except for 2016, when they experienced a minimal drop of less than 0.5 percent. EPE hospitals exhibit an overall performance increase of 1.1 percent, on average. PPP hospitals' performance reached the maximum value in 2015, and from then until 2017, it dropped by nearly 2 percent. Their performance increased from 2018 to 2019 by just 0.6 percent. Throughout this analysis, PPP hospitals exhibited a decrease in performance level, with an overall drop of 1.4 percent from 2015 to 2019.

Nonetheless, comparing both models, PPPs seem to outperform EPE hospitals every year, but that gap has been vanishing, according to this model: 2015 started with a clear difference in performance for the PPPs of more than 3 percent, until that difference converged to 0.7 percent in 2019.

Table 4.4 presents results from the statistical tests conducted on the average performance levels for every analysis year. The outputs obtained for both

Table 4.4 *Student's t-test for means and Kruskal–Wallis non-parametric test for distributions for the performance values of Models I m and II m*

Model *I m*						
	2015	2016	2017	2018	2019	2015–19
Student's t-test for means						
p-value	0.0000	0.0000	0.0000	0.0000	0.0017	0.0000
95% CI, lower bound	−0.0464	−0.0394	−0.0501	−0.0486	−0.0408	−0.0390
95% CI, upper bound	−0.0252	−0.0185	−0.0282	−0.0264	−0.0096	−0.0285
T statistic	−6.6238	−5.4395	−7.0296	−6.6467	−3.1799	−12.7032
Best performer	PPP	PPP	PPP	PPP	PPP	PPP
Kruskal–Wallis non-parametric test for distributions and medians						
p-value	0.0000	0.0000	0.0000	0.0000	0.0001	0.0000
Best performer	PPP	PPP	PPP	PPP	PPP	PPP

Model *II m*						
	2015	2016	2017	2018	2019	2015–19
Student's t-test for means						
p-value	0.0000	0.0000	0.0333	0.0695	0.4797	0.0000
95% CI, lower bound	−0.0440	−0.0455	−0.0265	−0.0255	−0.0255	−0.0263
95% CI, upper bound	−0.0195	−0.0198	−0.0011	0.0010	0.0120	−0.1390
T statistic	−5.1083	−4.9952	−2.1386	−1.8215	−0.7080	−6.3819
Best performer	PPP	PPP	PPP	similar	similar	PPP
Kruskal–Wallis non-parametric test for distributions and medians						
p-value	0.0000	0.0000	0.0063	0.0106	0.1271	0.0000
Best performer	PPP	PPP	PPP	PPP	similar	PPP

Note: Confidence interval (CI).

tests are very similar, with 2018 being the only exception. The Student's t-test rejected the null hypothesis of identical performance levels in 2015, 2016, 2017, and 2015–19 since the p-values are below the significance level of 5 percent. In those years, the best-performer group was the PPP hospitals. In 2018 and 2019, it was not possible to reject the null hypothesis in light of the statistical evidence, meaning that both types of hospital management exhibited similar performance levels. The Kruskal–Wallis test only differs from the t-test regarding the data for 2018, rejecting the null hypothesis in that year. In that case, PPP hospitals were the best performers.

Removing two PPP hospitals from the sample primarily affects the evolution of the performance of the PPP hospitals throughout the years. Whereas

REFERENCES

Alonso, J., Clifton, J., & Díaz-Fuentes, D. (2016). Public-private partnerships for hospitals: Does privatization affect employment? *Journal of Strategic Contracting and Negotiation*, *2*(4), 313–25.

Barbetta, G., Turati, G., & Zago, A. (2008). Behavioral differences between public and private not-for-profit hospitals in the Italian national health service. *Health Economics*, *1213*, 1207–1213.

Barros, P. P. (2019). *Economia da saúde* [Health economics]. Almedina.

Barros, P. P., Machado, S. R., & Simões, A. (2011). *Portugal health system review*. European Observatory on Health Systems and Policies.

Barros, P. P., & Martinez-Giralt, X. (2009). Contractual design and PPPs for hospitals: Lessons for the Portuguese model. *European Journal of Health Economics*, *10*(4), 437–53.

Caballer-Tarazona, M., Clemente-Collado, A., & Vivas-Consuelo, D. (2016). A cost and performance comparison of public-private partnership and public hospitals in Spain. *Health Economics Review*, *6*(1), 1–7.

Camanho, A. S., & Dyson, R. G. (2006). Data envelopment analysis and Malmquist indices for measuring group performance. *Journal of Productivity Analysis*, *26*(1), 35–49.

Caves, D. W., Christensen, L. R., & Diewert, W. E. (1982). The economic theory of index numbers and the measurement of input, output, and productivity. *Econometrica: Journal of the Econometric Society*, 1393–1414.

Cherchye, L., Lovell, C. K., Moesen, W., & Van Puyenbroeck, T. (2007a). One market, one number? A composite indicator assessment of EU internal market dynamics. *European Economic Review*, *51*(3), 749–79.

Cherchye, L., Moesen, W., Rogge, N., & Van Puyenbroeck, T. (2007b). An introduction to "benefit of the doubt" composite indicators. *Social Indicators Research*, *82*(1), 111–45.

Cherchye, L., Moesen, W., Rogge, N., & Van Puyenbroeck, T. (2011). Constructing composite indicators with imprecise data: A proposal. *Expert Systems with Applications*, *38*(9), 10940–9.

Comendeiro-Maaløe, M., Ridao-López, M., Gorgemans, S., & Bernal-Delgado, E. (2019). Public-private partnerships in the Spanish national health system: The reversion of the Alzira model. *Health Policy*, *123*(4), 408–411.

Cruz, C. O., & Marques, R. C. (2012). *O Estado e as parcerias público-privadas* [The state and public-private partnerships]. Sílabo.

Cruz, C. O., & Marques, R. C. (2013). Integrating infrastructure and clinical management in PPPs for health care. *Journal of Management in Engineering*, *29*(4), 471–81.

Despotis, D. K., (2005). A reassessment of the human development index via data envelopment analysis. *Journal of the Operational Research Society*, *56*(8), 969–80.

Entidade Reguladora da Saúde (ERS). (2016). *Estudo de avaliação das parcerias público-privadas na saúde*.

Ferreira, D. C., & Marques, R. C. (2015). Did the corporatization of Portuguese hospitals significantly change their productivity? *European Journal of Health Economics*, *16*(3), 289–303.

Ferreira, D. C., & Marques, R. C. (2016). Should inpatients be adjusted by their complexity and severity for efficiency assessment? Evidence from Portugal. *Health Care Management Science*, *19*(1), 43–57.

Ferreira, D. C., & Marques, R. C. (2018). Identifying congestion levels, sources and determinants on intensive care units: The Portuguese case. *Health Care Management Science*, *21*(3), 348–75.

Ferreira, D. C., & Marques, R. C. (2021). Public-private partnerships in health care services: Do they socially outperform public hospitals regarding quality and access? Evidence from Portugal. *Socio-Economic Planning Sciences*, *73*, 100798.

Ferreira, D. C., Marques, R. C., & Nunes, A. M. (2019). Pay for performance in health care: A new best practice tariff-based tool using a log-linear piecewise frontier function and a dual-primal approach for unique solutions. *Operational Research*, *21*, 2101–2146.

Ferreira, D. C., Marques, R. C., Nunes, A. M., & Figueira, J. R. (2018a). Patients' satisfaction: The medical appointments valence in Portuguese public hospitals. *Omega*, *80*, 58–76.

Ferreira, D. C., & Nunes, A. M. (2019). Technical efficiency of Portuguese public hospitals: A comparative analysis across the five regions of Portugal. *International Journal of Health Planning and Management*, *34*(1), e411–e422.

Ferreira, D. C., Nunes, A. M., & Marques, R. C. (2018b). Economies of scope in the health sector: The case of Portuguese hospitals. *European Journal of Operational Research*, *266*(2), 716–35.

Hollingsworth, B., & Peacock, S. J. (2008). *Efficiency measurement in health and health care*. Routledge.

Instituto Nacional de Estatística. (2019). *Estatísticas de saúde 2017* [Health statistics 2017]. Lisboa.

Kruse, F. M., Stadhouders, N. W., Adang, E. M., Groenewoud, S., & Jeurissen, P. P. (2018). Do private hospitals outperform public hospitals regarding efficiency, accessibility, and quality of care in the European Union? A literature review. *International Journal of Health Planning and Management*, *33*(2), e434–e453.

Kung, C. Y., & Wen, K. L. (2007). Applying grey relational analysis and grey decision-making to evaluate the relationship between company attributes and its financial performance—A case study of venture capital enterprises in Taiwan. *Decision Support Systems*, *43*(3), 842–52.

Marques, R. C., & Berg, S. (2011). Risks, contracts, and private-sector participation in infrastructure. *Journal of Construction Engineering and Management*, *137*(11), 925–32.

Marques, R. C., & Silva, D. (2008). As parcerias público-privadas em Portugal: Lições e recomendações [Public-private partnerships in Portugal: Lessons and recommendations]. *Tékhne - Revista de Estudos Politécnicos*, *10*, 33–50.

Matos, R., Ferreira, D. C., & Pedro, I. (2021). Economic analysis of Portuguese public hospitals through the construction of quality, efficiency, access, and financial related composite indicators. *Social Indicators Research*, *157*, 361–92.

McKee, M., Edwards, N., & Atun, R. (2006). Public-private partnerships for hospitals. *Bulletin of the World Health Organization*, *84*, 890–6.

Nunes, A. M., & Ferreira, D. C. (2018). Eficiência na assistência hospitalar em Portugal: Um estudo comparative [Efficiency in hospital care in Portugal: A comparative study]. *Jornal Brasileiro de Economia da Saúde*, *10*(3), 278–84.

Nunes, A. M., & Ferreira, D. C. (2019). The health care reform in Portugal: Outcomes from both the new public management and the economic crisis. *International Journal of Health Planning and Management*, *34*(1), 196–215.

Nunes, A. M., & Matos, A. A. (2017). Análise do desempenho dos hospitais em parceria público privada no serviço nacional de saúde Português [Analysis of the performance of hospitals in public-private partnership in the Portuguese national health service]. *Jornal Brasileiro de Economia da Saúde*, *9*(3), 304–309.

Pereira, M., Ferreira, D. C., & Marques, R. C. (2021). A critical look at the Portuguese public-private partnerships in healthcare. *International Journal of Health Planning and Management*, *36*(2), 302–315.

Reich, M. R. (2000). Public-private partnerships for public health. *Nature Medicine*, *6*(6), 617.

Roehrich, J. K., Lewis, M. A., & George, G. (2014). Are public-private partnerships a healthy option? A systematic literature review. *Social Science and Medicine*, *113*, 110–119.

Simões, J. (2004). As parcerias público-privadas no sector da saúde em Portugal [Public-private partnerships in the health sector in Portugal]. *Revista Portuguesa de Saúde Pública*, *4*, 79–90.

Torchia, M., Calabrò, A., & Morner, M. (2015). Public-private partnerships in the health care sector: A systematic review of the literature. *Public Management Review*, *17*(2), 236–61.

Tribunal de Contas. (2009). *Auditoria ao programa de parcerias público privadas da saúde – Primeira vaga de hospitais* [Audit of the public-private health partnerships program – First wave of hospitals].

Van Puyenbroeck, T. (2018). On the output orientation of the benefit-of-the-doubt-model. *Social Indicators Research*, *139*(2), 415–31.

Zaim, O., Färe, R., & Grosskopf, S. (2001). An economic approach to achievement and improvement indexes. *Social Indicators Research*, *56*(1), 91–118.

5. Addressing the performance advantages of PPPs in comparison to traditional public procurement and strictly private provision: evidence from sports stadiums built for the 2014 FIFA World Cup in Brazil

Claudio José Oliveira dos Reis and Sandro Cabral

INTRODUCTION[1]

Recently, public administration and strategy scholars have drawn attention to the interdependence between public and private actors and the need to understand the mechanisms that could lead to better (or worse) performance standards (Bel et al., 2014; Cabral et al., 2019; Hodge & Greve, 2017, 2019; Verweij & Van Meerkerk, 2020, 2021). In this sense, Public-Private Partnerships (PPPs) involving public authorities and private organisations have been largely invoked to foster public value creation by combining resources and capabilities dispersed among contracting parties (Lazzarini, 2020; Quelin et al., 2019; Verweij & Van Meerkerk, 2020, 2021; Dos Reis & Gomes, 2022). Given the recent implementation of PPPs in Brazil, few studies address the PPP implications in that context, especially in the sports and leisure sectors.

To fill this gap, we compared football stadiums built and renovated for the 2014 FIFA (Fédération Internationale de Football Association) World Cup in Brazil provided under PPPs, with those built and renovated under traditional public and private provision. Little is known about the performance of PPPs in sports facilities. Existing studies analyse how governments manage, for example, risks in PPP stadiums (Cabral & Silva, 2013), the perceptions of multiple stakeholders involved in PPPs in youth sport (Legg et al., 2018), the governance mechanisms of PPPs in sports infrastructure (Van den Hurk & Verhoest, 2015), and the PPP contracts for sports facilities (Van den Hurk &

Verhoest, 2017). In this vein, our study contributes to the PPP literature regarding sports facilities by investigating the implications of the three modes of provision (i.e., PPP, public, and private) adopted to provide football stadiums in the context of such a mega event: (i) five stadiums under PPP arrangements where the private partner (i.e., a concessionaire formed by for-profit firms) is in charge of the project implementation and execution via the Design–Build–Operate–Transfer (DBOT) model and where the public partner (i.e., a state government) is responsible for government sponsorship and monitoring the public service provision; (ii) four stadiums under traditional public procurement, which means that the state government holds the asset ownership and is responsible for the construction and operation phases of the stadium facilities; and (iii) three stadiums under private provision since a for-profit firm (i.e., a football club) holds the asset ownership and also is in charge of the stadiums' construction and operation.

In the Brazilian case, the choice of Brazil as a 2014 FIFA World Cup venue in October 2007 put the country in a prominent position in the international landscape due to the event's high visibility. However, major sporting events like the FIFA World Cup generally require high investments to construct or adapt a series of equipment to meet the standards demanded by FIFA (2011), most notably football stadiums and complementary infrastructure (Preuss et al., 2014). After selecting the tournament's 12 host cities in May 2009, the availability of stadiums in standards of excellence became a latent demand in the face of the decaying state of Brazilian sporting stadiums. The 9 out of 12 Brazilian football stadiums that hosted this mega event boasted outdated infrastructure averaging 55 years old.[2] Following the tradition of other large-scale sporting events (Cabral & Silva, 2013; Preuss et al., 2014; Roche, 2000), the Brazilian public sector played a critical role in providing public investments in sports infrastructure for the World Cup.

However, due to the need for huge investments, Roche (2000) stresses that it is often necessary to involve institutions from the public and private sectors in the organisation for these events to combine efforts to carry them out successfully. Public subsidies for the construction of new sports stadiums are commonly justified by the generation of economic benefits for the local economy (Siegfried & Zimbalist, 2000), and the presence of externalities and long-term effects brought by major sporting events (Mules, 1998). Thus, many governments have subsidised the construction of sports stadiums, claiming that such projects generate valuable public assets and positive externalities for the local economy, although these benefits are difficult to measure (Johnson & Whitehead, 2000). On the other hand, literature regarding mega sporting events does not provide a consensus on the scope of potential legacies, making it difficult to measure aspects affected by mega events (Preuss, 2007). Examples of unfavourable legacies are highlighted in the literature: the elevated costs for constructing sports equipment, investments in unnecessary structures, and the debt within the public sector (Gursoy & Kendall, 2006; Malfas et al., 2004; Roche, 2000). Then, scholars have argued that governments can adopt PPPs to: (i) reduce public spending without compromising the mega events, (ii) share financial burden and risks with the private sector, and (iii) balance short-term and long-term sustainability of sports facilities (Cabral & Silva, 2013).

From this perspective, aiming to comprehend the role of PPPs in providing sports infrastructure for mega events, we employed a qualitative approach in an exploratory and comparative perspective through a multi-case study on the five stadiums provided by PPPs for the 2014 FIFA World Cup Brazil (Arena Fonte Nova, Arena Pernambuco, Arena das Dunas, Arena Mineirão, and Arena Castelão). We then compared these initiatives with the stadiums provided under the traditional public procurement (Arena Maracanã,[3] Arena Mané Garrincha, Arena da Amazônia, and Arena Pantanal) and strictly private provision (Arena Beira-Rio, Arena da Baixada, and Arena Corinthians). Thus, we examined the performance of the PPPs compared to public and private provision. To do so, we adopted two Value for Money (VfM) indicators (i.e., time and cost performance) that can be explained by three incentive structures (i.e., asset property rights, bundling method and performance measurement, and sharing of economic risks and gains). Our analytical framework is presented below.

LITERATURE BACKGROUND AND ANALYTICAL FRAMEWORK

Various contractual arrangements between public institutions and private enterprises can be adopted to provide public assets and services, including sports-related facilities. In this sense, governments began to look for alternative provision modes with the involvement of private actors supplying public assets and services. In this context, PPPs arise as a hybrid organisational arrangement (Ménard, 2013, 2021), formed with formal arrangements between the public sector and the private initiatives (Osborne, 2010), and by combining public and private characteristics, such as economic- and social-based incentives (Kivleniece et al., 2017).

Thus, the joint action by the private sector with the public sector via PPPs is considered to generate a greater VfM[4] when compared to traditional public procurement (European Commission, 2003; International Monetary Fund [IMF], 2004; World Bank, 2012). The rationale is that the private partner plays a crucial role in adding multiple values (Kivleniece & Quelin, 2012) and capabilities (Quelin et al., 2019), so that the public-private arrangement may be economically superior to the traditional public offering. Following these premises, PPPs are advantageous when presenting (i) shorter deployment time and (ii) reduced costs (European Commission, 2003; IMF, 2004; O'Shea et al., 2019; Verweij & Van Meerkerk, 2020, 2021; World Bank, 2012).

Also, contractual features in PPPs shape private providers' incentives by encouraging adopting a holistic vision of the project's entire life-cycle and stimulating superior efforts in the provision (Hart, 2003). To this end, some sources of incentives (asset ownership, integration of construction/operations, and risk allocation) can add value to a PPP project because they affect the production efficiency in the provision of the public assets and services (European Commission, 2003; Hart, 2003; World Bank, 2012).

Our analytical framework thus highlights two essential aspects in understanding the potential of PPPs: VfM and incentive structures. The former is an aspect of performance that can be explained by the latter. Although multiple variables and factors may influence the performance of the PPPs (Hodge & Greve, 2007, 2017), our framework encompasses two VfM indicators (i.e., time and cost performance) and three incentive structures (i.e., asset property rights, bundling method and performance measurement, and sharing of economic risks and gains).

As to the PPPs' VfM indicators, scholars have posited that time performance is considered a critical success factor for infrastructure projects (Atmo et al., 2017; O'Shea et al., 2019; Verweij & Van Meerkerk, 2021). For example, a failure to comply with the execution schedule may increase the PPP's provision costs (Cabral & Silva, 2013). Then, the cost performance is also a critical factor in the provision of infrastructure (Atmo et al., 2017; Cabral & De Azevedo, 2008; Daito & Gifford, 2014; Verweij & Van Meerkerk, 2020, 2021) since the lower the provision costs, the higher the cost savings by the public administration and, in turn, the better the public value of such initiatives (Cabral et al., 2019; Lazzarini, 2020; Dos Reis & Gomes, 2022).

The incentive structures can influence the VfM indicators as follows. The first potential source of incentives relates to asset ownership. In a PPP, the private partner can hold large portions of property rights throughout the project's life-cycle. The concentration of property and decision rights in the private partner sphere can induce better time and cost performance in the presence of contractual incompleteness due to managerial flexibility (Hart, 2003; Tirole, 1999). In this case, the private partner has the motivations to carry out new investments to improve such performances. However, innovations for improving implementation time- and cost-efficiency can happen at the expense of reduced quality (Hart et al., 1997), which requires monitoring mechanisms by the public sector to curb self-interested behaviour by private stakeholders (Cabral et al., 2010).

Concerning the second potential source of incentives, PPP projects often have a higher integration of activities in the private sector encouraging productive efficiency (European Commission, 2003; IMF, 2004; World Bank, 2012).

Hart (2003) contends that the Build–Operate–Transfer (BOT) and DBOT models are associated with the fact that the private partner is responsible at the same time for the construction of the equipment and operation of the public service, which is often called bundling. The World Bank (2012) claims that bundling made possible by PPPs encourages the private partner to complete each phase of the project (construction, operation, and maintenance) with more operational efficiency, minimising the total costs incurred in the provision of equipment and public service and, in turn, improving the PPPs' cost performance. The integration between construction and operation creates additional incentives to mitigate behaviours that lead to a deterioration in ex-post quality (Cabral et al., 2013).

Lastly, the third potential source of incentives lies in allocating and distributing risks and benefits between the partners. Bing et al. (2005) argue that the public entity should identify the risks inherent to the PPP project, establishing the most relevant problems for each step, the probability of an occurrence of each risk event, and the potential financial consequences. This is needed so that the responsible public entity can define the type and number of risks that should be transferred to the private partner. In this sense, one of the main sources of risk in PPP projects is demand risk (Iossa & Martimort, 2012). Objected to a rigorous analysis by PPP project lenders, the uncertainties associated with demand can induce governments to offer minimum cash flow guarantees to make PPP projects more attractive (Cabral & Silva, 2013; Carbonara & Pellegrino, 2018). Thus, the adoption of an efficient risk allocation process can improve the cost performance and generate additional VfM for PPPs (Bing et al., 2005; Oudot, 2005).

METHODOLOGY

We adopted a qualitative approach in an exploratory, comparative, and descriptive perspective (Flick, 2014). We then performed analyses of the PPP, public, and private stadiums adopted in the provision of sports venues for the 2014 FIFA Brazil World Cup (Table 5.1).

We also adopted case-study methods to deepen our knowledge regarding the similarities and differences of PPP projects, seeking to distil the empirical knowledge through the theoretical systematisation of this study's theme (Eisenhardt, 1989; Yin, 2013). To do so, we employed three phases for data collection and analysis: documental analysis, semi-structured interviews, and content analysis.

As to secondary data collection, we first embraced an exploratory documentary analysis relating to all sports stadiums (public, private, and PPP). For that, we have assessed the following documents: public bidding documents and contracts for PPP projects and public projects, economic proposals of bid

Table 5.1 Summary of the sports stadium cases in Brazil

Nº	Sports Stadiums	Host City	Asset Ownership	Type of Action	Provision Method	Interview Code	Interviewer Code	Interviewer Position	Institutions
1	Arena Fonte Nova	Salvador	Public	Reconstruction	PPP	E1	Public Manager #1	State Secretary	Bahia State Government (Secopa-BA)
						E2	Private Manager #1	President	Arena Fonte Nova
						E3	Private Manager #2	Director	Bahia Sports Club
						E4	Private Manager #3	Director	Bahia Sports Club
2	Arena Pernambuco	Recife	Public	Construction	PPP	E5	Public Manager #2	State Secretary	Pernambuco State Government (Secopa-PE)
						E6	Private Manager #4	President	Arena Pernambuco
3	Arena das Dunas	Natal	Public	Reconstruction	PPP	E7	Public Manager #3	State Secretary	Rio Grande do Norte State Government (Secopa-RN)
4	Arena Mineirão	Belo Horizonte	Public	Renovation	PPP	E8	Public Manager #4	Chief of Staff	Minas Gerais State Government (Secopa-MG)
						E9	Private Manager #5	Manager	Arena Mineirão
5	Arena Castelão	Fortaleza	Public	Renovation	PPP	E10	Public Manager #5	State Secretary	Ceará State Government (Secopa-CE)
						E11	Private Manager #6	Manager	Arena Castelão
						E12	Private Manager #7	President	Lagardère/Arena Castelão
						E13	Private Manager #8	Director	Ceará Sporting Club
						E14	Private Manager #9	Construction Supervisor	Galvão Engenharia

Nº	Sports Stadiums	Host City	Asset Ownership	Type of Action	Provision Method	Interview Code	Interviewer Code	Interviewer Position	Institutions
6	Arena Maracanã	Rio de Janeiro	Public	Renovation	Public	E15	Private Manager #10	Director	Arena Maracanã
7	Arena Mané Garrincha	Brasília	Public	Reconstruction	Public	E16	Public Manager #6	District Secretary	Government of the Federal District (UGP Copa)
						E17	Public Manager #7	Director	Arena Mané Guarrincha
8	Arena da Amazônia	Manaus	Public	Reconstruction	Public	E18	Public Manager #8	UGP Copa Coordinator	Amazonas State Government (UGP Copa)
						E19	Public Manager #9	Director	Arena da Amazônia
9	Arena Pantanal	Cuiabá	Public	Reconstruction	Public	E20	Public Manager #10	State Secretary	Mato Grosso State Government (Secopa-MT)
						E21	Public Manager #11	Manager	Arena Pantanal
10	Arena Beira-Rio	Porto Alegre	Private	Renovation	Private	E22	Public Manager #12	State Secretary	Rio Grande do Sul State Government (Secretary of Sports)
						E23	Public Manager #13	Coordinator UGP Copa	Rio Grande do Sul State Government (UGP Copa)
						E24	Private Manager #11	Manager	Arena Beira-Rio/Sport Club Internacional

Nº	Sports Stadiums	Host City	Asset Ownership	Type of Action	Provision Method	Interview Code	Interviewer Code	Interviewer Position	Institutions
11	Arena da Baixada	Curitiba	Private	Renovation	Private	E25	Public Manager #14	Municipal Secretary	Curitiba Municipal Government—PR (Secopa)
						E26	Private Manager #12	President	Arena da Baixada/ Atlético Paranaense Club
12	Arena Corinthians	São Paulo	Private	Construction	Private	E27	Public Manager #15	Executive Coordinator	São Paulo State Government (World Cup Committee)
						E28	Public Manager #16	Consultant	City of São Paulo (World Cup Steering Committee)
						E29	Private Manager #13	President	Arena Corinthians/Sport Club Corinthians
						E30	Private Manager #14	Sports Specialist	Jornal Agora São Paulo

winners, business plans, economic feasibility studies, project performance indexes, and financing agreements. We also examined balance sheet reports on the 2014 FIFA World Cup provided by the Brazilian transparency portal, reports of the Car Wash (*Lava Jato*) operation, a major task force to investigate corruption schemes in Brazil, and reports on the stadiums by external control agencies, such as Brazilian Federal Audit Court (*Tribunal de Contas da União*).

We then conducted 30 semi-structured interviews with the public and private stakeholders involved in constructing the 12 sports stadiums (16 public officials and 14 private managers), totalling 28 hours and 48 minutes of recorded audio interviews (see Table 5.1).[5] We chose key stakeholders to be interviewed based on their formal position in public and private institutions involved in managing the stadiums' projects (see Table 5.1). Naturally, the availability of the key participants limited any expansion of the sample, which was compensated by the documentary analysis.

Lastly, we deployed content analysis combining bibliographical material, documental sources, and transcripts from the interviews. To do so, we coded the VfM (i.e., time and cost performance) and the contractual incentives (i.e., asset property rights, bundling method and performance measurement, and sharing of economic risks and gains) to examine the sports stadiums data. Finally, we adopted data triangulation to enhance the reliability of the research findings (Jick, 1979), using the NVivo software for the coding, analysis, and application of the content analysis.

DESCRIPTION OF THE PPP CASES

This section provides the main characteristics of the PPP cases regarding (i) bidding method, (ii) concession period, (iii) context and public need for PPP projects, (iv) risk management and allocation, (v) financial modelling, and (vi) operational modelling.

All PPP stadiums adopted the international bidding method, making it possible for bidding consortia to associate with foreign companies with expertise in managing multipurpose sports facilities. On the other hand, the PPP stadiums adopted different concession periods: Arena Fonte Nova (35 years),[6] Arena Pernambuco (30 years),[7] Arena das Dunas (20 years),[8] Arena Mineirão (27 years), and Arena Castelão (8 years).

Regarding the context and public need for PPPs, the research revealed that the primary motivating factors for implementing the projects are related to (i) expectations on generating potential legacies for the host city and state, and (ii) the feasibility of the construction or renovation of modern multipurpose sports venues to meet the technical requirements of FIFA's specifications. Two factors stand out regarding the reasons for choosing a particular PPP arrangement: (i) the absence of public financial resources for direct investments, and (ii) the search for a better VfM for governments.

As to the risk management and allocation process, different organisational arrangements between the public sector and the private sector were established, particularly regarding rules for sharing the demand risks and additional gains in PPP projects (Table 5.2).

As to the financial modelling of PPPs, we examined the different organisational arrangements between the public and private partners concerning (i) financing structure, (ii) structure of the guarantees offered by the public entity, and (iii) methodology for financial rebalancing (Table 5.3).

As to the operational modelling, our research also shows the difference in the organisational arrangements between the PPP parties, especially regarding the payment mechanisms of public compensation (fixed and variable) and for assessing the performance of the PPPs' private partners (see Table 5.3).

We argue that some lessons can be drawn from all PPP cases studied. For instance, the existence of contractual variations presented among the PPPs may influence the performance of such projects and, in turn, the generation of VfM for the public administration, as demonstrated regarding the dimensions of risk allocation, financial modelling, and operational modelling. We underscore the following potential implications: (i) an increase in provision costs as a result of the high risk assumed by some public partners, (ii) an increase in public debt in cases where the state governments have assumed almost the total or all of the project financing, and (iii) low potential for penalising the private partners on inefficiencies during the contract execution, in cases where mechanisms for measuring the PPP's performance are absent.

ANALYSIS

Evaluation of the VfM for PPP Projects

Time performance

We first analysed the time performance of the PPP, public, and private stadiums (Table 5.4). The results suggest that the PPP projects performed better in terms of implementation time than public and private provision, except for the PPP project in Bahia, which showed a minor delay of three months.

The Arena Fonte Nova was the only PPP project that exceeded the estimated initial implementation period. This is because FIFA's new requirements for the stadiums were launched after signing the PPP agreement (FIFA, 2011), leading to an increase in such PPP costs. On the other hand, the PPPs in Pernambuco and Ceará completed their work ahead of schedule due to a political decision by their governors to anticipate their stadiums' construction period to apply as a host city for the 2013 FIFA Confederations Cup in Brazil. This anticipation

Table 5.2 Rules for sharing the demand risks and additional gains in the PPP projects

Nº	PPP cases	Demand Risk Methodology		Rules for Sharing Additional Gains	
		Event triggering the sharing of demand risk	Methodology for the sharing of demand risk	Event triggering the sharing of additional gains	Methodology for sharing additional gains
1	Arena Fonte Nova	Variations taking place in the annual operating revenue earned by the private partner, the least, verified below 100% of the corresponding annual operating income of the base case	Share the loss of operational revenue between public and private partners in a 50% ratio for each party	Variations in the real annual operating revenue earned by the private partner, the greater, verified above at 100% of the base case's operating income (R$23.76 million)	Sharing of additional gains between public and private partners, at 50% for each party that exceeds 100% of the operating revenue
2	Arena Pernambuco	Variations taking place in the annual operating revenue earned by the private partner, the least, verified between 90% and 50% of the annual operating income of the base case	Share the loss of operational revenue between public and private partners in a 50% ratio for each party	Variations in the real annual operating revenue earned by the private partner, the greater, verified above at 110% of the base case's operating income (R$73.26 million)	Sharing of additional gains between public and private partners, at 50% for each party that exceeds 110% of the operating revenue
		Variations taking place in the annual operating income earned by the private partner, the least, verified below 50% of the annual operating income of the base case in less than six months	Share the loss of operational revenue between public and private partners in a 50% ratio for each party	—	—
		Variations taking place in annual operating income earned by the private partner, the least, verified below 50% of the base year's annual operating income in six consecutive months	100% of the corresponding losses will be the responsibility of the public partner	—	—

Nº	PPP cases	Demand Risk Methodology		Rules for Sharing Additional Gains	
		Event triggering the sharing of demand risk	Methodology for the sharing of demand risk	Event triggering the sharing of additional gains	Methodology for sharing additional gains
3	Arena das Dunas	—	The private partner assumes 100% of the level of demand risks	The calculation of complementary and ancillary revenues by the private partner	Sharing of complementary and ancillary revenues at 50% for each of the parties
4	Arena Mineirão	—	The private partner assumes 100% of the level of demand risks	Variations in the real annual operating revenue earned by the private partner, the greater, verified above at the monthly payment of R$3.7 million (Reference Value—VRR), whose value was established by the private partner itself in the bidding process	Sharing of additional gains between public and private partners, at 50% for each party that exceeds the Reference Value (VRR)
5	Arena Castelão	—	The private partner assumes 100% of the level of demand risks	The calculation of complementary and ancillary revenues by the private partner	Sharing of complementary and ancillary revenues at 50% for each of the parties

Table 5.3 Summary of the financial and operational modelling of the PPP projects

Nº	Sports Stadiums	Financing Structure		Structure of the Guarantees offered by the Public Entity	Methodology for Financial Rebalancing	Variable payment amount (USD)	Variable per total payment (%)	Variable payment (%)	Negative implications
		Public Partner	Private Partner						
1	Arena Fonte Nova	The public partner assumed 61% of the PPP's total value (R$689.4 M), using: (1) financing with the Brazilian National Development Bank (BNDES) ProCopa line of credit at R$323.6 M; (2) contribution of their resources of R$97.7 M from the State Treasury	The private partner assumed 39% of the PPP's total value, using R$250 M of financing with the Northeast Development Bank (BNB) and R$18 M from their resources	Transfer of 12% of financial resources from the State Participation Fund (FPE) for the Bahia State Development Bank (Desenbahia) instituted as a guarantor agent	Based on the sharing of demand risks	$3.3 M	7.30%	60%	Low absolute value of variable public payment
2	Arena Pernambuco	The public partner assumed 75% of the total value of PPP (R$532.6 M), using R$392.8 M of financing from BNDES ProCopa line of credit	The private partner assumed 25% of the PPP's total value, using R$218 M of financing with the BNB (part of this financing was paid by the state) and R$34.6 M from financial institutions and their resources	(1) The state of Pernambuco contracted financing from BNDES Pro-Copa to repay the loan initiated by the concessionaire with the BNDES and part of the financing with BNB; (2) This state also created a guaranteed account for a six-month guarantee of public payment	Based on the sharing of demand risks	$1.6 M	100%	5%	Low absolute value + Low maximum percentage limit for a reduction of variable payment

Nº	Sports Stadiums	Financing Structure		Structure of the Guarantees offered by the Public Entity	Methodology for Financial Rebalancing	Variable payment amount (USD)	Variable per total payment (%)	Variable payment (%)	Negative implications
		Public Partner	Private Partner						
3	Arena das Dunas	—	The private partner assumed 100% of the value of PPP, using R$396.6 M of financing from BNDES ProCopa and R$3.4 million from their resources	(1) Guarantor Fund for PPPs in the Rio Grande do Norte (FGPPP/RN) with a minimum value of R$70 M, and the state may use FPE resources; (2) Offer of public assets, totalling R$412 M	Based on the premise that the private partner is fully responsible for all the risks inherent in the construction (time and costs) and operation (demand) of public sports venues	$6.8 M	15%	86%	Low absolute value of variable public payment
4	Arena Mineirão	—	The private partner assumed 100% of the PPP's total value, using R$400 M of financing with the BNDES ProCopa and R$277.3 M from financial institutions and their resources	(1) Credit rights from the Development Incentive Fund (Findes), in the amounts of R$386.8 M (Pro-Invest) and R$406.7 M (Pro-Giro); (2) Securities from federal public debt in the amount of R$100 M	Based on the premise that the private partner is fully responsible for all the risks inherent in the construction (time and costs) and operation (demand) of the public sports venue	$18.3 M	38%	60%	—
5	Arena Castelão	The public partner assumed 100% of the total value of the PPP, using: (1) financing with BNDES ProCopa of R$351.5 M; (2) provision of its funds of R$167 M from the State Treasury	—	(1) Full assumption of the payment for the construction of public sports venues by the state of Ceará; (2) Creation of an escrow account with the Federal Bank Caixa Econômica Federal (PPP contract does not specify value offered in guarantee)	Based on the premise that the private partner is fully responsible for all the risks inherent in the construction (time and costs) and operation (demand) of public sports venues and that the state has fully paid the cost of construction of the stadium in the delivery of the project	$0.16 M	100%	38%	Low absolute value + low maximum percentage limit for a reduction of variable compensation

Table 5.4 *Time performance of the 12 sports stadiums*

Nº	Sports Stadiums	Type of Provision	Type of Intervention	Contract Signing Date	Start of Work	Delivery Schedule Outlined in the Contract	Actual Delivery Schedule	Total Estimated Time (months)	Total Actual Time (months)	Var. (%)
1	Arena Fonte Nova	PPP	Reconstruction	Jan. 2010	Jun. 2010	Dec. 2012	Mar. 2013	36	39	108%
2	Arena Pernambuco	PPP	Construction	Jun. 2010	Jan. 2011	Jun. 2013	Apr. 2013	36	34	94%
3	Arena das Dunas	PPP	Reconstruction	Apr. 2011	Aug. 2011	Dec. 2013	Dec. 2013	32	32	100%
4	Arena Mineirão	PPP	Renovation	Dec. 2010	Jan. 2011	Dec. 2012	Dec. 2012	24	24	100%
5	Arena Castelão	PPP	Renovation	Nov. 2010	Dec. 2010	Apr. 2013	Dec. 2012	29	24	83%
6	Arena Maracanã	Public	Renovation	Aug. 2010	Aug. 2010	Feb. 2013	May 2013	30	33	110%
7	Arena Mané Garrincha	Public	Reconstruction	Jul. 2010	Jul. 2010	Dec. 2012	Jun. 2013	30	36	120%
8	Arena da Amazônia	Public	Reconstruction	Jul. 2010	Jul. 2010	Jun. 2013	Mar. 2014	36	45	125%
9	Arena Pantanal	Public	Reconstruction	Apr. 2010	May 2010	Dec. 2012	May 2014	32	49	153%
10	Arena Beira-Rio	Private	Renovation	Not published	Jul. 2010	Dec. 2013	Feb. 2014	41	43	105%
11	Arena da Baixada	Private	Renovation	Not published	Oct. 2011	Jun. 2013	May 2014	21	30	143%
12	Arena Corinthians	Private	Construction	Not published	May 2011	Dec. 2013	Apr. 2014	31	35	113%

was not previously estimated and contributed to an increase in PPP costs in Pernambuco. As to the Arena Mineirão and Arena das Dunas, their private partners managed to complete the stadiums' construction within the deadlines established in the initial schedule, which the contractual modelling of both PPPs can justify.

We underline that there was a faster execution of PPP projects because of the flexibility and managerial agility by the private partners, coupled with the strong involvement of the public partners in implementing the projects (Boyer et al., 2016). The need for the government's involvement becomes clear in the strictly private projects of Arena Corinthians and Arena da Baixada. The reason is that they had significant delays in their stadiums' implementation schedules, despite having the same benefits as the PPPs regarding the flexibility and managerial agility of the private actors. In this sense, our findings suggest that the impossibility of the state government to take financing for the strictly private projects (e.g., as they did in the PPP projects) impacted the private stadiums' larger fundraising processes, resulting in delays in such projects' implementation. As to the public projects, we highlight that the managerial rigidity imposed by the Brazilian Federal Procurement Law (No. 8666 of 1993) generated delays and increased project costs.[9]

> We had some obstacles to taking the BNDES ProCopa line of credit because the stadium ownership belongs to our private football club,[10] and we did not have a solid guarantee to offer the bank… So, the local public development bank had to be our intervening party in this BNDES financing. (Private Manager #12, Arena da Baixada)

> We were only able to speed up the work schedule because it was a PPP. If it had been a project through Federal Law No. 8666, we would not have had time to quickly execute the project because we would not have the flexibility to adapt the construction process by implementing modern engineering techniques that had not been initially foreseen. (Private Manager #9, Arena Castelão)

Another potential advantage of the PPP stadiums that contributed to better time performance was its bidding process. We compared the bidding processes between PPP and public stadiums (see Table 5.5).[11] Our findings suggest that almost all PPPs showed a shorter bidding execution time than traditional public procurement in terms of the difference between the date of releasing the public tender notice and the date of signing the contract. It is worth noting that the Fonte Nova and Mineirão stadiums were the only PPP projects that adopted the inversion mechanism between the bidding phases of eligibility and the judgement for the technical/economic proposals, following the Brazilian Law of PPPs (Federal Law 11 079 of 2004). Such mechanisms contribute to accelerating the PPP's bidding process, making it possible only to analyse the eligibility of the winning bidder. This practice is an economic advantage

Table 5.5 *Implementation time and competitiveness level of the bidding processes of PPP and public sports stadiums*

Nº	Sports Stadiums	Implementation Time for the Bidding Process					Competitiveness Level of the Bidding Process	
		Type of Provision	Bidding Types of Competition	Publication date of Public Bid	Contract Signature Date	Implementation Time (months)	Number of Firms or Consortia Bidders	Estimated Cost per Seat at Start of Contract (US$)
1	Arena Fonte Nova	PPP	International	Oct. 2009	Jan. 2010	3	1	4430
2	Arena Pernambuco	PPP	International	Feb. 2010	Jun. 2010	4	2	3386
3	Arena das Dunas	PPP	International	Dec. 2010	Apr. 2011	4	1	3922
4	Arena Mineirão	PPP	International	Jun. 2010	Dec. 2010	6	1	4490
5	Arena Castelão	PPP	International	Jan. 2010	Nov. 2010	10	4	3352
6	Arena Maracanã	Public	National	Mar. 2010	Aug. 2010	5	2	3698
7	Arena Mané Garrincha	Public	National	Jul. 2009	Jul. 2010	12	8	3945
8	Arena da Amazônia	Public	National	Nov. 2009	Jul. 2010	8	2	4628
9	Arena Pantanal	Public	National	Oct. 2009	Apr. 2010	6	6	4823

in implementing infrastructure projects through PPP, as the total execution period of a project directly influences its provision costs (Ahadzi & Bowles, 2004). This is an essential factor in the context of mega sporting events like the FIFA World Cup, characterised by a strict schedule that needs to be rigorously complied with in order for the competitions to be held on time (FIFA, 2011).

Cost performance

Second, we examined the cost performance of the PPP, public, and private stadiums (Table 5.6). We then assessed the provision costs' compliance with the costs initially forecasted and the cost-per-seat indicator of the stadiums. From this perspective, our findings indicate that two of the three sports stadiums built under the private firm's logic (Arena Beira-Rio and Arena da Baixada) showed a lower cost of provision per seat than sports stadiums built under the logic of the PPPs and the traditional public procurement. However, the lesser degree of physical intervention in these renovation projects should be accounted for compared to other projects in which new facilities were built. In comparing PPP projects with traditional public provision projects, we reveal that PPPs performed better in terms of the cost-per-seat indicator and the first forecast budget. It is worth noting that the Mané Garrincha and Maracanã

Table 5.6 *Cost performance of the 12 sports stadiums*

Nº	Sports Stadiums	Provision Type	Intervention Type	Total Capacity (Fixed + Temporary)	Total Cost Expected in the Contract (US$)	Total Real Cost (US$)	Var. (%)	Estimated Cost Per Seat (US$)	Real Cost per Seat (US$)	Var. (%)
1	Arena Fonte Nova	PPP	Reconstruction	55 045	243 873 879	284 170 171	117%	4430	5162	117%
2	Arena Pernambuco	PPP	Construction	46 154	156 313 445	219 511 189	140%	3386	4756	140%
3	Arena das Dunas	PPP	Reconstruction	42 024	164 860 075	164 860 075	100%	3922	3922	100%
4	Arena Mineirão	PPP	Renovation	62 170	279 171 175	286 444 380	103%	4490	4607	103%
5	Arena Castelão	PPP	Renovation	63 763	213 743 560	213 743 560	100%	3352	3352	100%
6	Arena Maracanã	Public	Renovation	78 639	290 808 698	495 297 643	170%	3698	6298	170%
7	Arena Mané Garrincha	Public	Reconstruction	72 777	287 123 804	592 915 318	207%	3945	8146	207%
8	Arena da Amazônia	Public	Reconstruction	44 480	205 872 606	275 934 550	134%	4628	6203	134%
9	Arena Pantanal	Public	Reconstruction	44 335	213 864 732	278 619 489	130%	4823	6284	130%
10	Arena Beira-Rio	Private	Renovation	49 989	136 009 561	150 970 613	111%	2720	3020	111%
11	Arena da Baixada	Private	Renovation	42 381	96 443	161 356 798	167%	2275	3807	167%
12	Arena Corinthians	Private	Construction	68 000	337 963 153	445 122 202	132%	4970	6545	132%

stadiums—both renovated under the traditional public procurement—were the stadiums that obtained the highest respective costs of provision, and both presented indications of over-invoicing according to external control agencies (Tribunal de Contas da União, 2013; Tribunal de Contas do Distrito Federal, 2013).

However, despite evidence of costs overrun and signs of over-invoicing on the part of some public sports facilities, the provision costs for Brazilian stadiums are consistent with the costs of similar stadiums built in other countries (e.g., the 2006 FIFA World Cup in Germany), most likely because of the tireless performance of Brazilian external control agencies. Comparing similar stadium projects provided in both mega sporting events (Germany and Brazil), Cabral and Silva (2014) found that the Munich stadium had higher costs (capacity 68 000 seats and US$7797 per seat) than the strictly private Arena Corinthians (capacity 68 000 seats and US$6545 per seat),[12] although both had similar seat capacities. In turn, the Cologne stadium (capacity 50 000 seats and US$7048 per seat) presented a higher cost than the cost for the Arena Fonte Nova (capacity 50 000 seats and US$5162 per seat).[13] On the other hand, these authors also demonstrate that even the purely public Arena da Amazônia (US$6203 per seat), whose real budget was higher than expected, had a provisioning cost that was consistent with the stadiums built in Germany. Brasília's strictly public stadium (US$8146 per seat) was the worst-performing in terms of costs, suggesting that the purely public stadiums have higher costs than strictly private or PPP stadiums.

As a complementary explanation regarding operating cost performance, we underscore the possibility of diversifying revenue by the PPP and private stadiums that can help improve their VfM. Our study shows that PPP and private stadiums have a great potential for generating alternative operating revenues beyond football tickets, such as revenues from non-sports events (e.g., mega concerts, conferences, and cultural events) and other revenues (e.g., naming rights, advertising and marketing, parking, bar, and restaurants). For instance, concerning the PPP stadiums, the Arena Fonte Nova and Arena Pernambuco signed a ten-year naming rights deal, valued at R$100 million, with the same brewery firm at the beginning of their operations (before the 2014 FIFA World Cup in 2013). As to the private stadiums, the Arena Corinthians also signed a 20-year naming rights deal with a private pharmaceutical company, valued at R$300 million (after the 2014 FIFA World Cup in 2020). On the other hand, sports stadiums under traditional public management cannot charge additional revenue for the commercial operation of public equipment due to the limits imposed by the Brazilian Procurement Law. In this way, the PPP and private stadiums can reduce the uncertainties and demand risk associated with operating revenues from the football ticket office (Cabral & Silva, 2013). Thus, we emphasise that obtaining these complementary revenues requires a business structure whose competencies are rarely found within traditional public administration, demonstrating the potential of PPPs compared to traditional public procurement.

Finally, we also underline the level of competitiveness in the stadiums' biddings (see Table 5.5), which can serve as another complementary explanation of their cost performance. This is because the bidding competitiveness is considered a critical success factor in infrastructure projects since it is expected that the higher the number of firms/consortia bidders, the better the cost performance (Tiong, 1996). However, as shown in Table 5.5, almost all PPP and public stadiums presented a low level of competitiveness in their bidding process, which may have influenced the stadiums' cost performance (e.g., the estimated cost per seat). In this sense, we highlight some possible negative implications on the VfM of almost all stadiums. Ten out of twelve sports stadiums, including all PPP projects, were in the spotlight of the Car Wash (*Lava Jato*) operation because of possible cases of malfeasance (Ministério Público Federal, 2021),[14] which may explain the low competition in almost all stadiums' bids and, in turn, their cost performance. In this vein, as a lesson for future PPP projects, we claim that effective public accountability mechanisms (Forrer et al., 2010; Grimsey & Lewis, 2005; Reeves, 2013) can contribute to mitigating such issues and enhance the VfM and public value of these initiatives (Cabral et al., 2019; Lazzarini, 2020; Reynaers, 2014; Dos Reis & Gomes, 2022).

The Implications of Incentive Structures in the Implementation of PPP Projects

Our findings suggest that the contractual incentive structures found in PPP projects contribute to generating VfM for the public administration. This is because such incentives are not provided for in public stadiums contracts, which are prepared based on the Brazilian Procurement Law. Thus, in this section, we discuss the following economic incentives: (i) asset property rights, (ii) bundling method and performance measurement, and (iii) sharing of economic risks and gains.

Property rights

First, as to the asset property rights (Hart et al., 1997), we argue that this economic incentive granted to the private partner throughout the contractual execution contributed to a gain of managerial flexibility in managing the contract and, in turn, better time and cost performance. The rationale is that the PPP's private partner has a margin of autonomy for the execution of the construction and operation of the stadium without the need for bidding procedures for each specific type of investment as required for the public stadiums. This encourages the private partner to carry out new investments in public sports facilities due to its greater autonomy to solve potential contingencies that could occur during the construction and operation of the stadium, also minimising the potential risks arising from the possibility of contractual incompleteness in the execution of the contract (Tirole, 1999). Conversely, this cannot be done in sports venues under the traditional public procurement model, given the need to hold bidding procedures for each type of contracted product and service, as determined by the Brazilian Procurement Law, which is configured in the absence of contractual flexibility in the implementation of the project (De Brito & Silveira, 2005).[15] For example, in the specific case of sporting facilities constructed under the logic of traditional public procurement, several bidding processes were conducted to procure different contractual objectives, which contributed to the occurrence of delays in the implementation schedule and, consequently, boosting the costs in the provision of public projects. To illustrate the influence of property rights on time and cost performance, we highlight two exemplary cases: Arena Mané Garrincha (public stadium) versus Arena Castelão (PPP stadium).

> Under the Federal Law 8666, we had to undertake different bids to each of the stadium's structures, for example, the concrete structure, bleachers, and grass... So, the need of realising different bids for providing different parts of the stadium contributed to increasing our implementation schedule and provision costs. (Public Manager #7, Arena Mané Garrincha)

> As it is a PPP and the responsibility as a private partner for the execution of the project is ours, we had the flexibility and agility to carry out the work. If the project had been under Federal Law 8666, this process would be hampered because we would have to ask the government's approval for every change we might need to make throughout the project, which could result in months of delays... So, we can attribute our efficiency to the aspects of flexibility in executing the engineering and structure of the PPP contract. (Private Manager #9, Arena Castelão)

Bundling method and performance measurement

Second, concerning the contractual incentives from the bundling method and the performance measurement, we underscore that the private partners of the five PPP projects received a greater incentive for improved performance on the indicators of the implementation time and stadium provision costs. The reason is that the private concessionaire's poor performance in the construction and operation of public equipment influences the payment value of the variable public compensation, which could suffer a reduction depending on the performance measured. Contrarily, the sports stadiums built under the traditional public logic are characterised by unbundling, as the private agent responsible for building the stadium (through the bidding procedure in Federal Procurement Law) is different from the agent that will operate the sports facilities—the public entity itself. Therefore, the stadium-building consortium does not earn future benefits or sanctions due to its performance in the stadium's construction, which does not create any incentive mechanism for better performance in the construction phase of public facilities (Hart, 2003). We underline two exemplary cases to demonstrate the effect of bundling method on time and cost performance: Arena Maracanã (built under the traditional public procurement and later granted to private initiatives via PPP in the operational phase) versus Arena Mineirão (PPP stadium).

> The interesting aspect about the Maracanã is that this stadium has some peculiarities. The construction was done by another firm under traditional public procurement. After that, we won the bid to manage the stadium's operations via PPP concession… We were not responsible for the Maracanã's construction. If so, perhaps we would have had better performance in the construction phase due to our managerial flexibility as we now have in the Maracanã's operation phase. (Private Manager #10, Arena Maracanã)[16]

> During the stadium construction phase, we had the possibility of getting both penalties as well as bonuses. Although these penalties are not immediately financial, this penalty could apply during the facility's future operation. Therefore, we realised that we could not only think about the facility's construction but also think about both the construction and the operation throughout the concession. (Private Manager #5, Arena Mineirão)

Sharing of economic risks and gains

Finally, regarding the critical process of risk-sharing between the parties (Bing et al., 2005; Grimsey & Lewis, 2002; Iossa & Martimort, 2012; Oudot, 2005), we discuss the different organisational arrangements adopted by the PPP stadiums, particularly those related to construction risks (implementation time and the provision costs) and operation of such sports facilities (demand risk). Our study suggests that PPPs have an improved risk allocation between the parties. Unlike the public stadiums, our findings suggest that the distribution of the PPP risks between the public and private partners facilitated the generation of VfM and contributed to enhancing the PPPs' performance. Incentives in terms of both rewards (e.g., whether the PPP achieves a better time, cost, and operational performance) and contractual penalties (e.g., contrary to the previously presented situations) were key. We underscore the following exemplary cases to show the impact of risk allocation on time and cost performance: Arena Pantanal (public stadium) versus Arena Fonte Nova (PPP stadium).

> We are responsible for all construction risk because it is a traditional public procurement based on Federal Law 8666, although we can apply fines and penalties to the private contractor in charge of carrying out the construction work in case he fails to comply with any clause of the contract… Regarding the stadium's operation, we

> also bear all demand risks since the state government operates the sports facilities. (Public Manager #10, Arena Pantanal)

> With PPP, if we divide the risks in a way that does not overwhelm any of the partners, both parties will engage in a more balanced and equitable manner for the success of implementing the venture. (Public Manager #1, Arena Fonte Nova)

As to the sharing of economic gains, PPP projects have mechanisms to stimulate the reduction of public payment over the contractual execution of the projects so that the greater the gains earned by private partners, the smaller the public compensation payments will be. This is due to the possibility of sharing the parties' operational revenues if the private partner gains operating revenues above a certain limit set in the PPP projects, despite the potential problems identified and already discussed about the Fonte Nova and Pernambuco Stadiums. Thus, regarding a win–win model of revenue guarantee (Carbonara & Pellegrino, 2018), we argue that the PPP projects contributed to higher public funding allocation efficiency on public administration and greater production efficiency by the private partners. On the other hand, the Brazilian projects executed under the traditional public management logic do not have any type of contractual mechanism that establishes the possibility of decreasing public payments during the operation of public facilities (De Brito & Silveira, 2005). Finally, we emphasise two exemplary cases to show how sharing economic gains can influence cost performance: Arena da Amazônia (public stadium) versus Arena Mineirão (PPP stadium).

> We are in charge of operating all sports facilities and renting the stadium to football clubs to play a specific match… So, we charge rental fees of about 10 per cent of the total revenue of the football tickets of such matches… We are responsible for the monthly operating costs of the stadium. (Public Manager #9, Arena da Amazônia)

> Among the many advantages of PPP, one that we can cite is that, depending on the performance of the private partner, the state government can reduce its disbursement in public compensation throughout the contract execution, thanks to the possibility of sharing the additional gains with the private partner. (Public Manager #4, Arena Mineirão)

CONCLUSION

Regarding the debate over public and private efficiency in the provision of public assets and services (Hart et al., 1997; Shleifer, 1998), our study investigated the behaviour of the PPPs used for the construction of stadiums for the 2014 FIFA World Cup in comparison to the traditional public procurement and the strictly private provision. Although it cannot be considered a panacea, our findings show that PPP projects for providing new sports stadiums generated a better VfM than public stadiums in terms of time performance (implementation time delay) and cost performance (difference between estimated and realised cost per seat), which is in line with the PPP literature (e.g., O'Shea et al., 2019; Verweij & Van Meerkerk, 2020, 2021). Our findings suggest that the PPPs achieved better performance and VfM due to economic incentive structures, specifically, the flexibility and lower restrictions imposed on the private partner in carrying out the contract. Notwithstanding, considering the complexities associated with the performance differences between such modes of provision, our study reveals that the performance advantages of PPPs may vary due to different sources of incentives (i.e., asset property rights, bundling method and performance measurement, and sharing of economic risks and gains) regarding different performance criteria (i.e., time and cost performance).

In such a context, we contribute to the growing debates on public-private interactions in the fields of public administration and strategy in organisations (Cabral et al., 2019; Lazzarini, 2020; Mahoney et al., 2009). Some theoretical and practical implications can be drawn from this research. Specifically, examining PPPs in Brazilian football stadiums can contribute as part of educating public and private agents in the structuring and delivery of future PPP projects. In other words, the experiences and capabilities accrued by those involved in the structuring of projects designed for football stadiums are likely to be explored in other public utilities, enabling a generation of public value (Cabral et al., 2019; Kivleniece & Quelin, 2012; Lazzarini, 2020; Dos Reis & Gomes, 2022). Additionally, the PPPs analysed here can provide spillover for other public- and private-sector projects through the accumulation of idiosyncratic capabilities related to the management of public-private interactions (Boyer et al., 2016; Cabral et al., 2013; Quelin et al., 2019).

However, our study also demonstrates that PPPs can potentially have negative impacts on public administration, underlined by the possibilities of: (i) shifts in the optimal financing structure due to the critical timetable for implementing the major sports facilities projects; (ii) greater assumption of risk for the project by the public partners to attract the private sector to the PPP bids, leaving governments in an unfavourable position in terms of bargaining with private partners; (iii) higher public indebtedness due to the low contribution of private financial resources concerning the total cost of the PPPs; and (iv) the need to build capabilities in the public sector to monitor the behaviour and evaluate the effective performance of the PPPs (cf. Casady et al., 2020; Casady, 2021; Casady & Peci, 2021). Future research projects focusing on PPP experiences in other sectors and countries can verify whether the previous propositions are confirmed or refuted.

NOTES

1. This chapter is an updated version of the original article by Dos Reis and Cabral (2017) in the *Brazilian Journal of Public Administration.*
2. This descriptive statistic was generated by the authors based on the arithmetic mean of the age of the nine public stadiums used in the mega-event.
3. The Arena Maracanã was built under traditional public procurement and later granted to private initiatives via PPP in the operational phase. However, we only examined its construction phase under public provision.
4. The expression 'Value for Money' (VfM) is used in the PPP literature to express an improved economic advantage for the public administration in relation to the traditional public procurement.
5. The interviews held in the 12 host cities were subsidized with funding from the Ministry of Sports and the National Council for Scientific and Technological Development (CNPq).
6. In 2021, the State Government of Bahia reduced the concession period from 35 to 18 years and the annual public payment compensation.
7. In 2016, the State Government of Pernambuco decided to terminate the concession contract due to contract management issues by the private partner and took over the stadium's operational management.
8. In 2021, the Public Prosecutor's Office of the Rio Grande do Norte State filed a lawsuit against the private partner due to contract management issues.
9. Former Brazilian Law of Traditional Public Procurement. Recently, a new law was enacted in Brazil: Federal Law No. 14.133 of 2021.
10. A line of credit offered by the Brazilian National Development Bank (BNDES) for the construction of sports stadiums for the 2014 FIFA World Cup in Brazil.
11. The private stadiums were not included in this analysis because they are not subject to a public bidding process as the PPP and public stadiums are.
12. In their original study, Cabral and Silva (2014) evaluated the German stadiums based on EUR currency. However, to compare German with Brazilian stadiums, we convert it to USD currency regarding the same quotation data of 31 January 2014.
13. The Arena Fonte Nova was built with a fixed capacity of 50 000 seats. However, during the 2014 FIFA World Cup games, the private partner added 5000 temporary seats to attend the FIFA's requirement (Fédération Internationale de Football Association, 2011).
14. The Brazilian Car Wash operation was a federal investigation conducted by the Federal Public Ministry and Federal Police from 2014 to 2021 regarding malfeasance in the public administration. The Petrobras S.A. (a Brazilian federal state-owned enterprise in the petroleum sector) was the initial target of the operation. However, some of the stadiums' construction firms were also involved in Petrobras's case. In comparative terms, the Brazilian Car Wash operation is similar to the Italian *Mani Pulite* Operation.
15. It is worth highlighting that the public stadiums were built under the former Brazilian Law of Traditional Public Procurement (Federal Law No. 8666 of 1993). However, despite its recent improvements regarding the bidding process aspects, the new Brazilian Law of Traditional Public Procurement (Federal Law No. 14 133 of 2021) still lacks the offering of contractual flexibility to the implementation and operational phases of public projects.

16. The Maracanã operator is the same firm responsible for constructing Arena Fonte Nova via PPP concession, whose contract integrated both the construction and operation phases.

REFERENCES

Ahadzi, M., & Bowles, G. (2004). Public-private partnerships and contract negotiations: An empirical study. *Construction Management and Economics*, *22*(9), 967–78.

Atmo, G. U., Duffield, C., Zhang, L., & Wilson, D. I. (2017). Comparative performance of PPPs and traditional procurement projects in Indonesia. *International Journal of Public Sector Management*, *30*(2), 118–36.

Bel, G., Brown, T., & Warner, M. (2014). Editorial overview: Symposium on mixed and hybrid models of public service delivery. *International Public Management Journal*, *17*(3), 297–307.

Bing, L., Akintoye, A., Edwards, P. J., & Hardcastle, C. (2005). The allocation of risk in PPP/PFI construction projects in the UK. *International Journal of Project Management*, *23*(1), 25–35.

Boyer, E. J., Van Slyke, D. M., & Rogers, J. D. (2016). An empirical examination of public involvement in public-private partnerships: Qualifying the benefits of public involvement in PPPs. *Journal of Public Administration Research and Theory*, *26*(1), 45–61.

Cabral, S., & De Azevedo, P. F. (2008). The modes of provision of prison services in a comparative perspective. *Brazilian Administration Review*, *5*(1), 53–69.

Cabral, S., Lazzarini, S. G., & De Azevedo, P. F. (2010). Private operation with public supervision: Evidence of hybrid modes of governance in prisons. *Public Choice*, *145*(1–2), 281–93.

Cabral, S., Lazzarini, S. G., & De Azevedo, P. F. (2013). Private entrepreneurs in public services: A longitudinal examination of outsourcing and statization of prisons. *Strategic Entrepreneurship Journal*, *7*(1), 6–25.

Cabral, S., Mahoney, J. T., McGahan, A. M., & Potoski, M. (2019). Value creation and value appropriation in public and non-profit organizations. *Strategic Management Journal*, *40*(4), 465–75.

Cabral, S., & Silva, A. F. A. (2013). An approach for evaluating the risk management role of governments in public-private partnerships for mega-event stadiums. *European Sport Management Quarterly*, *13*(4), 472–90.

Cabral, S., & Silva, A. F. A. (2014). A verdade sobre os custos dos estádios da copa [The truth about World Cup stadium costs]. *A Tarde: Caderno Opinião* [The afternoon: Notebook opinion].

Carbonara, N., & Pellegrino, R. (2018). Revenue guarantee in public-private partnerships: A win–win model. *Construction Management and Economics*, *36*(10), 584–98.

Casady, C. B. (2021). Examining the institutional drivers of public-private partnership (PPP) market performance: A fuzzy set qualitative comparative analysis (fsQCA). *Public Management Review*, *23*(7), 981–1005.

Casady, C. B., Eriksson, K., Levitt, R. E., & Scott, W. R. (2020). (Re)defining public-private partnerships (PPPs) in the new public governance (NPG) paradigm: An institutional maturity perspective. *Public Management Review*, *22*(2), 161–83.

Casady, C. B., & Peci, F. (2021). The institutional challenges of public-private partnerships (PPPs) in transition economies: Lessons from Kosovo. *Economic Research-Ekonomska Istraživanja*, *34*(1), 1949–65.
Daito, N., & Gifford, J. L. (2014). U.S. highway public-private partnerships: Are they more expensive or efficient than the traditional model? *Managerial Finance*, *40*(11), 1131–51.
De Brito, B. M. B., & Silveira, A. H. P. (2005). Parceria público-privada: Compreendendo o modelo brasileiro. *Revista Do Serviço Público*, *56*(1), 7–21.
Dos Reis, C. J. O., & Cabral, S. (2017). Public-private partnerships (PPP) in mega-sport events: A comparative study of the provision of sports arenas for the 2014 FIFA World Cup in Brazil. *Brazilian Journal of Public Administration*, *51*(4), 551–79.
Dos Reis, C. J. O., & Gomes, R. C. (2022). Public value creation and appropriation mechanisms in public–private partnerships: How does it play a role? *Public Administration*. https://doi.org/10.1111/padm.12826
Eisenhardt, K. M. (1989). Building theories from case study research. *Academy of Management Review*, *14*(4), 532–50.
European Commission. (2003). *Guidelines for Successful Public-Private Partnerships*.
Fédération Internationale de Football Association. (2011). *Football Stadiums: Technical Recommendations and Requirements*.
Flick, U. (2014). *The Sage handbook of qualitative data analysis*. SAGE.
Forrer, J., Kee, J. E., Newcomer, K. E., & Boyer, E. (2010). Public-private partnerships and the public accountability question. *Public Administration Review*, *70*(3), 475–84.
Grimsey, D., & Lewis, M. K. (2002). Evaluating the risks of public-private partnerships for infrastructure projects. *International Journal of Project Management*, *20*(2), 107–118.
Grimsey, D., & Lewis, M. K. (2005). Are public-private partnerships value for money? *Accounting Forum*, *29*(4), 345–78.
Gursoy, D., & Kendall, K. W. (2006). Hosting mega events: Modeling locals' support. *Annals of Tourism Research*, *33*(3), 603–623.
Hart, O. (2003). Incomplete contracts and public ownership: Remarks, and an application to public-private partnerships. *The Economic Journal*, *113*(486), 69–76.
Hart, O., Shleifer, A., & Vishny, R. W. (1997). The proper scope of government: Theory and an application to prisons. *Quarterly Journal of Economics*, *112*(4), 1127–61.
Hodge, G. A., & Greve, C. (2007). Public-private partnerships: An international performance review. *Public Administration Review*, *67*(3), 545–58.
Hodge, G. A., & Greve, C. (2017). On public-private partnership performance: A contemporary review. *Public Works Management & Policy*, *22*(1), 55–78.
Hodge, G. A., & Greve, C. (2019). *The logic of public-private partnerships: The enduring interdependency of politics and markets*. Edward Elgar.
International Monetary Fund (IMF). (2004). *Public-private partnerships*.
Iossa, E., & Martimort, D. (2012). Risk allocation and the costs and benefits of public-private partnerships. *RAND Journal of Economics*, *43*(3), 442–74.
Jick, T. D. (1979). Mixing qualitative and quantitative methods: Triangulation in action. *Administrative Science Quarterly*, *24*(4), 602–611.
Johnson, B., & Whitehead, J. (2000). Value of public goods from sports stadiums: The CVM approach. *Contemporary Economic Policy*, *18*(1), 48–58.
Kivleniece, I., Cabral, S., Lazzarini, S. G., & Quelin, B. V. (2017). Public-private collaboration: A review and avenues for further research. In L. F. Mesquita, R.

Ragozzino, & J. J. Reuer (Eds.), *Collaborative strategy: Critical issues for alliances and networks* (pp. 224–33). Edward Elgar.
Kivleniece, I., & Quelin, B. V. (2012). Creating and capturing value in public-private ties: A private actor's perspective. *Academy of Management Review*, *37*(2), 272–99.
Lazzarini, S. G. (2020). The nature of the social firm: Alternative organizational forms for social value creation and appropriation. *Academy of Management Review*, *45*(3), 620–45.
Legg, E., Jones, G. J., & White, M. (2018). Whose job is it anyway? Public-private partnerships in youth sport. *Managing Sport and Leisure*, *23*(4–6), 261–76.
Mahoney, J. T., McGahan, A. M., & Pitelis, C. N. (2009). Perspective—The interdependence of private and public interests. *Organization Science*, *20*(6), 1034–52.
Malfas, M., Theodoraki, E., & Houlihan, B. (2004). Impacts of the Olympic Games as mega-events. *Proceedings of the Institution of Civil Engineers – Municipal Engineer*, *157*(3), 209–220.
Ménard, C. (2013). Hybrid modes of organization: Alliances, joint ventures, networks, and other "strange" animals. In R. Gibbons & J. Roberts (Eds.), *The handbook of organizational economics* (pp. 1066–1108). Princeton University Press.
Ménard, C. (2021). Hybrids: Where are we? *Journal of Institutional Economics*, 18(2), 297–312.
Ministério Público Federal. (2021). *Relatório da operação lava jato* [Operation Car Wash report].
Mules, T. (1998). Taxpayer subsidies for major sporting events. *Sport Management Review*, *1*(1), 25–43.
O'Shea, C., Palcic, D., & Reeves, E. (2019). Comparing PPP with traditional procurement: The case of schools procurement in Ireland. *Annals of Public and Cooperative Economics*, *90*(2), 245–67.
Osborne, S. P. (2010). *Public-private partnerships: Theory and practice in international perspective*. Routledge.
Oudot, J. M. (2005). *Risk-allocation: Theoretical and empirical evidences: Application to public-private partnerships in the defence sector* [Paper presentation]. The 9th Annual Conference of the Institutions of Market Exchange, Barcelona, Spain.
Preuss, H. (2007). The conceptualisation and measurement of mega sport event legacies. *Journal of Sport & Tourism*, *12*(3–4), 207–228.
Preuss, H., Solberg, H. A., & Alm, J. (2014). The challenge of utilizing the venues. In S. Frawley & D. Adair (Eds.), *Managing the football World Cup* (pp. 82–103). Palgrave Macmillan.
Quelin, B. V., Cabral, S., Lazzarini, S., & Kivleniece, I. (2019). The private scope in public-private collaborations: An institutional and capability-based perspective. *Organization Science*, *30*(4), 831–46.
Reeves, E. (2013). Mind the gap: Accountability and value for money in public-private partnerships in Ireland. In C. Greve & G. A. Hodge (Eds.), *Rethinking public-private partnerships: Strategies for turbulent times* (pp. 90–109). Routledge.
Reynaers, A. M. (2014). Public values in public-private partnerships. *Public Administration Review*, *74*(1), 41–50.
Roche, M. (2000). *Mega-events and modernity: Olympics and expos in the growth of global culture*. Routledge.
Shleifer, A. (1998). State versus private ownership. *Journal of Economic Perspectives*, *12*(4), 133–50.
Siegfried, J., & Zimbalist, A. (2000). The economics of sports facilities and their communities. *Journal of Economic Perspectives*, *14*(3), 95–114.

Tiong, R. L. K. (1996). CSFs in competitive tendering and negotiation model for BOT projects. *Journal of Construction Engineering and Management*, *122*(3), 205–211.

Tirole, J. (1999). Incomplete contracts: Where do we stand? *Econometrica*, *67*(4), 741–81.

Tribunal de Contas da União. (2013). *Acordão TCU TC-029.514/2013-4* [Agreement TCU TC-029.514/2013-4].

Tribunal de Contas do Distrito Federal. (2013). *Relatório de Auditoria permanente do estádio mané garrincha.*

Van den Hurk, M., & Verhoest, K. (2015). The governance of public-private partnerships in sports infrastructure: Interfering complexities in Belgium. *International Journal of Project Management*, *33*(1), 201–211.

Van den Hurk, M., & Verhoest, K. (2017). On the fast track? Using standard contracts in public-private partnerships for sports facilities: A case study. *Sport Management Review*, *20*(2), 226–39.

Verweij, S., & Van Meerkerk, I. F. (2020). Do public-private partnerships perform better? A comparative analysis of costs for additional work and reasons for contract changes in Dutch transport infrastructure projects. *Transport Policy*, *99*, 430–8.

Verweij, S., & Van Meerkerk, I. F. (2021). Do public-private partnerships achieve better time and cost performance than regular contracts? *Public Money & Management*, *41*(4), 286–95.

World Bank. (2012). *Public-private partnerships reference guide version 1.0.*

Yin, R. K. (2013). *Case study research: Design and methods*. SAGE.

6. A mixed-methods comparison of the performance of Dutch PPP and non-PPP infrastructure projects

Ingmar van Meerkerk, Mike Duijn, Rianne Warsen, Stefan Verweij, Erik-Hans Klijn, Joop Koppenjan, and Samantha Metselaar

INTRODUCTION

Over recent decades, Public-Private Partnerships (PPPs) have become increasingly popular in government rhetoric and in policy practice (European PPP Expertise Centre, 2015). This holds in particular for the development and management of transport infrastructure, such as highways and waterways (European PPP Expertise Centre, 2015). Two important reasons for procuring transport infrastructure through PPPs are the expectations that PPPs develop and manage transport infrastructure both at lower costs and on time (i.e., they are better able to meet initially planned and agreed-upon budgets and schedules; Hodge, 2010; Verweij & Van Meerkerk, 2021). At the same time, critical views on the future of PPPs and their rise in the delivery of long-term infrastructure projects are increasing in some countries. The complex and inflexible nature of the contracts, the excessive risks for private contractors, and—partly as a consequence thereof—the financial problems of several construction firms are some of the reasons underlying these critical views (Verweij & Van Meerkerk, 2021). For example, the United Kingdom decided to stop new Private Finance Initiative (PFI) and Private Finance 2 (PF2) contracts because of (perceived) disappointing performance (Global Construction Review, 2018).

Studies of the performance of PPPs present mixed results (see also Chapter 1 in this book). Evidence of a PPP performance advantage or disadvantage over regular procurement is weak. On the one hand, this is due to a lack of comparative research. Research on PPPs is dominated by single case studies (see Tang et al., 2010; Warsen, 2021). By definition, single case studies cannot provide evidence for a performance advantage of PPPs. Furthermore, large-N (quantitative) research on PPPs is often based on perceptual performance data of projects (e.g., Clifton & Duffield, 2006; Kort & Klijn, 2011; Warsen et al., 2018). Rarely does this type of research include hard measures of cost and time performance or compare PPPs with regular procurement. Making comparisons is highly challenging. Much of the existing comparative research involves business case projections or comparisons of ex-ante performance instead of materialized or realized performance (Petersen, 2019; Verweij & Van Meerkerk, 2021).

Recently, the number of studies attempting to assess the performance advantages of PPPs has increased (e.g., Atmo et al., 2017; O'Shea et al., 2019; Rodrigues & Zucco, 2018; Verweij & Van Meerkerk, 2021). In this chapter, we contribute to this stream of literature—in line with the central aim of this book—by comparing the cost and time performance of PPPs with that of regular procured projects. In particular, we add to the research by using three data sources for this comparison: "hard" project data on cost and time performance, perceptual data of managers involved in PPPs and regular procured projects, and interview data with involved managers and experts. Combining these data sources enables us to provide nuance and meaning to the performance assessment and to possible differences between PPPs and regular procured projects. This chapter builds on and expands previous research by Verweij and Van Meerkerk (2020, 2021) using the same project data but adding survey data and qualitative interview data to the analysis. By combining datasets, this study overcomes some of the methodological issues related to the use of a single data source. The use of a survey and interviews in addition to the "hard" project data allows us to go deeper into the perceptions and experiences of involved managers regarding cost and time performance.

In this contribution, we focus on public highway and waterway transport infrastructure projects in the Netherlands. Rijkswaterstaat is the major Dutch public procurer of these infrastructure projects. The two main contracts that it uses to procure transport infrastructure are Design and Construct (D&C) and Design–Build–Finance–Maintain (DBFM). Rijkswaterstaat considers DBFM as its default PPP option; in the Netherlands, D&C is not considered a type of PPP because it does not include private financing and a long-term public-private relationship (see also Rijkswaterstaat, 2021; Yescombe, 2013).[1] In this chapter, we analyze the cost and time performance differences of D&C and DBFM projects procured by Rijkswaterstaat.

In the next section, we first define PPPs in the Netherlands. Then, we address possible explanations for potential differences in cost and time performance between PPPs and regular procured infrastructure projects. In the third section, we elaborate on the data sources used for the comparative analysis. Subsequently, we discuss the findings of our study. We will synthesize and compare the findings based on the different data sources and discuss possible differences in results and what they mean for assessing the performance of PPPs in comparison with regular procured projects.

UNDERSTANDING PUBLIC-PRIVATE PARTNERSHIP PERFORMANCE

PPPs in this Chapter: DBFM Projects

As noted in Chapter 1 of this book, different conceptions and definitions of PPP exist. To compare PPPs with regular procured infrastructure projects, it is important to be clear on the definition of PPP. In this chapter—in line with the introduction of this book—we refer to PPPs as single projects (here: transport infrastructure projects) that have "a specific institutional and financial structure in place to initially fund and deliver construction works as well as operate the long-term facility" (Hodge & Greve, 2017, p. 58). Many definitions stress the long-term character of the relationship or contractual arrangement between public and private actors (Klijn & Teisman, 2003; Palcic et al., 2019). This means that partnerships not only include the D&C of infrastructure, but also the maintenance and/or operation (Hodge & Greve, 2017; Warsen, 2021). The inclusion of the maintenance and/or operation phase into the contract is expected to motivate the private consortium to take the full life-cycle into account when designing the project (Hodge & Greve, 2017). A second core aspect of PPPs that is often mentioned is the sharing of risks and, in particular, the private financing of the infrastructure (Hodge & Greve, 2017; Casady & Geddes, 2019). The shift of financial risks to the private partner is expected to create strong incentives to deliver and maintain the project within time, budget, and scope (Verweij & Van Meerkerk, 2021).

One of the most discussed and typical contract types used in PPP is the DBFM contract, also known as Design–Build–Finance–Operate (DBFO) or Design–Construct–Maintain–Finance (DCMF; Grimsey & Lewis, 2004; Monk et al., 2019; World Bank, 2017). In a DBFM contract, public actors procure the design, building, financing, and maintenance of a public infrastructure project from a private consortium for a longer period of time through an integrated contract. The private consortium sets up a Special Purpose Company (SPC). This SPC serves as the contract partner of the public procurer. Private investors and construction firms are usually the shareholders of the SPC. They make investments and arrange loans from banks. The SPC also has subcontracts with an engineering, procurement, and construction (EPC) company—responsible for the construction of the public work—and with a maintenance company (MTC)—responsible for the maintenance of the project (Ng & Loosemore, 2007; Demirag et al., 2011).

There are various reasons why DBFM projects are expected to deliver better cost and time performance compared to regular projects, such as those with a D&C contract. In the Netherlands, specifically, DBFM contracts are only considered for large infrastructure projects. As governments can normally borrow money at lower interest rates than private consortia, DBFM requires a certain project size to be a viable option (Leruth, 2012; Moore et al., 2017). In addition, due to the long timespans of these contracts, the uncertainty, associated risks, and complexity of infrastructure projects, DBFM is usually only considered in the Netherlands for projects with a contract worth over €60 million (Ministerie van Financiën, 2013). Before elaborating on the various reasons why DBFM is expected to lead to better cost and time performance, it is important to first define what we mean by cost and time performance in this chapter.

To compare DBFM projects with D&C projects in a meaningful way, we focus our comparative analysis on the implementation phase: from the moment the contract has been awarded until the opening of the infrastructure for its users. This is for both contract types comparable in terms of duration and the project activities that are performed. When comparing DBFM and D&C projects, we focus on both time and cost performance. Regarding time performance, projects and services are on time if they are delivered according to the initially planned or agreed-upon schedule and meet important project milestones (Hodge, 2010). As for cost performance, we focus on different aspects. As noted in the introduction of this book, cost performance generally concerns operational costs, capital costs, total (whole-life) project costs including D&C costs, and on-budget delivery (Hodge, 2010; Petersen, 2019). We focus predominantly on on-budget delivery and budget overruns. On the one hand, we do so by measuring the relative value of additional work costs as compared to the initial contract value (see also Verweij & Van Meerkerk, 2020, 2021). On the other hand, we build on the perceptions of project managers regarding the on-budget delivery of their projects. The latter may differ for public and private partners. The public actor often considers additional work costs as exceeding the initial budget (i.e., a cost overrun). For private partners, however, additional work costs could be an important way for covering investments. By including their perceptions of cost performance, return on investment for the private consortium is also considered.

PPPs as Principal–Agent Relationships

Although the term "partnership" may suggest otherwise, a key characteristic of PPPs is the contract between a principal (e.g., the state or a governmental organization) and an agent (a private consortium). The contract specifies the outputs that are to be delivered and the agreements made regarding this exchange, including agreements regarding performance, pay, monitoring, and sanctions. Principal–agent theory focuses on how this relationship works (De Palma et al., 2012). It departs from two key assumptions that can also be applied to the formation and monitoring of a PPP contract (De Palma et al., 2012):

- Information asymmetry: in general, the agent (the private contractor) has more information about its own actions and the so-called "state of nature" than the principal (public client).
- The agent pursues its own interests, which may run contrary to those of the principal.

In PPPs, it can be argued that public and private actors share some interests, but there are also important differences in interests. Whereas the public sector serves the public interest, a private partner strives to maximize its profits or at least has a keen eye on making sufficient profit in relation to the investments made. This can lead to moral hazard issues in which agents have the opportunity to take advantage of the situation due to information asymmetry (De Palma et al., 2012). This type of opportunistic behavior might occur, for example, when contractors falsely or opportunistically claim additional costs after a project has started or anticipate additional costs during the bidding process (Mohamed et al., 2011; Verweij & Van Meerkerk, 2021).

Given these assumptions, the incentive structure and the control and monitoring systems regulating the behavior of agents are considered to be highly important to avoid issues of opportunistic behavior and moral hazard. Transaction cost economics therefore postulates that the best results for the principal would be obtained with (De Palma et al., 2012):

- A fully specified, enforceable contract between the government and the consortium;
- Stable terms of contract over time;
- Measurable output indicators and monitoring mechanisms; and
- Credible punishment in case cheating is proven.

However, fulfilling most—let alone all—of these terms is impossible in practice. For example, Reynaers and Parrado (2017) have shown that the use of sanctions in Dutch Design–Build–Finance–Maintain–Operate (DBFMO) contracts is not always applied strictly. Contracts—especially in the context of complex, long-term infrastructure projects—are unavoidably incomplete (Brown et al., 2016). Both principal and agent are confronted with unforeseen events that are not covered in the contract or unanticipated disturbances due to gaps and omissions in the contract (Williamson, 2002).

In the next subsections, we further elaborate on cost and time performance of transport infrastructure projects. We argue that, due to the role of private financing, the risk allocation, and the integrated nature of the contract, the incentive structure for DBFM projects is different from that of D&C projects. This leads to different expectations regarding their cost and time performance.

Cost Performance

There are several arguments, rooted in principal–agent theory and transaction cost economics, why DBFM projects are expected to lead to better cost performance than D&C projects, at least from the public principal point of view (Verweij & Van Meerkerk, 2021).

First, there is the "economies of scope" argument (De Bettignies & Ross, 2004). In DBFM contracts, the responsibility for the infrastructure design, construction, and maintenance is transferred to the private partner. This provides strong incentives for the private partner to invest in durable designs and better constructions that will have lower maintenance costs (Martimort & Pouyet, 2008). The costs of the various phases are taken into account at the start of the project, which might help to prevent budget overruns. So, the business model in DBFM focuses on finding innovative and efficient solutions through integrated project designs and processes and life-cycle optimization (Lenferink et al., 2013), resulting in better cost performance. Investments in the D&C will also lead to fewer contract changes after contract closure, leading to lower additional work costs (Verweij & Van Meerkerk, 2020). In contrast, D&C contracts provide fewer incentives for the private contractor to develop improved designs that take the maintenance phase into account. After all, the private contractor is not responsible for maintenance costs occurring after project completion (Culp, 2011).

A second, yet related, argument is the "risk argument" in relation to the private financing of the project. In DBFM, risks related to design, construction, and maintenance are allocated to the private partner. Additional work that stems from these risks may have to be financed by the private partner. This increases uncertainty and transaction costs for the consortium. The private partner will therefore try to minimize any additional work that would lead to increased costs (Verweij & Van Meerkerk, 2021). In D&C contracts, in contrast, additional work is not privately financed. This means that the uncertainty and transaction costs associated with privately financing additional work are absent. Instead, there is a higher chance of moral hazard: claiming additional work at the expense of the public partner may increase the private partner's revenue and potentially their profit. So, the assumption is that DBFM contracts lead to lower additional work costs for the public partner which, consequently, will prevent budget overruns for the client.

Third, there is the "shadow of the banks" argument (Verweij & Van Meerkerk, 2021). The equity provider in DBFM, who finances the activities of the private consortium, demands high-quality risk management as a condition for investing in the project and providing the loans (Demirag et al., 2011). Financiers are risk-averse, and the role of the financiers generates "an added level of diligence for effective project execution" (Culp, 2011, p. 237). The argument is that this leads to a better identification, allocation, and mitigation of risks. To obtain the loans, private contractors need to reserve space in their budgets to mitigate potential risks, which decreases the risk of budget overruns. Moreover, the improved risk management is expected to lead to lower additional work costs. More attention to, and explication of, risk management plans, skills, and strategies during the tendering phase of the project will also decrease some of the information asymmetry in relation to the principal. This shadow of the banks for the private consortium is absent in projects with a D&C contract.

Time Performance

The bundling of the design, build, and maintain phases of infrastructure projects, combined with the transfer of risks to the private partners in PPPs, is also expected to result in better time performance.

First, a major difference between DBFM and D&C contracts concerns the output that is expected. In DBFM projects, the private consortium is expected to deliver a service: the availability of a road or waterway. This concerns the so-called availability criterion. In contrast, in D&C projects, the private consortium is expected to design and construct a product: an infrastructure, such as a road or sluice, for which "functional specifications" are set by the principal. In addition, in DBFM projects, performance-dependent payment is an essential element. This basically means that the public partner pays the private partner if the availability criterion is met. Payment is made either via user fees or via availability payments (Lawther & Martin, 2014). In case of the latter, the public client pays the private contractor only if the product is available. This provides an incentive for the private contractor to deliver on time. After all, delayed delivery of the infrastructure means that the contractor will not be paid for the time the road or waterway was not available.

Next to the overall availability, important project milestones may be set. This strongly incentivizes the private consortium to deliver their output on time (Culp, 2011; Verweij & Van Meerkerk, 2021). After all, their revenue structure is highly dependent on the payment stream from the public partner. When the private consortium does not comply with the agreed output specifications, or fails to meet important milestones, it may be fined and cut short on payments. It consequently may not be able to meet its debt service obligations, as the project financing consists of multiple short- and long-term loans. This will have a negative effect on the companies' creditworthiness and its profits may decrease (Ng & Loosemore, 2007).

Although there can be fierce discussions between public and private partners about contract omissions and changes in both DBFM and D&C projects, the performance-dependent payments in combination with the private financing of the project, as well as the availability criterion, put strong pressure on the private consortium in DBFM projects to meet the given deadlines and deliver the project on time (O'Shea et al., 2019). This mechanism is absent in D&C projects.

DATA AND METHODS

The data presented in this chapter were collected as part of an evaluation study on the performance of DBFM projects in the Netherlands (Koppenjan et al., 2020). This evaluation study was commissioned by Rijkswaterstaat—the executive agency of the Ministry of Infrastructure and Water Management—and *Bouwend Nederland*, which is the Dutch association of project developers, construction, and/or maintenance companies. As part of the evaluation, we collected and analyzed both quantitative and qualitative data using a mixed-methods design (Koppenjan et al., 2020). In this chapter, three datasets are used to study cost and time performance. First, using the project database of Rijkswaterstaat, we collected "hard" project data regarding project completion and additional work costs of both DBFM and D&C projects (N = 30). Second, we conducted a survey of project managers and members directly involved in the DBFM and D&C projects (N = 163). Both professionals working for the public client and the private consortium participated in this survey. Finally, interviews were held with public and private partner respondents involved in implementing mainly DBFM projects and respondents from financial institutions financing these projects (N = 34).

In the next subsections, we elaborate on the methods and techniques used in collecting and analyzing the three datasets, with a particular focus on cost and time performance. Table 6.1 provides an overview of the indicators used for cost and time performance. It also presents the data sources used to measure these indicators. In the next subsections, we explain these methods further.

Hard Project Data on Cost and Time Performance

Hard project data were collected from the project database of Rijkswaterstaat between September 2019 and November 2019. Sufficient data regarding cost and time performance were available for 12 DBFM projects and 49 D&C projects. As Rijkswaterstaat usually only considers DBFM—through the

Table 6.1 *Overview of data and measurements*

Performance	Indicators	Data source
Cost performance	Additional costs during the implementation phase for the public partner	Information collected from the project database of Rijkswaterstaat
	Perceptions on whether: – The costs of the project stayed within the set bandwidth agreed upon at the beginning of the project – The benefits of the project are in general larger than the costs	These are two survey items in the survey for public and private project managers
	– On-budget realization of the project – A reasonable return on investments for private partners – The role of private financing in realizing the project on budget	These topics were included in the interviews with public and private project managers and financiers If available, financial data from private consortia were used to verify the findings
Time performance	Performance of the project compared to the defined recommissioning milestone	Information collected from the project database of Rijkswaterstaat
	Perceptions on whether: – The infrastructure has been realized within the predetermined time frame	This is a survey item in the survey for public and private project managers
	Comparison of DBFM and D&C projects in their stimulus to deliver on time	This topic was included in the interviews with public and private project managers and financiers

application of a Public-Private Comparator (PPC)—for projects with a contract worth at least €60 million (Ministerie van Financiën, 2013), we focused our comparative analysis on the 18 D&C projects with a contract value of more than €60 million. These larger D&C projects are better comparable with the 12 DBFM projects in the database—in terms of their size and complexity—than the smaller D&C projects.

The database provides data on additional work costs in the implementation phase as one of the key indicators used in this study for cost performance (see Table 6.1). Specifically, additional work was measured using the sum of the costs for additional work (in Euros) caused by contract changes that occurred after the contract was signed. We divided these costs by the contract value, resulting in a percentage (Verweij et al., 2015). High percentages indicate high additional work costs and, thus, lower cost performance from a public-sector perspective. Contract value is measured as the initial contract value of the project (i.e., the value of the contract at the moment of contract close), as reported in the project database.

In addition, the database provides data on time performance. We counted the days in the period between the moment the contract was awarded and the moment of full recommissioning of the infrastructure after the construction activities were finished. This number is subtracted from the number of days initially planned—at the moment the contract was awarded—for the construction phase of the project. The resulting number is expressed as a percentage of the planned duration of the construction phase. A negative percentage indicates a delay in the project (i.e., no on-time delivery), whereas a positive percentage indicates an acceleration of the completion of the construction phase ahead of schedule.

As the hard project data (contract size, additional work costs, time performance) are not normally distributed, we use the non-parametric Mann–Whitney U test to compare the cost and time performance between the DBFM and D&C projects. The test is suitable for comparing groups that are relatively small and not normally distributed (Nachar, 2008), which is the case in this study.

Perceptions of Cost and Time Performance

For the survey, in collaboration with Rijkswaterstaat and Bouwend Nederland, we compiled a list of public and private respondents who are or have been involved in Dutch transport infrastructure projects using either a DBFM or a D&C contract. This resulted in a list of 396 respondents to whom the survey was sent. The survey data were collected from October 2019 to February 2020. We received 163 completed questionnaires, resulting in a response rate of 41 percent. The response rates of public-sector (N = 71, 44 percent) and private-sector respondents (N = 92, 39 percent) were similar. The distribution of the 163 responses over contract type is as follows: 110 responses for DBFM projects, 51 responses for D&C projects, and two responses for Design–Build–Maintenance (DBM) projects. The dataset included respondents working in both small and large DBFM and D&C projects, although the dataset contains relatively more small D&C projects (< €50 million) than small DBFM projects. Large projects (> €225 million) are more often DBFM.

Each respondent was asked to complete the survey for a specific project in which they were involved. The survey contained two items on cost performance and one item on time performance, measured on a seven-point Likert scale ranging from "totally disagree" (1) to "totally agree" (7). To better interpret the results, we transformed this scale to a ten-point scale. The three items are listed below:

- The costs of the project stayed within the set bandwidth and norms (cost performance);
- The benefits of the project are in general larger than the costs (cost performance); and
- The availability of the infrastructure developed in this project has been realized within the predetermined agreed time frame (time performance).

For the analysis, we use both descriptive statistics as well as independent t-tests to test whether any differences between the mean scores of the two groups were significant—for example, the mean scores on perceived cost and time performance for DBFM and D&C projects, for public- and private-sector respondents, and for combinations of the two (e.g., public-sector respondents involved in DBFM projects versus private-sector respondents involved in D&C projects).

Qualitative Data on Cost and Time Performance

The qualitative data used for understanding the performance of these projects are based on semi-structured interviews conducted between December 2019 and March 2020. We conducted 34 interviews of approximately 1.5 hours each with persons closely involved in the organization and implementation of the DBFM projects, both from the public sector as well as private-sector organizations. Six respondents worked for Rijkswaterstaat, 22 respondents for construction firms, and six respondents for private financiers involved in the projects. Respondents were selected based on their expertise and experience with DBFM projects; the aim was to arrive at a sample that was representative of the DBFM projects procured by Rijkswaterstaat.

In these interviews, the performance of DBFM projects was assessed on various levels. Cost and time performance were two key topics in the conversations. Where possible and relevant, respondents were asked to compare their experience on cost and time performance in DBFM projects with D&C projects. The semi-open interview strategy enabled us to gain deeper insights into the experienced incentives, pressures, and risks in relation to cost and time performance. They also helped in understanding the findings from the analyses of the other two datasets. The interview transcripts were coded with ATLAS.ti using "cost performance" and "time performance" as the two main relevant codes regarding this topic. Other codes included "flexibility" and the "role of financiers." Assigning multiple codes to a text fragment was possible. Based on the coded text, the experiences and perceptions on each variable were compared to find differences and commonalities within the three respondent groups and across the groups.

COMPARATIVE ANALYSIS OF DBFM AND D&C PROJECTS

Findings on Cost Performance

Analyzing cost performance using hard project data

The analysis of the data from the project database of Rijkswaterstaat, presented in Table 6.2,[2] shows that the 12 DBFM projects had an average contract value of €267 million and the 18 D&C projects had an average contract value of €168 million. Overall, the DBFM projects have a larger size than the D&C projects. The DBFM projects had, on average, lower additional work costs as a percentage of the initial contract value (13.59 percent) than the D&C projects (27.78 percent). This difference is statistically significant ($p < .05$). In this respect, DBFM projects thus had a better cost performance than D&C projects. This confirms the results of previous studies using comparable datasets (see Verweij & Van Meerkerk, 2020, 2021).

Table 6.2 Comparative analysis of additional work costs performance

	DBFM	D&C	Significance
N	12	18	
Average contract value in millions of €	267.006	168.051	
Average additional work costs in %	13.59%	27.78%	Difference is significant ($p < .05$; $U = 61$)
Standard deviation	9.52%	23.29%	

Note: Significance tests are two-tailed: $p \leq .05$; based on Mann–Whitney U test.

Analyzing cost performance using survey data

From an aggregate point of view, the survey data show few differences between D&C and DBFM (Table 6.3). The differences between the two types of projects regarding the question of whether costs stayed within the bandwidth are not significant. DBFM projects received an average score of 5.4 out of 10, whereas D&C projects scored 6.1 out of 10. In contrast, the differences between public and private partner respondents are striking and significant: public partner respondents score this item for DBFM projects with an average of 7.1 out of 10, while private respondents score DBFM with a 4.1 out of 10. Hence, the low score of DBFM projects regarding cost performance is mainly due to the perceptions of private respondents. Public respondents score DBFM projects, on average, even a bit higher than D&C projects, though this differ-

Table 6.3 Comparative analysis of cost performance based on survey data

Item	N	Mean	Significance
The costs of the project stayed within the bandwidth and norms			
DBFM	110	5.4	Differences are not significant
D&C	51	6.1	
Public partner	71	7.0	Differences are significant
Private partner	90	4.5	($t = 5.040$, $df = 161$, $p < .01$)
Public partner/DBFM	46	7.1	Differences are not significant
Public partner/D&C	25	7.0	
Private partner/DBFM	64	4.1	Differences are not significant
Private partner/D&C	26	5.3	
Total	161	5.6	—
The benefits of the project are larger than the costs			
DBFM	110	6.1	Differences are not significant
D&C	51	6.5	
Public partner	71	7.5	Differences are significant
Private partner	90	5.2	($t = 6.167$, $df = 155$, $p < .01$)
Public partner/DBFM	46	7.7	Differences are not significant
Public partner/D&C	25	7.2	
Private partner/DBFM	64	4.9	Differences are not significant
Private partner/D&C	26	5.7	
Total	161	6.2	—

ence is very small (7.1 for DBFM versus 7.0 for D&C). Private respondents are less positive regarding the cost performance for both types of projects. Still, they score DBFM projects lower than D&C projects (4.1 for DBFM versus 5.3 for D&C). This difference is not significant. Overall, private respondents are clearly less satisfied about cost performance than are their public-sector counterparts.

Likewise, when asked if the benefits of the projects are larger than the costs, the differences between DBFM and D&C are small and not significant. Again, the DBFM projects scored overall a bit lower (6.1 out of 10) than the D&C projects (6.5 out of 10). There is also a significant difference between the perceptions of public and private respondents. Private respondents score lower on the cost–benefit balance than public respondents for both types of projects. They score DBFM projects with a 4.9 out of 10. D&C projects score somewhat higher, with 5.7 out of 10, even though the difference is not significant. For public respondents, this is reversed. On average, they score DBFM projects a 7.7 out of 10 and D&C projects a 7.2 out of 10. Clearly, public respondents are more positive regarding this item.

We can conclude that, even though DBFM scores lower on the items for cost performance, the differences between DBFM and D&C projects are nonsignificant. There is, however, a significant difference between the perceptions of public and private respondents. The latter are less positive regarding the cost performance of transport infrastructure projects.

Analyzing cost performance using interview data

The interview data can shed more light on the perceptions and experiences of public and private project managers in relation to the cost performance of these infrastructure projects and the mechanisms behind it. According to the respondents, DBFM leads to cost savings for the public partner. A potential reason for this is the competition between private consortia. Whereas the client (i.e., Rijkswaterstaat) sets a maximum project budget, competition between private consortia often results in lower bids. This is, of course, under the assumption that the maximum project budget is a realistic estimation for the investments in the intended infrastructural works.

> The private companies must offer below that ceiling price [set by Rijkswaterstaat]. Then you could directly see that there are strong differences between the ceiling price and the price for which the private companies offer. All in all, I believe that in 2016 or 2017, €1.5 billion was saved that way. So, I believe DBFM has worked out well for the public principal. (Private-Sector Respondent, R20)

Moreover, many respondents share the impression that DBFM leads to better manageable projects in terms of the additional work claimed. Because of the inclusion of the private finance component in the DBFM contract—something that is absent in D&C contracts—respondents suggested that there are fewer claims for additional work costs. This is in line with our findings in the section above, "Analyzing cost performance using hard project data." The private consortium has a strong incentive to prevent contract changes due to the involvement of banks as financiers of the project. This is very different from a D&C project.

> I've always said, when I take a DBFM, I want zero [contract] changes… because a DBFM in itself is already exciting… I think a DBFM essentially has in it that the public principal is aware… that there will be no changes, because with those banks you have an agreed deadline.… Within a D&C you can make more trouble. In a worst-case scenario, it's going to run out of time, but if it's going to run out of time, and the public principal is responsible, he will have to pay for it in time and money. And then I sit back, until I'm proved right or until I come up with a solution that I decide together with the principal. But in such a case, there is no pressure of the bank on me. (Private-Sector Respondent, R13)

Although the involvement of private financiers is a strong incentive to avoid additional work costs and thus realize projects, as much as possible, in line with predetermined budgets, there is also a downside. According to several respondents, it offers less flexibility to make changes along the way. Both public and private partners recognize this drawback.

> And also, for RWS [Rijkswaterstaat], right, scope is scope, so don't add or change things anymore [after contract closure]... That was different in a D&C contract... Then you just said: "Well, while you're at it, add this too or do that as well." That is absolutely killing in a DBFM. (Public-Sector Respondent, R2)

> I think the main bottleneck is the flexibility in the contracts. And the fact that Rijkswaterstaat actually wants to have a lot more say in the maintenance phase. So, for example, faster overlaying of asphalt. That's where a DBFM gets in the way. Because that is still running for 20 years and there is really nothing you can actually do about it. (Financier, R30)

With respect to the return on investments for the private partners, it proved difficult to clearly determine the performance of the projects, mainly because of the complex, fragmented, and opaque nature of the financial arrangements between the various private parties involved. Still, the respondents confirmed that DBFM projects provide a rather safe return on investments for the banks. Financial investors, who accept a higher risk, received an internal rate of return of approximately 11 percent (Koppenjan et al., 2020).

For the construction and maintenance companies, the financial results fluctuated strongly between projects. A few projects faced major financial losses, but in general the respondents had the impression that members of the EPC made a small profit: "Excessive profits are definitely not made. Projects that do not receive media attention probably have a profit margin between zero and 2 percent" (Financier, R34).

As most Dutch DBFM projects just entered the maintenance phase (for an overview, see Koppenjan et al., 2020), it is not yet possible to measure financial performance over the entire project life-cycle. Respondents indicated, though, that they expect that return on investment would improve during the maintenance phase, when the benefits of the life-cycle approach become manifest and smart practices might reduce maintenance costs. This might nuance the findings of the survey, in which private respondents score DBFM quite low when it comes to the balance between costs and benefits. Whereas D&C projects do not include the maintenance phase, DBFM projects might allow for improving return on investment for the private partner in that phase of the project. With regard to profitability and continuity of revenues, the experiences with DBFM projects are moderately positive. Nevertheless, several respondents point out that the DBFM regime—of achieving milestones and fulfilling the requirements of availability—combined with the competition mechanism, might lead to private partners taking on more risk than they would for regularly tendered projects: "The risk is bigger that, under commercial pressure, private consortia are tempted to accept risks that they shouldn't take on. I think that this is the source of many complaints in the construction sector right now" (Private-Sector Respondent, R17).

Consortium partners often participate in both the SPC, EPC, and the MTC, although they are not necessarily composed in the same manner. This means that the risk for private partners may vary. In general, EPCs will run the largest financial risks during the realization of the projects. This estimation is emphasized by respondents of the construction firms and confirmed by respondents of the financial institutions.

> Well, the basis of a SPC is that it doesn't have any risks... And the MTC doesn't have to run any risks either if the EPC functions in the right way... In the end, it all comes down to the functioning of the EPC. Yes, all risks are actually located at the EPC. (Private-Sector Respondent, R7)

This implies that there can be large differences in the perceived performance of the project. The involved private parties do not all carry the same risks. For some, the project stayed within budget, while others faced budget overruns. However, the SPC and MTC are also affected negatively when the EPC has to take financial losses. Consequently, different respondents—mainly from construction companies—emphasize that it is desirable that the composition of the SPC and the EPC, but also of the EPC and MTC, should be similar. This might lead to a more balanced distribution of financial risks among the private parties involved in a DBFM project and decrease the chance of problems in managing and coordinating the private consortium. A more balanced constellation of the three "DBFM vehicles" might help to compensate potential losses in, for example, the EPC, by the profits of the SPC or MTC. The constellation with an SPC, EPC, and MTC does not exist in D&C projects. Therefore, compared to D&C projects, it might be more complex to get an unambiguous image of the performance of DBFM projects. Moreover, the coordination between the various private partners and the three "DBFM vehicles" (EPC, SPC, and MTC) offers both risks and opportunities for on-budget performance. On the one hand, private parties carrying more risks are in danger of budget overruns. On the other hand, there is the possibility that losses in one vehicle can be compensated in another.

Synthesis of findings on cost performance

The different data sources present some interesting findings regarding the cost performance of DBFM and D&C projects. Combining the various data sources, three observations can be made.

First, the data from the project database of Rijkswaterstaat show that DBFM projects perform better than D&C projects in terms of additional work costs. This is in line with our expectations building on principal–agent theory and transaction costs economics (Verweij & Van Meerkerk, 2021). The analysis of the interviews confirms these findings, stressing the importance within DBFM contracts of not making contract changes. The private financing components (i.e., the involvement of the banks to deliver on time, meet payment obligations, and avoid additional risks) and the limited flexibility of the contract are strong incentives to avoid additional work in DBFM projects. D&C contracts do not have such strong incentives.

Second, the survey findings provide a different picture. There are no significant differences between the cost performance of DBFM and D&C projects when it comes to the two indicators included in the survey. This is in line with the interview data, where respondents are not univocal regarding the potential performance advantage of DBFM over D&C projects. Some of these different perceptions can be related to the difference in perceived performance among public and private parties in these projects. The survey shows that public-sector respondents are more positive regarding the cost performance (for both DBFM and D&C) compared to their private counterparts. Public-sector respondents score DBFM projects, on average, slightly higher than D&C projects, although these differences are not found to be statistically significant.

Third, the significant difference in perceptions between public and private parties regarding cost performance is reflected in the interviews. Public partners are able to reduce costs with DBFM, compared to traditionally procured projects, in case private consortia, due to competition, offer a lower bid than the ceiling price set by Rijkswaterstaat. For private parties, however, DBFM usually implies higher risk than regularly tendered projects such as D&C projects. This might affect their financial performance. The competition among private parties during tendering is an incentive to bear more risks. Despite potential differences regarding cost performance between the SPC, EPC, MTC, and between construction firms and banks, DBFM does lead to some return on investments.

All in all, the findings regarding cost performance are mixed. The hard project data seem to suggest that DBFM performs better than D&C in terms of additional work costs. However, the survey data show that private-sector respondents are clearly less satisfied concerning cost performance, for both DBFM and D&C projects, compared to their public-sector counterparts. DBFM projects score lower, on average, than D&C projects, although these differences are not statistically significant. The interviews confirm the varying perceptions regarding cost performance, suggesting that, from a public-sector perspective, DBFM performs better than D&C in terms of cost performance. For private parties, the profitability of the project differs considerably. For banks and investors, DBFM provides a relatively safe market with predictable returns, while construction companies in the EPC and MTC sometimes work with small margins. The impression is that a limited profit is achieved by most companies, although not as much as intended, and that a number of projects have suffered losses. This might explain the relatively low scores in the survey from private-sector respondents on the cost performance items.

Findings on Time Performance

Analyzing time performance using hard project data

The analysis of the data from the project database of Rijkswaterstaat, presented in Table 6.4,[3] shows that the seven DBFM projects, for which sufficient data on the achievement of the recommissioning milestone were available, had an average *acceleration* of 18.89 percent of the planned duration of the project implementation period between contract award and full commissioning of the infrastructure. In comparison, the 12 D&C projects for which data were available had an average *delay* of 6.84 percent. Hence, overall, the DBFM projects performed significantly better regarding time performance. This confirms the expectations based on the literature that PPPs should be able to improve on-time delivery of public infrastructure (Hodge & Greve, 2017).

Table 6.4 Comparative analysis of achievement of the recommissioning milestone

	DBFM	D&C	Significance
N	7	12	
Average acceleration in %	18.89%	−6.84%	Difference is significant ($p < .05$; $U = 69$)
Standard deviation	14.76%	25.19%	

Note: Significance tests are two-tailed: $p \leq .05$; based on Mann–Whitney U test.

Analyzing time performance using survey data

From an aggregate point of view, the survey data show only a very small difference between D&C and DBFM regarding time performance (Table 6.5). The differences between the two types of projects, regarding the question whether the infrastructure was developed within the agreed time period, are statistically insignificant. DBFM projects received an average score of 7.7 out of 10, whereas D&C projects scored a 7.5 out of 10.

Table 6.5 Comparative analysis of time performance based on survey data

Item	N	Mean	Significance
The availability of the developed infrastructure is realized within the agreed time period			
DBFM	110	7.7	Differences are not significant
D&C	51	7.5	
Public partner	71	8.2	Differences are significant
Private partner	92	7.1	($t = 2.310$, $df = 158.479$, $p < .05$)
Public partner/DBFM	46	8.4	Differences are not significant
Public partner/D&C	25	7.9	
Private partner/DBFM	64	7.1	Differences are not significant
Private partner/D&C	26	7.1	
Total	161	7.6	—

In contrast, the differences between public-sector and private-sector respondents are again significant. Although both groups, on average, assess the time performance of both DBFM and D&C projects to be good, the public-sector respondents are more satisfied about the on-time delivery (8.2 out of 10) compared to private-sector respondents (7.1 out of 10). Moreover, public-sector respondents score DBFM projects on average a bit higher than D&C projects (8.4 for DBFM projects versus 7.9 for D&C projects), even though this difference is not significant. Private-sector respondents assess DBFM and D&C projects similarly (both 7.1 out of 10).

Analyzing time performance using interview data

The interview data are also in line with the data from the project database and are more convincing than the survey data. Both public-sector and private-sector respondents share similar perceptions and experiences about the time performance of DBFM projects.

The interviews clearly show that DBFM puts more pressure on achieving on-time delivery of the projects, at the agreed date of availability, than D&C. Timely delivery occurs in almost all DBFM projects that were included in this study. In addition, in the projects that have suffered from delay, respondents indicate that this delay would probably be greater if the project was implemented within a D&C contract.

> If you look at a D&C [project], in—I believe—nine months' time you could be delayed by three years. In the context of a DBFM, you would have solved that really quickly with each other… It gives a positive pressure to solve issues. If you have a real big problem, it [the pressure] can become unhealthy. I'll admit that right away. During the issues that normally occur, it is good that there is a time limit to solve it together. (Private-Sector Respondent, R16)

> I think the DBFM contracts resulted in projects that are much more on time. Relatively speaking. Of course, there is some delay of these projects. We work on one which is also publicly known... it is heavily delayed. I think that if it would have been a D&C contract, the delay would have been many times longer. So, the fact that a DBFM contract lies behind it, made sure that the delay is limited. (Private-Sector Respondent, R12)

According to the respondents, the main reason for the timely delivery of DBFM projects lies in the severe financial consequences for not meeting the agreed deadlines: "I think that the most important added value of the F-component is the focus on timely delivery. This makes a difference between DBFM and D&C and regular contract forms; once you realize that the construction stage will take more time... it will immediately hurt in financial terms" (Financier, R35).

For DBFM projects, timely delivery is not only stimulated by the public client, but also from the financial component of this contract type. The contracted loans force private parties to fulfill the present repayments in time, and this can only be achieved by meeting the agreed milestones in the project's development process. An all-important milestone is the availability of the project. Private parties experience severe pressure to accomplish timely availability because this is vital for the financing of the project and the project's financial performance.

> From the moment you are running out of time, you need to renew the financial arrangements and then you are stuck with whatever preconditions you need to fulfil to get these new financial means... If you are running out of time, it will cost money, and these costs will increase because of the new financial arrangements you need to engage. So... the negative financial impact of running out of time doubles. (Private-Sector Respondent, R9)

The pressure on timely delivery is so severe that even at moments of discussion (e.g., between client and contractor) about potential project changes, the work in a DBFM project continues as much as possible. This is different in D&C projects, where the financial consequences of stopping construction are less severe. This mechanism in DBFM contracts makes investment decisions by financial institutions easier because of the absolute "must" for contractors to meet the present deadlines on time.

DBFM clearly contains a strong incentive for time performance that D&C is lacking. However, this incentive also has some negative effects. Some respondents indicate that the severe time pressure that flows from the financial arrangements in a DBFM might pose a risk for the project's quality or pose risks for the long run. For instance, time pressure might lead to a decision to proceed with building activities at unfavorable moments (e.g., laying asphalt at low temperatures), which might negatively affect a road's quality and durability. Other respondents point to the "perverse stimulus" to offer unrealistic planning schemes in the procurement stages in order to win the bid. Finally, some respondents indicate that there is a tension between a high project pace and timely delivery on the one hand, and sustainability and reasonable work pressure on the other. With regard to the negative effect of this incentive, much has been learned from previous projects, as several respondents stated that measures are taken to avoid "unhealthy" time pressure.

Synthesis of findings on time performance

Comparing the findings from the three data sources, the first thing that stands out is that the data from the project database and the interviews are very much in line with each other. Both show clearly that DBFM projects perform better than D&C projects concerning on-time delivery. The data stemming from the survey present less convincing evidence in this respect, showing a small yet nonsignificant difference in favor of DBFM projects. To understand the findings of the project database and the survey, the interview data present the underlying mechanisms of DBFM contracts resulting in higher time performance. Respondents attributed the difference in time performance between DBFM and D&C contracts to the severe financial consequences for DBFM projects if on-time delivery (meeting the availability criterion) is not realized. The effects of this mechanism are not only positive (e.g., construction is not stopped in case of disagreements) but can also be negative, such as a risk of lower quality and increased work pressure.

CONCLUSION AND DISCUSSION

Based on a mixed-methods study, we compared DBFM projects with D&C projects regarding their cost and time performance. The evidence stemming from three data sources is not completely conclusive. Nevertheless, the findings show that, on average, DBFM projects perform better than D&C projects in terms of on-time delivery. As expected, private financing in combination with the availability criterion creates strong incentives for the private consortium to deliver on time. This mechanism does not exist in D&C projects. Regarding time performance, there is a performance advantage for PPP projects, compared to regularly tendered infrastructure projects with D&C contracts.

In terms of cost performance, the findings are a bit more nuanced. On the one hand, DBFM projects have clearly lower additional work costs for the public principal compared to D&C projects (Verweij & Van Meerkerk, 2020, 2021). In this respect, DBFM outperforms D&C. However, the interview and survey data showed that from a private-sector perspective, DBFM has different implications. Private-sector respondents in general assessed the cost performance far more critically than their public counterparts; but they were also more negative about the cost performance of DBFM projects compared to D&C projects. Although DBFM is a safe investment for banks and private investors, the profits for contractors are marginal and uncertain while the risks are high. This may explain the more negative perceptions regarding cost performance expressed in the survey by private respondents compared to public respondents.

At the same time, the findings confirm that the shadow of the banks and the transfer of various risks to the private partner—both of which come with DBFM contracts—indeed play an important role in explaining cost and time performance of DBFM on a project level—at least from a public-sector perspective. It, however, also raises questions about the long-term sustainability of these contracts for the construction sector. In this respect, the evaluation study of Koppenjan et al. (2020) shows that relational governance mechanisms, as well as institutional learning, play an important role in making PPPs work better for both public and private partners. All respondents in the interviews, both public and private, indicated that an important reason for the rather positive performance of DBFM projects is that the public and private partners have now learned to collaborate much better than during the early years of DBFM in the Netherlands. In this respect, good performance of PPPs is obviously dependent on a combination of contractual arrangements as well as relational governance mechanisms (Warsen et al., 2019). During the 15 years in which DBFM was used, partners have learned to manage the contract better and that collaboration and flexibility are more important than sticking to the contract. This is especially true in times of crisis (Casady & Baxter, 2020). So, there are strong indications that learning and more intense collaboration between project partners (and actively addressing problems and pitfalls during the project) have been very important for the performance advantage of DBFM.

NOTES

1. See https://www.rijkswaterstaat.nl/zakelijk/zakendoen-met-rijkswaterstaat/werkwijzen/werkwijze-in-gww/contracten-gww (accessed 14 February 2022).
2. Adapted from Verweij et al. (2020).
3. Adapted from Verweij et al. (2020).

REFERENCES

Atmo, G. U., Duffield, C., Zhang, L., & Wilson, D. I. (2017). Comparative performance of PPPs and traditional procurement projects in Indonesia. *International Journal of Public Sector Management*, *30*(2), 118–36.

Brown, T. L., Potoski, M., & Van Slyke, D. (2016). Managing complex contracts: A theoretical approach. *Journal of Public Administration Research and Theory*, *26*(2), 294–308.

Casady, C. B., & Baxter, D. (2020). Pandemics, public-private partnerships (PPPs), and force majeure | COVID-19 expectations and implications. *Construction Management and Economics*, *38*(12), 1077–85.

Casady, C. B., & Geddes, R. R. (2019). Private participation in US infrastructure: The role of regional PPP units. In R. E. Levitt, W. R. Scott, & M. J. Garvin (Eds.), *Public-private partnerships for infrastructure development: Finance, stakeholder alignment, governance* (pp. 224–42). Edward Elgar.

Clifton, C., & Duffield, C. F. (2006). Improved PFI/PPP service outcomes through the integration of alliance principles. *International Journal of Project Management*, *24*(7), 573–86.

Culp, G. (2011). Alternative project delivery methods for water and wastewater projects: Do they save time and money? *Leadership and Management in Engineering*, *11*(3), 231–40.

De Bettignies, J. E., & Ross, T. W. (2004). The economics of public-private partnerships. *Canadian Public Policy*, *30*(2), 135–54.

Demirag, I., Khadaroo, I., Stapleton, P., & Stevenson, C. (2011). Risks and the financing of PPP: Perspectives from the financiers. *British Accounting Review*, *43*(4), 294–310.

De Palma, A., Leruth, L. E., & Prunier, G. (2012). Towards a principal–agent based typology of risks in public-private partnerships. *Reflets et Perspectives de la Vie Économique*, *51*(2), 57–73.

European PPP Expertise Centre. (2015). *PPP motivations and challenges for the public sector: Why (not) and how*. European Investment Bank.

Global Construction Review. (2018). Bye-bye, PFI: UK signals effective end of private finance initiative. *Global Construction Review*.

Grimsey, D., & Lewis, M. K. (2004). *Public-private partnerships: The worldwide revolution in infrastructure provision and public finance*. Edward Elgar.

Hodge, G. A. (2010). Reviewing public-private partnerships: Some thoughts on evaluation. In G. A. Hodge, C. Greve, & A. E. Boardman (Eds.), *International handbook on public-private partnerships* (pp. 81–112). Edward Elgar.

Hodge, G. A., & Greve, C. (2017). On public-private partnership performance: A contemporary review. *Public Works Management and Policy*, *22*(1), 55–78.

Klijn, E. H., & Teisman, G. R. (2003). Institutional and strategic barriers to public-private partnership: An analysis of Dutch cases. *Public Money & Management*, *23*(3), 137–46.

Koppenjan, J. F. M., Klijn, E. H., Duijn, M., Klaassen, H. L., Van Meerkerk, I. F., Metselaar, S. A., Warsen, R., & Verweij, S. (2020). *Leren van 15 jaar DBFM-projecten bij RWS: Eindrapport* [Learning from 15 years of DBFM projects at RWS: Final report]. Rijkswaterstaat en Bouwend Nederland.

Kort, M., & Klijn, E. H. (2011). Public-private partnerships in urban regeneration projects: Organizational form or managerial capacity? *Public Administration Review*, *71*(4), 618–26.

Lawther, W. C., & Martin, L. (2014). Availability payments and key performance indicators: Challenges for effective implementation of performance management systems in transportation public-private partnerships. *Public Works Management & Policy*, *19*(3), 219–34.

Lenferink, S., Tillema, T., & Arts, J. (2013). Towards sustainable infrastructure development through integrated contracts: Experiences with inclusiveness in Dutch infrastructure projects. *International Journal of Project Management*, *31*(4), 615–27.

Leruth, L. E. (2012). Public-private cooperation in infrastructure development: A principal–agent story of contingent liabilities, fiscal risks, and other (in)pleasant surprises. *Networks and Spatial Economics*, *12*(2), 223–37.

Martimort, D., & Pouyet, J. (2008). To build or not to build: Normative and positive theories of public-private partnerships. *International Journal of Industrial Organization*, *26*(2), 393–411.

Ministerie van Financiën. (2013). *Handleiding publiek-private comparator* [Public-private comparator manual].

Mohamed, K. A., Khoury, S. S., & Hafez, S. M. (2011). Contractor's decision for bid profit reduction within opportunistic bidding behavior of claims recovery. *International Journal of Project Management*, *29*(1), 93–107.

Monk, A. H. B., Levitt, R. E., Garvin, M. J., South, A. J., & Carollo, G. (2019). Public-private partnerships for infrastructure delivery. In R. E. Levitt, W. R. Scott, & M. J. Garvin (Eds.), *Public-private partnerships for infrastructure development: Finance, stakeholder alignment, governance* (pp. 19–34). Edward Elgar.

Moore, M. A., Boardman, A. E., & Vining, A. R. (2017). Analyzing risk in PPP provision of utility services: A social welfare perspective. *Utilities Policy*, *48*(C), 210–218.

Nachar, N. (2008). The Mann–Whitney U: A test for assessing whether two independent samples come from the same distribution. *Tutorials in Quantitative Methods for Psychology*, *4*(1), 13–20.

Ng, A., & Loosemore, M. (2007). Risk allocation in the private provision of public infrastructure. *International Journal of Project Management*, *25*(1), 66–76.

O'Shea, C., Palcic, D., & Reeves, E. (2019). Comparing PPP with traditional procurement: The case of schools procurement in Ireland. *Annals of Public and Cooperative Economics*, *90*(2), 245–67.

Palcic, D., Reeves, E., & Siemiatycki, M. (2019). Performance: The missing "P" in PPP research? *Annals of Public and Cooperative Economics*, *90*(2), 221–6.

Petersen, O. H. (2019). Evaluating the costs, quality, and value for money of infrastructure public-private partnerships: A systematic literature review. *Annals of Public and Cooperative Economics*, *90*(2), 227–44.

Reynaers, A. M., & Parrado, S. (2017). Responsive regulation in public-private partnerships: Between deterrence and persuasion. *Regulation and Governance*, *11*(3), 269–81.

Rijkswaterstaat. (2021). *Contracten GWW*.

Rodrigues, B., & Zucco, C. (2018). A direct comparison of the performance of public-private partnerships with that of traditional contracting. *Brazilian Journal of Public Administration*, *52*(6), 1237–57.

Tang, L. Y., Shen, Q., & Cheng, E. W. L. (2010). A review of studies on public-private partnership projects in the construction industry. *International Journal of Project Management*, *28*(7), 683–94.

Verweij, S., & Van Meerkerk, I. F. (2020). Do public-private partnerships perform better? A comparative analysis of costs for additional work and reasons for contract changes in Dutch transport infrastructure projects. *Transport Policy*, *99*, 430–8.

Verweij, S., & Van Meerkerk, I. F. (2021). Do public-private partnerships achieve better time and cost performance than regular contracts? *Public Money & Management*, *41*(4), 286–95.

Verweij, S., Van Meerkerk, I. F., & Klaassen, H. L. (2020). *De performance van DBFM bij Rijkswaterstaat: Een kwantitatieve analyse van projectendata* [The performance of DBFM at Rijkswaterstaat: A quantitative analysis of project data]. Rijksuniversiteit Groningen en Erasmus Universiteit Rotterdam.

Verweij, S., Van Meerkerk, I. F., & Korthagen, I. A. (2015). Reasons for contract changes in implementing Dutch transportation infrastructure projects: An empirical exploration. *Transport Policy*, *37*, 195–202.

Warsen, R. (2021). *Putting the pieces together: Combining contractual and relational governance for successful public-private partnerships.* Erasmus University Rotterdam.

Warsen, R., Klijn, E. H., Koppenjan, J. F. M. (2019). Mix and match: How contractual and relational conditions are combined in successful public-private partnerships. *Journal of Public Administration and Theory*, *29*(3), 375–93.

Warsen, R., Nederhand, J., Klijn, E. H., Grotenbreg, S., & Koppenjan, J. F. M. (2018). What makes public-private partnerships work? Survey research into the outcomes and the quality of cooperation in PPPs. *Public Management Review*, *20*(8), 1165–85.

Williamson, O. E. (2002). The theory of the firm as a governance structure: From choice to contract. *Journal of Economic Perspectives*, *16*(3), 171–95.

World Bank. (2017). *Public-private partnerships: Reference guide*. World Bank.

Yescombe, E. R. (2013). PPPs and project finance. In P. de Vries & E. B. Yehoue (Eds.), *The Routledge companion to public-private partnerships* (pp. 227–46). Routledge.

7. The performance of PPP and publicly procured road projects: evidence from India

Akash Deep, Mojahedul Islam Nayyer, and Thillai Rajan A.

OVERVIEW OF INDIA'S ROADS SECTOR

The importance of transportation infrastructure for economic growth is well recognized. The ability of road infrastructure to cater to individual needs and provide connectivity to remote areas makes road transport a preferred choice for users. Roads also provide trunk as well as last-mile connectivity for other modes of transport, such as airways, railways, and waterways. Road transport remains the dominant segment in India's transportation sector, accounting for about 87 percent of passenger traffic and 60 percent of freight traffic (Ministry of Road Transport and Highways [MoRTH], 2021a). Totaling over 6 million km, India's road network is the second-largest in the world (MoRTH, 2021b). Roads in India can be broadly classified into two categories, depending upon the agency responsible: national roads and state roads. National roads, also called national highways, are implemented by the central government. State roads—consisting of state highways, district roads, urban roads, and village roads—are implemented by their respective state governments. National highways comprise 2 percent of the total road network in the country but carry about 40 percent of the total road traffic, forming the backbone of India's road infrastructure. In terms of road network length, the share of rural roads is the highest (71 percent), followed by district roads (10 percent), urban roads (9 percent), and state highways (3 percent). Two-thirds of India's road network consists of surfaced roads (MoRTH, 2021a).

India's road sector has witnessed significant growth in recent years. Total investment in road construction increased from ₹519.3 billion in 2015 to ₹1727.7 billion in 2020, an average annual growth rate of 27 percent (Department of Economic Affairs [DoEA], 2021). In 2019, roads accounted for one-fifth of the country's total infrastructure investment of ₹10 trillion

(DoEA, 2020). In terms of road networks, the total road length increased at the average annual rate of 4 percent (from 5.5 million km in 2015 to 6.4 million km in 2019), but the length of national highways grew at almost double that pace, increasing from 97 991 km to 132 500 km (MoRTH, 2021a).

Procurement of Road Projects

The selection of an appropriate procurement model is fundamental to the success of a road project. Procurement of road projects in India can be broadly classified into two categories: public procurement and Public-Private Partnerships (PPPs).

Public procurement takes two forms: item rate contracts—which are pure construction contracts where the engineering design is provided to the contractor—and Design–Build (DB) contracts—where the construction company designs and builds the road project. In India, public procurement has been gradually moving away from item rate contracts to DB contracts, which are also called Engineering, Procurement, and Construction (EPC) contracts.

In India's road sector, PPPs have largely taken two forms: Build–Operate–Transfer (BOT)-Toll and BOT-Annuity. In both formats, the private concessionaire designs, builds, finances, and operates the road for a predetermined period of time before transferring ownership to the government. The difference lies in how the concessionaire recovers its investment. In the BOT-Toll format, fees (tolls) are collected from road users. Conversely, BOT-Annuity arrangements rely on fixed payments from the government agency (annuities or availability payments).

In the public procurement approach, even though a private contractor is entrusted with the responsibility of constructing the project, it is the public sector that bears the majority of risks that the project may face over its life. In contrast, under the PPP model, the private sector usually bears significant risks related to construction, operations and maintenance, level of usage, and the financing of the infrastructure project. A major goal of PPP projects is the optimal sharing of risks between the public agency and the private sector (DoEA, 2016). For example, the public sector might be better placed to mitigate risks relating to land acquisition, approvals, clearances, and shifting utilities (Singh, 2019). On the other hand, the private sector is typically better equipped to mitigate risk related to the project's design, construction, and operation.

In public procurement, project specifications are provided by the public agency; the responsibility of the private contractor ends with development and construction and does not include operation and maintenance of the asset. Therefore, the contractor has little incentive to consider the life-cycle costs of the project, such as choosing a more expensive but higher-quality asset

Table 7.1 *Road sector financing in India in millions of ₹*

	10th Five-Year Plan (2002–2007)		11th Five-Year Plan (2007–2012)		12th Five-Year Plan (2012–2017)	
	Public	Private	Public	Private	Public	Private
National roads	647990	85750	1745240	742420	1247890	544950
State roads	724290	26180	1839600	134470	3034920	998130
Total	1372280	111930	3584840	876960	4282810	1543080

Source: Planning Commission (2013, 2014).

construction option that would lower asset maintenance costs. However, PPP projects are not only about creating assets but also about delivering a level of service to end-users. Most PPP contracts have clauses to suspend toll collections if the quality of the road does not meet prescribed standards (see MoRTH, 2008). PPPs also bring a higher level of autonomy in the design, financing, construction, operation, and maintenance of the projects, thereby providing greater opportunities for benefiting from private-sector innovation and efficiency.

Public procurement projects are financed by the government through budgetary allocations, and the contractor receives milestone payments upon achievement of prespecified milestones. In PPP contracts, payments to the private sector are generally not made during the construction phase. The private sector recovers its investment during the operation phase, either in the form of contractually agreed annuity payments from the government agency or by collecting tolls from the road users. Since the government does not incur upfront costs for project procurement in the case of most PPP variants, procurement through PPPs is often recommended as a financing mechanism to overcome short-term fiscal constraints faced by governments.

Traditionally, public procurement was the dominant, if not the only, route for developing road projects in India. However, since the early 2000s, the government has extensively adopted the PPP approach. Table 7.1 illustrates this shift in road procurement toward PPP between 2002 and 2017.

The numbers in Table 7.1 represent the source of funding from the perspective of governments. The share of private-sector investment increased from about 8 percent in the 10th Five-Year Plan to 26 percent in the 12th Five-Year Plan. While the compounded average growth in public-sector investment in roads was 76 percent between the 10th and 12th Five-Year Plans, the growth of private-sector investments for the corresponding period was 271 percent. This indicates the increased role of private investment in the road sector. The growth of private-sector financing was seen in both national roads and state roads. While private-sector financing increased by 152 percent for national roads between the 10th and 12th Five-Year Plan periods, the corresponding increase was 517 percent for state roads. Between 2000 and 2020, a total of 516 national and state highway road PPP projects were delivered, comprising a total length of 144 070 lane-kilometers (lane-km) and investment of ₹2575 billion. In comparison, 481 national and state highway road projects comprised of 65 341 lane-km with a total investment of ₹834 billion had been completed through traditional public procurement in the same period. These numbers underline the important role and contribution of PPPs for road development in India. The next section describes the evolution of the different forms that these PPPs have taken in India.

PUBLIC-PRIVATE PARTNERSHIPS IN INDIAN ROADS

Policy initiatives to promote private-sector investment in the roads sector started in 1995, with the amendment of the National Highway Act (1956) to allow private investment in road projects. The first policy framework for PPP was introduced in 1997 and, since then, the Indian road sector has grown to become one of the largest PPP road programs in the world in terms of the number of road stretches being developed through the PPP model. The PPP framework also constantly evolved to sustain the interest of private developers, such as the introduction of Viability Gap Funding (VGF) for BOT-Toll projects and the BOT-Annuity model (for details, see Haldea, 2006).[1] By 2020, the PPP forms being used in India consisted of: BOT-Toll, BOT-Annuity, Hybrid Annuity Model (HAM), and Toll–Operate–Transfer (TOT).[2]

BOT-Toll

In this format, the concessionaire recovers the initial investment through toll fees from road users. The concessionaire bears not only the construction and the maintenance risks, but also the entire commercial risk with respect to toll income (Anant & Singh, 2009; Mangu et al., 2021). This has been the preferred PPP model for the government due to the high extent of risk sharing with the private sector. However, the interest of the private sector in BOT-Toll projects has been low when traffic demand is uncertain, resulting in high revenue risk.

BOT-Annuity

In this format, the concessionaire is assured of a pre-agreed return on the initial investment. While the concessionaire bears the construction and maintenance risks, the revenue and financial risks are mitigated because of the fixed payments from the government agency (Anant & Singh, 2009; Mangu et al., 2021). Since BOT-Annuity does not provide any upside to the developer, even if the traffic growth exceeds projections, it is used only for those projects where the traffic demand is highly uncertain.

Hybrid Annuity Model

Bidders' interest in Indian PPP road projects started to decline around 2015 because many existing PPP projects were experiencing financial difficulties. To rekindle private-sector interest, governments proposed the HAM approach, which envisaged significant financial support from the government. In the HAM model, a significant part of the project cost (between 40 percent and 60 percent) is paid to the developer during the construction stage. The remaining payments are made through availability and performance payments during the operation phase over an extended period of 7 years–10 years (Peri et al., 2019).

Toll–Operate–Transfer

This format is used for operating roads with well-established traffic and does not involve any major development and construction work. In this format, the concessionaire has to make an upfront, lump-sum payment to the government. The concessionaire is required to maintain and operate the road during the concession period and, in return, enjoys the right to collect tolls from the road users over the same period. This model helps to operate and maintain previously constructed public projects and those PPP projects that have been transferred back to the government at the end of their concession periods.

BOT-Toll and BOT-Annuity have been the most common PPP models for the road sector in India for more than 20 years. The first BOT-Toll road project in India commenced in 1996, while the BOT-Annuity format was first implemented in 2001 (PPP Cell, 2022). By 2020, about 340 national and state highway road projects comprising a total length of 108 895 lane-km (and investments exceeding ₹1857 billion) had been completed on a BOT-Toll basis (PPP Cell, 2022). About 172 national and state highway road projects comprising a total length of 29 341 lane-km (and investments exceeding ₹643 billion) had been completed on a BOT-Annuity basis (PPP Cell, 2022). The first HAM project and TOT models commenced in 2014 and 2018, respectively (MoRTH, 2019).[3] At the time of writing this chapter, the number of projects implemented in these latter two formats were very few, and data were limited. Therefore, the analysis in this chapter focuses only on BOT-Toll and BOT-Annuity projects.

LIFE-CYCLE OF ROAD PROJECTS

Irrespective of the type of procurement, a typical road project consists of three phases: development, construction, and operation and maintenance

Table 7.2 Major activities in the life-cycle of road projects

Number	Activities
	Panel A: Development Phase
1	Project identification to meet service needs
2	Project pre-feasibility analysis (economic, technical, social, etc.)
3	Demand forecast and financial viability
4	Procurement option analysis depending on the pre-feasibility report (PPP or EPC)
5	Complete feasibility study (demand analysis, social and environmental impact assessment, financial viability, economic feasibility, risk assessment, risk sharing, etc.)
6	PPP model (Toll, Annuity, HAM, etc.) selection depending on the full feasibility report
7	Land acquisition
8	Procurement strategy (international competitive bidding, national competitive bidding, limited competitive bidding, unsolicited proposal, Swiss challenge, etc.)
9	Procurement design (bid evaluation criteria, single-stage RFP or multi-stage EOI, RFQ, RFP)
10	Expression of Interest (EOI): market sounding
11	Request for Qualification (RFQ): shortlisting of the qualified bidder
12	The final draft of the agreement
13	Request for Proposal (RFP) and bid evaluation
14	Contract finalization and award
15	Public disclosure of the contract
16	Financial closure
17	Permits and clearances
	Panel B: Construction Phase
1	Final permits and clearances for the project to start construction
2	Finalize design and manage changes in the design
3	Manage risk (land acquisition, environment, social, legal, etc.)
4	Construction of the road
5	Construction completion and hand-over to the operation team
	Panel C: Operation and Maintenance Phase
1	Revenue collection
2	Repair and maintenance of the asset to meet the specified quality of service
3	Transfer of the asset to the public sector at a specified quality standard as per the agreement at the end of the concession period

Source: DoEA (2010a).

(Vilventhan & Kalidindi, 2012). An overview of the major activities in each of the phases is provided in Table 7.2.

Development Phase

In this phase, often referred to as the "drawing board" phase, the main features of the project are finalized, such as length, alignment, and other technical and commercial features, as well as the type of procurement (i.e., public procurement or PPP, as well as the specific type of PPP). Since decisions made during this phase cannot be modified easily over the life of the project, the development phase is critical for effective risk management (Beckers et al., 2013). The complexity of collaboration necessitates a large number of activities during the development phase, all the way from project selection to financial close and the obtainment of permits. If financial close cannot be reached, the procurement process fails; if technology risks are deemed to be significant, a project may be delayed or aborted during this phase (Boshuizen, 2015). Panel A in Table 7.2 provides an overview of the major activities during the development phase.

Irrespective of the type of procurement, government agencies play a dominant role during the development phase, which not only includes pre-feasibility studies and project preparation but also land acquisition, provision of forest and environment clearances, and assistance with the obtainment of approvals from various central and state government departments. The development phases of public procurement and PPP projects differ from each other in the following ways:

- Since PPP projects are financed by private capital, the project's financial viability is of paramount importance. A detailed traffic demand and forecast study is a necessary prerequisite for PPP projects.
- The construction of PPP projects does not begin until the project reaches financial close, which is the responsibility of the concessionaire. The extent of financial burden may not be so high in the case of public procurement projects; it is usually adequate for the contractor to arrange for short-term working capital since milestone payments are expected to be received from the public agency.
- The outcomes of the development phase include various agreements among the stakeholders. In the case of PPP projects, the extent of contracting far exceeds the contractual requirements of public procurement projects. Consequently, the development phase of PPP projects is usually characterized by higher transaction costs (see Dudkin & Välilä, 2006).

In summary, the development phase of PPP road projects may take longer than that of public procurement projects because of the need for traffic forecast studies and the necessity of reaching financial close. The process of achieving financial close can begin only after the concessionaire has been identified.

Construction Phase

After the development phase, the construction begins during the "ground-breaking" phase. It is during this phase that significant capital expenditure is incurred. Panel B in Table 7.2 lists the major activities during the construction phase of a road project. The construction phases of public procurement and PPP projects vary from each other in the following ways:

- The degree of freedom for project design is higher for the private sector in PPP projects. Using value engineering and principles of life-cycle costing is not only encouraged from the concessionaire but largely expected.
- PPP projects are characterized by a higher level of monitoring since there is additional oversight by the lenders' engineer and the government to ensure construction quality. In addition, the cost is also scrutinized at the bidding stage before the project is approved.
- Delays in project completion due to delays in milestone payments is not unusual in the case of public procurement projects. PPP projects generally do not suffer delays for want of capital because financing is secured before construction begins.
- The concession duration for PPP projects includes both the construction phase and the operation and maintenance phase (MoRTH, 2008). Since the concessionaire seeks to maximize the toll collection period, there is strong incentive to reach the commercial operations date as early as possible by completing construction quickly. The incentive for timely completion exists even in BOT-Annuity projects, where the concessionaire is rewarded for early completion with bonus payments. Concessionaires deal with events that are likely to cause time overruns (e.g., changes in scope) in a tactical manner to complete construction in a timely manner. While PPP concessionaires may assume additional financial risk to complete construction quickly, the contractor in public procurement is unlikely to take on such risks. It is therefore hypothesized that the construction phase for PPP projects would be shorter, and time overruns would also be lower.

Chapter 1 of this book lists some of the previous studies that indicate the superior time performance of PPP projects across sectors. Whittington (2012), Verweij and Van Meerkerk (2021), and Verweij et al. (2020) also specifically confirm this hypothesis for the road sector. Using data from road projects in the United States for the period 1998–2005, Whittington (2012) found that PPP projects took less time and were completed earlier. Verweij and Van

Meerkerk (2021) and Verweij et al. (2020) also arrived at a similar result based on their study of Dutch transport infrastructure projects.

Operation and Maintenance Phase

The operation and maintenance phase starts when the road is opened to traffic; it is the longest phase in the project life-cycle. Performance of the road during the operations phase is very closely watched and can be politically and socially sensitive. It can affect the reputation of the nodal agency, developer, contractor, and the government (Boshuizen, 2015). Panel C in Table 7.2 lists the significant activities during the operation and maintenance phase of a road project. The operation phases of public procurement and PPP projects vary from each other in the following salient ways:

- The concessionaire in a PPP contract has to ensure the quality of the road by doing routine and periodic maintenance for the entire duration of the concession. Defaulting on maintenance would impact toll collections in the case of BOT-Toll projects or suspended annuity payments in the case of BOT-Annuity.[4] However, the maintenance requirements are not so onerous in a public procurement contract, typically requiring the contractor to maintain the road for a short initial period after completion of construction.[5] After the initial period, maintenance of the road becomes the responsibility of the public authority.
- The quality of service for the end-users has been found to be superior in the case of PPP projects when compared to the public road projects because of a well-defined maintenance schedule (Singh, 2019). A road of inferior quality or one that has poor service would also have an adverse impact on traffic and affect revenues. Such pressures are not felt for public procurement projects.
- PPP concessionaires are more proactive in implementing measures that minimize travel discomfort. For example, waiting time for toll payment has been a major problem in toll roads, resulting in user irritability. Many PPP developers were quick to shift to electronic toll collection systems when technology became available to minimize toll collection times.

A REVIEW OF PPP ROAD PROJECT PERFORMANCE

A detailed review of the literature on the performance of PPP projects in different sectors is provided in Chapter 1. This section therefore provides a short review of the performance of PPP projects only in the roads sector. Past research comparing the performance of public procurement and PPP road projects has primarily focused on developed economies. Many of these studies have examined performance during the construction phase, and specifically on cost and time overruns. Using data from 12 PPP projects in North America, Chasey et al. (2012) performed benchmarking with previous studies and found that PPP projects had lower cost and time overruns. Iacobacci (2010) obtained similar results based on data from 19 PPP projects from Canada. He found that time and costs are lower in PPP projects when compared to traditional procurement. A similar incidence of superior time and cost performance of PPP projects was found in the UK (Grimsey & Lewis, 2007) and Australia (Infrastructure Partnerships Australia, 2007). These studies indicated that the results from developed economies have consistently indicated the superior performance of PPP projects.

However, research findings on the performance of PPP projects in developing countries have varied. Rajan et al. (2014), in an empirical analysis of 521 road projects implemented in India, found that the cost overruns for PPP projects were higher than those of publicly procured projects. Singh (2019), too, had a similar finding from an analysis of 313 national highway projects in India: PPP projects had 34 percent higher cost overrun than public procurement projects. However, Meduri and Annamalai (2013), in another empirical analysis of road projects in India, found that PPP projects were larger in size, and the unit cost of PPP road projects was lower when compared to that of publicly procured projects. Regression analysis showed that PPP projects could achieve lower unit costs because of the benefit from economies of scale.

Rajan et al. (2014) and Singh (2019) also found that time overruns for PPP projects were lower than those of public procurement projects. The average time overrun for PPP projects was approximately 13 percent, and it was 75 percent for public procurement projects (Rajan et al., 2014). Taken together, these findings from both developed and developing economies indicate PPP projects' superior on-time performance across countries, whereas the evidence on cost overruns is mixed. This is consistent with the results of the systematic review by Petersen (2019) and those in the review provided in Chapter 1 of this book. While the overall performance of PPPs in terms of cost, time, and project overruns has been well studied, attributing the performance differences on dimensions of cost, time, and service quality to different stages of the project life-cycle has been limited. This chapter addresses this gap.

Life-Cycle Performance Indicators for Infrastructure Projects

Based on a review of the PPP India Toolkit,[6] we identified indicators that can be used as measures of performance for different phases of the project life-cycle. Table 7.3 details these measures.

Table 7.3 Performance indicators across phases

Number	Measure	Performance Indicator
Development Phase		
1	Estimated construction cost	Construction cost benchmark
2	Estimated construction time	Construction time benchmark
3	Duration of the development phase	Actual development time
Construction Phase		
4	Project management	Project size (lane-length)
5	Unit time	Actual construction time per lane-km
6	Unit cost	Actual construction cost per lane-km
7	Time overrun	Time-effectiveness of PPP
8	Cost overrun	Cost-effectiveness of PPP
Operation and Maintenance Phase		
9	Average speed of the vehicle and delay time experienced by the user	Service quality
10	The number of accidents reported and accident response time	Service quality
11	Road roughness indicator	Service quality

DATA AND METHODS

Data pertaining to national and state highway projects implemented in India during 1996–2017 were used in our analysis. The data were obtained from the Integrated Database on Indian Infrastructure Projects (IDIP),[7] which is a curated comprehensive data set of infrastructure projects in India from the following sources: the Indian DoEA of the Ministry of Finance, the Ministry of Statistics and Program Implementation, National Highway Authority of India (NHAI), and respective state government websites. The final dataset used in this study consisted of 997 projects: 481 developed using public procurement and 516 PPP projects. Among the PPP projects, 344 were BOT-Toll and 172 were BOT-Annuity. Since the data cover a 21-year period, all financial values were converted to 2017 values in our analysis.

This study adopts a mixed-methods approach. To compare the performance of publicly procured and PPP projects during the development and construction phases, paired project comparison was done. Since limited data were available for the operations and maintenance phase, an evidence summary was

Table 7.4 Variables and their descriptions

Type of Variable	*Unit*	*Description*
Size Variable		
Length	km	Length of the stretch of the road
Number of lanes	—	Number of lanes in the newly constructed road
Lane-length	Lane-km	Length × number of lanes
Time Variable		
Construction start date	Date	Date of start of construction
Scheduled construction completion date	Date	Estimated date of completing the construction
Actual construction completion date	Date	Actual date of completing construction
Scheduled project completion time	Month	Scheduled construction completion date − construction start date
Actual project completion time	Month	Actual construction completion date − construction start date
Time overrun	Month	Actual project completion time − scheduled project completion time
Percentage time overrun	—	$\left(\frac{\text{Time overrun}}{\text{scheduled project completion time}}\right)\times 100$
Scheduled unit time	Days/lane-km	$\frac{\text{Scheduled project completion time}}{\text{lane} - \text{length}}$
Actual unit time	Days/lane-km	$\left(\frac{\text{Actual project completion time}}{\text{lane} - \text{length}}\right)$
Cost Variable		
Project budgeted cost	₹ million	Estimated cost of the project at the bidding phase
Project actual cost	₹ million	Actual cost incurred at the end of the construction phase
Cost overrun	₹ million	Project actual cost − project budgeted cost
Percentage cost overrun	—	$\left(\frac{\text{Cost overrun}}{\text{project budgeted cost}}\right)\times 100$
Budgeted unit cost	₹ million/ lane-km	$\frac{\text{Project budgeted cost}}{\text{lane} - \text{length}}$
Actual unit cost	₹ million/ lane-km	$\frac{\text{Project actual cost}}{\text{lane} - \text{length}}$

completed. Table 7.4 presents the list of variables and their descriptions in the comparative analysis.

FINDINGS AND DISCUSSION: DEVELOPMENT AND CONSTRUCTION PHASES

Data Description and Means Comparison

Table 7.5 provides a description of the data for public procurement and PPP projects. The findings indicate that there are significant differences between public procurement and PPP road projects. The data show that PPP projects tend to be larger than public procurement projects, both in terms of the length of roads and the number of lanes. Since road project costs are directly dependent on lane-length, the budgeted project costs are also significantly different. The project length also affects the unit costs, because of economies of scale. The t-test results in Table 7.5 show significant differences in the means for public procurement and PPP projects, indicating large differences between the two types of projects. Therefore, to make the performance comparison meaningful, a matched-pair analysis was done. Since project length and budgeted costs do not reflect the complexity of the road (terrain, bridges, etc.), we used budgeted unit cost and scheduled unit time to identify comparable projects

Table 7.5 Comparison of public procurement and PPP projects (independent-sample t-test)

	Public Procurement	PPP	p-value
Number of projects	481	516	—
Size Variables			
Length (km)	58.6	74.9	0.000***
Average number of lanes	2.5	3.6	0.000***
Lane-length (lane-km)	135.8	279.2	0.000***
Development Phase			
Project budgeted cost (₹ million)	1828.7	7254.4	0.000***
Budgeted unit cost (₹ million per lane-km)	15.7	24.5	0.000***
Scheduled project completion time (months)	23.2	24.8	0.070*
Scheduled unit time (days per lane-km)	8.1	5.3	0.000***

Note: *** $p < .01$; ** $p < .05$; * $p < .10$.

Matched-Pair Analysis

To offer robust conclusions, we followed the overall mean comparisons with a paired-sample t-test. The main factors affecting development and construction in the case of road projects are road length and complexity. Since budgeted unit cost and scheduled unit time are indications of both length and complexity, both of these were used in the matched-pair comparison. The results are shown in Table 7.6. The key findings are as follows.

Development phase

Project size

The size variables in Table 7.6 (Panels A and B) indicate that PPP projects are larger than those that use public procurement for budgeted unit cost and scheduled unit time. When matched on budgeted unit cost, the average length of a PPP road was 68.1 km and 53.2 km for public procurement. When matched on scheduled unit time, the difference in length was not statistically significant, but the difference in average lane-length between PPP (193.0 lane-km) and public procurement (147.2 lane-km) was significant. This indicates that PPP projects have better economies of scale and are able to handle complexity more effectively. While procuring road projects through the PPP route was a relatively new concept during the late 1990s, in the last two decades, there have been concerted efforts toward capacity building for preparing PPP projects. Projects with a longer stretch or with a higher number of lanes are complex and require a higher level of technical and managerial skills during the development phase. Our finding indicates that the private sector has, over the years, acquired the management and operational expertise to successfully develop longer road projects (Meduri & Annamalai, 2013).

Scheduled unit time

Table 7.6 (Panel A) shows that for projects that have comparable unit costs, the average number of days to construct 1 lane-km of the road was 6.4 days for PPP whereas it was 8.4 days for public procurement. This indicates that, on average, scheduled unit time is 23 percent lower for a PPP project. The shorter duration can be attributed to the strength of PPP developers in project management and the inbuilt incentive to complete the project quickly to maximize the toll collection period.

Budgeted unit costs

Table 7.6 (Panel B) shows that for projects that have comparable unit time, average budgeted unit costs for PPP roads was ₹21.7 million, whereas the corresponding figure for publicly procured roads was ₹13.5 million. Our results indicate that the average budgeted unit costs for PPP roads are 61

Table 7.6 *Matched-pair analysis*

	Public Procurement	PPP	p-value
Panel A: Confounding for Budgeted Unit Cost			
Number of projects	336	258	—
Size Variables			
Length (km)	53.2	68.1	0.000***
Average number of lanes	2.4	3.0	0.000***
Lane-length (lane-km)	124.2	208.6	0.000***
Development Phase			
Budgeted unit cost (₹ million per lane-km)	15.3	16.1	0.225
Scheduled unit time (days per lane-km)	8.4	6.4	0.002***
Construction Phase			
Actual unit cost (₹ million per lane-km)	15.9	18.3	0.026**
Actual unit time (days per lane-km)	12.3	7.3	0.000***
Percentage cost overrun	10.6	13.9	0.215
Percentage time overrun	67.3	30.0	0.000***
Panel B: Confounding for Scheduled Unit Time			
Number of projects	264	224	—
Size Variables			
Length (km)	67.8	62.5	0.275
Average number of lanes	2.3	3.3	0.000***
Lane-length (lane-km)	147.2	193.0	0.002***
Development Phase			
Budgeted unit cost (₹ million per lane-km)	13.5	21.7	0.000***
Scheduled unit time (days per lane-km)	6.0	5.6	0.227
Construction Phase			
Actual unit cost (₹ million per lane-km)	14.5	25.3	0.000***
Actual unit time (days per lane-km)	9.9	6.9	0.000***
Percentage cost overrun	11.9	18.4	0.091
Percentage time overrun	72.1	32.6	0.000***

Note: *** $p < .01$; ** $p < .05$; * $p < .10$.

percent higher when compared to publicly procured roads. We hypothesize various reasons for this finding. First, higher unit costs for PPP projects can be attributed to the higher risk faced by the developers and the corresponding higher financing costs (see Blanc-Brude & Strange, 2007). Second, the higher estimated costs for the initial PPP projects come from the concessionaire's focus on minimizing project life-cycle costs, resulting in higher initial costs. It has also been observed that the quality of PPP roads is better than that of publicly procured roads (Singh, 2019). To ensure better quality of PPP roads, the budgeted cost is relatively higher. Third, the higher unit costs can also be partly attributed to the intention of the developers to complete the project quickly, resulting in higher costs. Additional studies are needed to confirm these hypotheses.

Table 7.7 Average time taken for key events in PPP road projects

Activities	Time Taken (Days)
Concession agreement to financial closure	222
Financial closure to construction commencement	59
Concession agreement to construction commencement	262

Duration development phase

Notwithstanding the evidence on time and costs, the development phase of PPP projects is expected to be longer because of the need to achieve financial close before construction can begin. Table 7.7 shows that the average time taken to achieve financial close in PPP projects is more than seven months, which is significant. However, construction commences within two months after achieving financial close. Since the requirement for financial close does not arise in the case of public procurement, the development phase of the PPP project is longer.

Construction phase

Cost overrun

When matched on budgeted unit cost (Panel A in Table 7.6), the cost overrun was 13.9 percent for PPP roads and 10.6 percent for publicly procured roads. Though the cost overrun percentage was higher for PPP roads, the difference was not statistically significant. When matched on scheduled unit time (Panel B in Table 7.6), the cost overrun for was 18.4 percent PPP roads versus 11.9 percent for publicly procured roads. Once again, the difference is not statistically significant. However, cost overrun trends broadly follow the trends in actual and budgeted unit cost. The reasons for higher unit costs for PPP roads were explained in the section on the development phase.

Practitioners opined that cost overruns are usually the result of delays in getting project clearances, changes of scope, and so on. In such instances, the concessionaire is eligible for compensation from the agency. Since approvals for such compensation can be delayed, the concessionaire usually goes ahead and absorbs the costs so that construction can be completed on schedule. Subsequently, the concessionaires tend to recover the cost from the agency through an arbitration or legal process. Thus, while some of the overrun costs would be recovered eventually, the project records will continue to show an incidence of overrun as of project completion.

Time overrun

The performance difference between PPP and publicly procured roads is most significant for time overrun. When projects were matched on budgeted unit cost (Panel A in Table 7.6), the time overrun for PPP roads was 30.0 percent, and it was 67.3 percent for publicly procured roads. When projects were matched on scheduled unit time (Panel B in Table 7.6), the time overrun was 32.6 percent for PPP roads and 72.1 percent for publicly procured roads. In both instances, the difference was significant ($p < .10$).

Lower unit time and time overruns in PPP projects can be directly attributed to the incentive structure of PPP contracts. Since the concession period is fixed, there is an inbuilt incentive for the developers to complete the construction faster so they can start collecting tolls quicker. Any delays in construction would directly result in lost toll collections. Therefore, PPP procurements are not only characterized by faster project completion time but also have lower time overruns.

As an additional robustness check, the matched-pair analysis was done after controlling for both budgeted unit cost and scheduled unit time simultaneously. While the number of observations were lower as a result of the more restricted matching, the results were consistent with those given in Table 7.6.

Does type of PPP impact performance?

To determine whether the performance difference between public procurement and PPP projects persists for the two types of road PPPs (i.e., BOT-Toll and BOT-Annuity), matched-pair analysis was performed separately for the two types of PPP projects. Table 7.8 contains the results.

Public procurement and BOT-Annuity

The results in Table 7.8 (I) indicate that although the road lengths of public procurement and BOT-Annuity are not significantly different, the lane-lengths of BOT-Annuity projects are higher and significantly different, whether the matching was based on budgeted unit cost or scheduled unit time. When controlling for budgeted unit cost, scheduled unit times were not significantly different between the two project types. When controlling for scheduled unit time, budgeted unit costs were higher for BOT-Annuity roads. Cost overrun was not significantly different between the two types of projects, whereas percentage time overrun was significantly different, irrespective of the matching. When matching was done on budgeted unit cost, the average percentage time overruns for BOT-Annuity and publicly procured roads were 0.2 percent and

Table 7.8 *Comparison of public procurement with BOT-Toll and BOT-Annuity procurement*

	(I) Public Procurement versus BOT-Annuity			(II) Public Procurement versus BOT-Toll		
	Mean			Mean		
	Public Procurement	BOT-Annuity	p-value	Public Procurement	BOT-Toll	p-value
Panel A: Confounding for Budgeted Unit Cost						
Number of projects	167	104	—	211	146	—
Size Variables						
Length (km)	46.3	48.9	0.536	56.0	83.7	0.000***
Average number of lanes	2.4	2.6	0.068*	2.4	3.3	0.000***
Lane-length (lane-km)	106.8	134.8	0.028**	132.7	282.3	0.000***
Development Phase						
Budgeted unit cost (₹ million per lane-km)	14.6	15.7	0.295	15.3	16.5	0.217
Scheduled unit time (days per lane-km)	8.4	9.4	0.306	8.3	3.9	0.000***
Construction Phase						
Actual unit cost (₹ million per lane-km)	15.0	16.2	0.372	16.2	19.4	0.031**
Actual unit time (days per lane-km)	12.01	8.7	0.005***	12.8	5.6	0.000***
Percentage cost overrun	7.6	5.8	0.451	11.7	20.4	0.061*
Percentage time overrun	59.2	0.2	0.000***	72.2	46.2	0.009***

	(I) Public Procurement versus BOT-Annuity			(II) Public Procurement versus BOT-Toll		
	Mean			Mean		
	Public Procurement	BOT-Annuity	p-value	Public Procurement	BOT-Toll	p-value
Panel B: Confounding for Scheduled Unit Time						
Number of projects	177	109	—	186	149	—
Size Variables						
Length (km)	60.5	54.7	0.285	79.1	81.3	0.749
Average number of lanes	2.4	3.4	0.000***	2.3	3.6	0.000***
Lane-length (lane-km)	137.1	172.5	0.032**	171.1	298.4	0.000***
Development Phase						
Budgeted unit cost (₹ million per lane-km)	14.8	25.2	0.000***	11.9	23.2	0.000***
Scheduled unit time (days per lane-km)	6.1	6.3	0.666	4.7	4.4	0.386
Construction Phase						
Actual unit cost (₹ million per lane-km)	15.9	27.1	0.000***	12.9	28.8	0.000***
Actual unit time (days per lane-km)	10.1	7.6	0.004***	7.6	6.1	0.024**
Percentage cost overrun	9.0	7.5	0.562	13.5	28.7	0.009***
Percentage time overrun	72.8	15.3	0.000***	75.5	44.8	0.001***

Note: *** $p < .01$; ** $p < .05$; * $p < .10$.

59.2 percent, respectively. When matching was done on scheduled unit time, the corresponding figures were 15.3 percent and 72.8 percent, respectively.

Public procurement and BOT-Toll

The results in Table 7.8 (II) indicate that the road lengths of public procurement and BOT-Toll roads are significantly different when matched on budgeted unit costs, not just in length but also in the number of lanes. When the matching was done on scheduled unit time, the differences were significant for the number of lanes and lane-length. When controlling for budgeted unit cost, scheduled unit times were significantly different between the two project types. The average scheduled unit time for BOT-Toll was 3.9 days, whereas for public procurement it was 8.3 days. When controlling for scheduled unit time, the average budgeted unit cost was higher for BOT-Toll roads: ₹23.2 million for BOT-Toll versus ₹11.9 for public roads. Cost overruns were significantly different between the two types of projects under both matchings, with BOT-Toll roads having higher cost overrun percentages. The trend was reversed for time overrun. The average time overrun was higher for publicly procured roads when compared to BOT-Toll roads. When projects were matched on budgeted unit costs, the percentage time overruns for public procurement and BOT-Toll roads were 72.2 percent and 46.2 percent, respectively. When projects were matched on scheduled unit time, the corresponding numbers were 75.5 percent and 44.8 percent, respectively.

Comparing the performance of public procurement with that of PPP roads separated by type of PPP shows that although both BOT-Toll and BOT-Annuity projects differed significantly from publicly procured roads, the parameter values of BOT-Annuity projects are closer to public projects than to BOT-Toll projects. For example, the mean difference in length of publicly procured roads and BOT-Annuity roads was not significant, though it was significant when compared on lane-length. Even when the differences were significant, the magnitude of the difference was considerably higher for public procurement versus BOT-Toll roads than for public procurement versus BOT-Annuity. Both BOT-Toll and BOT-Annuity had significantly lower time overruns, whereas the difference in cost overruns were significant only for BOT-Toll versus public procurement. Therefore, our results show that time overruns are lower for PPP projects irrespective of the type of PPP, whereas cost overruns are only significant when comparing public procurement against BOT-Toll projects.

PERFORMANCE DURING THE OPERATION AND MAINTENANCE PHASE

For road projects, various parameters are used to analyze performance during the operation and maintenance phase. These include the speed of travel, number of accidents, quality and smoothness of the road, roadside support for vehicle repair and breakdowns, and so on. There is a large number of dimensions to performance, although they could be broadly grouped under the dimension of service quality, as identified in Chapter 1.

However, unlike the development and construction phases, performance data during the operation and maintenance phase are very limited in our dataset. Therefore, we rely on empirical evidence documented by other researchers and the findings of public audit reports scrutinizing the Indian road sector. In addition, the main drivers of the differential performance of PPPs and publicly procured roads over the operating and maintenance phase are illustrated by drawing upon some prominent examples from the Indian road sector.

Available empirical evidence sheds light on how PPPs have performed compared to publicly procured roads in India. For example, Singh (2019) compared the quality of Indian roads procured using PPP and non-PPP contracts using the International Roughness Index (IRI) as an indicator of quality. Based on IRI data for 84 projects, the study found that PPP projects had a better IRI when compared to non-PPP roads. This implies that the quality of the PPP roads was better than that of the non-PPP roads, even after controlling for the age of the road.

In another study, Gopalkrishna and Karnam (2015) performed a qualitative Value for Money (VfM) analysis for road users of four PPP projects in the State of Karnataka in India and compared this with old public roads. Using a survey from 200 end-users (50 from each of the four projects), they measured the quality of the road projects during the operation phase. The users reported key performance variables, such as travel time, fuel efficiency, consistency in reaching the destination, road safety in driving, vehicle operation and maintenance costs, average driving speed, and potholes. Survey results revealed that, on average, travel time reductions ranged from 30 percent to 50 percent. An average travel speed of 80 km/h (as specified in the contract agreement) was achieved in all four projects, indicating that the construction supported the desired performance. All categories of regular road users reported improvement in the fuel mileage by about 30 percent. The road users also reported consistency in reaching the destination. All four roads were also free of potholes, and potholes were repaired within 24 hours of when they appeared, per the contract guidelines. Road users also conceded that vehicle operation and maintenance costs came down.

The superior quality of PPP roads was also corroborated by the reports from the Comptroller and Auditor General (CAG) of India on the National Highways Development Program. CAG reports indicated that most of the government projects (i.e., non-PPPs) were found to be deficient in quality. For example, a quality audit by the CAG of 21 completed projects and 11 ongoing projects found that out of these 32 stretches, seven of the stretches were of sub-standard quality (CAG, 2005). The quality of most of the PPP projects has been satisfactory. For example, in another quality audit of six PPP projects conducted by the CAG, it was found that the pavement surface condition was satisfactory in all the projects (CAG, 2008). The roughness levels were tested at 932 locations in these projects and all of them were at the acceptable level. Moreover, in 348 out of these 932 locations, the quality standard was more than the acceptable level, and they we declared to have achieve the "desirable" levels of roughness.[8]

Underlying this difference in operating performance of PPPs relative to publicly procured roads are some distinguishing features of PPP projects. These features are best illustrated using specific examples of PPPs in the Indian road sector.

Use of Contracts

In the Tuni Anakapalli Annuity Road Project, the quality of the service during the operation phase was ensured through contractual obligations, such as reduction or non-payment of annuity by NHAI, in case of non-availability of the road for reasons that can be attributed to the concessionaire (DoEA, 2010b). This project involved the widening and strengthening of the existing two-lane 59-km highway into a four-lane expressway. As one of the first BOT-Annuity projects to be implemented in India, road operations commenced in 2004, and the concession was transferred back to the NHAI in 2019. However, the NHAI retained a sum of ₹74 million from the last four annuity payments preceding the expiry of the concession period to ensure that the concessionaire completed the last periodic maintenance before the road was transferred back to the public authority (ICRA, 2020).

Being Responsive to User Difficulties

The 28-km Delhi Gurgaon Expressway involved the expansion of a four-lane highway to an eight-lane expressway connecting the national capital of Delhi and its satellite city Gurgaon. However, the actual traffic far exceeded the projected traffic expectations, growing at 9 percent every year, making it the densest highway in India (Kaur, 2014). Consequently, there was heavy queuing at the toll station because tolls were being collected through cash payments. It appeared that the very purpose of the expressway—to reduce travel time, fuel cost, and congestion—failed. However, this issue was managed by deploying various traffic management techniques. Cash payment of tolls was replaced by introducing electronic payment through sensors. Asia's largest toll station of 32 lanes was constructed to avoid any loss of time due to queuing.

Focus on Construction for Better Performance during Operation Phase

Better design and engineering during the construction phase also improves performance during the operation and maintenance phase. The Vadodara Halol Toll Road, one of India's first state PPPs in the State of Gujarat, involved the widening and strengthening of the existing two-lane 32-km highway into a four-lane expressway. Some of the main service improvements were the contiguous and parallel intermediate service roads on both sides of the expressway to avoid accidents; the introduction of noise barriers, subways, and compound walls; and the planting of 550 trees across the highway to comply with the emissions norms (DoEA, 2010b).

In the case of the Delhi Gurgaon Expressway, significant improvements in operating performance (i.e., increased average travel speed from 26 km/h to 66 km/h, the reduction of travel time from Delhi to Gurgaon from 65 to 25 minutes, and improved safety) were the result of a reduction in the number of intersections from 20 to 10, with grade separators (flyovers) at the intersections (DoEA, 2010b).

Finally, some of the other prominent features of the Tuni Anakapalli Annuity Road Project included the replacement of two existing railway-level crossings with overbridges, thereby eliminating a delay of 1088 vehicle hours (NHAI, 2000). The dual carriageway highway improved safety and raised average speed from 32 km/h to 53 km/h (Miyazaki, 2006). To ensure high-quality performance during the operation and maintenance phase, the concessionaire entered into an operation and maintenance contract with the construction contractor (DoEA, 2010b).

These examples illustrate the noteworthy performance of PPP roads in India during the operation and maintenance phase and its prominent drivers. A common example (though an extreme case) used to highlight the better performance of PPP roads during the operation and maintenance phase is the 93-km National Highway from Poonamallee to Walajahpet in the South Indian State of Tamil Nadu. This stretch was implemented as a PPP project initially. However, due to the slow progress made in widening it to a six-lane road and other defaults, NHAI terminated the concession agreement in 2016 (Projects Today, 2016) and took over operations and maintenance of the stretch. In

2019, the lack of maintenance was cited as the reason for two fatal accidents that occurred in the stretch along with long travel time delays (ToI, 2019). In December 2020, the High Court of Tamil Nadu penalized NHAI for poor maintenance of the stretch and directed toll plazas to collect only 50 percent of the toll fee for two weeks (ToI, 2020).

CONCLUSION AND IMPLICATIONS

Typical infrastructure projects mainly have three phases: development, construction, and operation. Each phase has its own significance and contributes to the overall success of the project. Activities in one phase feed the activities of the subsequent phase and, hence, monitoring performance throughout the project life-cycle is vital for project success. This edited volume discusses the performance of PPP projects across three dimensions: cost, time, and service quality. We posit that the relative importance of these three dimensions varies across the three phases: time is more relevant than cost during the development phase, whereas during the construction phase, both time and cost would be equally relevant. In the operations phase, service quality is the most relevant dimension of performance.

Highway projects are generally procured using two types of contracts: public procurement and PPP. Since PPP contracts are long-term in nature, concessionaires adopt a life-cycle approach and are able to assume a higher level of risk that results in better project performance. Our analysis shows that PPP projects are larger in size and that they are implemented faster than publicly procured projects. In terms of cost, the PPP and publicly procured projects are not significantly different.

The development phase is shorter for publicly procured projects than for PPP projects because of the need to achieve financial close before construction can begin in the latter case. The time taken for financial close can be significant, though it can vary depending on the developer. Therefore, PPP projects take a longer time to begin construction. During the construction phase, PPP projects demonstrate a superior capacity to complete projects in scheduled time. The percentage of time overruns are significantly lower for PPP projects when compared to publicly procured projects. While there is no significant difference on cost overruns between the two types of procurement, budgeted unit costs are higher for PPP projects. We thus conclude that while PPP projects show superior performance on time during the construction phase, this is not the case with respect to cost. We hypothesize that a major reason for the higher unit cost is the greater cost of capital for PPP projects.

The performance of a road project during the operation phase can be assessed on multiple parameters, such as reduced accidents, time taken for the journey, road roughness, maintenance costs incurred, and others. All of these parameters could be broadly classified as contributing to service quality. The case studies presented here, as well as past research reviewed, indicate that the service quality of PPP roads is superior to that of public roads. Industry experts indicated that contractual conditions, better construction, and responsiveness to user needs ensure superior service quality performance in PPP roads. Since the duration of the operation and maintenance phase is the longest in the project life-cycle, achieving superior performance during the operation and maintenance phase is critical. The variations in performance of PPP projects on cost and time during the development and construction phases should therefore be seen from that perspective.

ACKNOWLEDGMENTS

The authors would like to acknowledge the helpful comments and suggestions of Dr. Esther Malini Victor, General Manager at L&T Infrastructure Development Projects Limited on the draft version of the chapter. The authors would also like to acknowledge the review comments of the editors for the draft version of the chapter.

NOTES

1. VGF is a mechanism to provide capital support to PPP projects that would not otherwise be financially viable. It has the effect of reducing the revenue required to recover costs and provide a financially attractive return for the private sector (DoEA, 2016).
2. One recent development has been the creation of Infrastructure Investment Trusts (InvITs). Though it is strictly not a form of PPP, InvITs have helped individual as well as institutional investors to invest in operating road assets. Developers bundle existing road assets under a trust and sell units of the trust to the investors. InvITs help developers to exit from the project and attract new investors during the operations and maintenance phase (DoEA, 2020).
3. Traditionally, newer PPP models are first rolled out in national highway projects. However, HAM was first implemented in a state highway project in the Indian State of Madhya Pradesh (Garg & Dayal, 2020). The first HAM project in national highway commenced in 2016 (PPP Cell, 2022).
4. Article 17 of the Model Concession Agreement (MCA) for BOT projects says that "the concessionaire shall procure that at all times during the operation period, the project highway conforms to the maintenance requirements set forth." Furthermore, Article 36 states that "upon occurrence of a concessionaire default, the authority shall be entitled, without prejudice to its other rights and remedies under this agreement including its rights of termination hereunder, to (i) suspend all rights of the concessionaire under this agreement including the concessionaire's right to collect fee, and other revenues pursuant hereto, and (ii) exercise such rights itself and perform the obligations hereunder or authorise any other person to exercise or perform the same on its behalf during such suspension" (MoRTH, 2008). MCA lays down the standard terms relating to the allocation of

risks, contingent liabilities and guarantees, as well as service quality and performance standards. MCA have been developed by MoRTH for implementing PPP road projects in India.

5. Article 14 of the EPC agreement states that "the contractor shall maintain the project highway for a period of two years commencing from the date of the provisional certificate. For the performance of its maintenance obligations, the contractor shall be paid a total amount equal to 1.5 percent of the contract price for the first year of maintenance, and 2 percent of the contract price for the second year of maintenance" (MoRTH, 2012).
6. The PPP Toolkit is a web-based resource that has been designed by the Indian DoEA of the Ministry of Finance. The toolkit is for use by PPP practitioners across India in both the public and private sectors.
7. The IDIP can be accessed at http://www.idip.co.in.
8. The performance deficiency of public roads is also corroborated by the meagre budget allocation for maintenance. The annually available fund for maintenance and repair of national highways has been only about 35 percent–40 percent of the estimated fund requirement as per the norms for maintenance of national highways. The allocation of funds for the repair and maintenance has been in a range of 1 percent–5 percent of the annual allocation to the Ministry during the period 2017–22, which is far less than in developed countries.

REFERENCES

Anant, T. C. A., & Singh, R. (2009). *Distribution of highways public-private partnerships in India: Key legal and economic determinants*. CDDRL Working Papers, Stanford University. https://cddrl.fsi.stanford.edu/publications/distribution_of_highways_public_private_partnerships_in_india_key_legal_and_economic_determinants

Beckers, F., Chiara, N., Flesch, A., Maly, J., Silva, E., & Stegemann, U. (2013). *A risk-management approach to a successful infrastructure project: Initiation, financing, and execution*. McKinsey & Company.

Blanc-Brude, F., & Strange, R. (2007). How banks price loans to public-private partnerships: Evidence from the European markets. *Journal of Applied Corporate Finance*, *19*(4), 94–106.

Boshuizen, S. (2015). *Infrastructure development*. Marsh.

Comptroller and Auditor General (CAG). (2005). *Report no. 7 of 2005 for the period ended March 2004 performance audit of – Review on National Highways Authority of India (M/O Road Transport and Highways)*. Comptroller and Auditor General of India.

CAG. (2008). *Report no. PA 16 of 2008 for the period ended March 2007 – Public-private partnership in implementation of road project by National Highways Authority of India (PSU)*. Comptroller and Auditor General of India.

Chasey, A. D., Maddex, W. E., & Bansal, A. (2012). Comparison of public-private partnerships and traditional procurement methods in North American highway construction. *Transportation Research Record: Journal of the Transportation Research Board*, *2268*(1), 26–32.

Department of Economic Affairs (DoEA). (2010a). *PPP toolkit for improving PPP decision-making processes*. Department of Economic Affairs, Ministry of Finance, Government of India.

DoEA. (2010b). *Public-private partnership projects in India: Compendium of case studies*. Department of Economic Affairs, Ministry of Finance, Government of India.

DoEA. (2016). *PPP guide for practitioners*. Department of Economic Affairs, Ministry of Finance, Government of India.

DoEA. (2020). *National infrastructure pipeline: Report of the task force*. Department of Economic Affairs, Ministry of Finance, Government of India.

DoEA. (2021). *Economic survey 2020–21*. Department of Economic Affairs, Ministry of Finance, Government of India.

Dudkin, G., & Välilä, T. (2006). Transaction costs in public-private partnerships: A first look at the evidence. *Competition and Regulation in Network Industries*, *1*(2), 307–330.

Garg, S., & Dayal, M. (2020). Road learnings: Evolution of public-private partnerships in the Indian highway sector. *Transportation Research Procedia*, *48*, 2488–2510.

Gopalkrishna, N., & Karnam, G. (2015). Performance analysis of national highways public-private partnerships in India. *Public Works Management and Policy*, *20*(3), 264–85.

Grimsey, D., & Lewis, M. (2007). Public-private partnerships and public procurement. *Agenda*, *14*(2), 171–88.

Haldea, G. (2006). *Financial support to public-private partnerships*. The Secretariat for the Committee on Infrastructure.

Iacobacci, M. (2010). *Dispelling the myths: A pan-Canadian assessment of public-private partnerships for infrastructure investments*. The Conference Board of Canada.

ICRA. (2020). *GMR Tuni Anakapalli Expressways Limited: Long-term rating withdrawn, short-term rating assigned for non-fund based facilities*. ICRA Limited (formerly known as the Investment Information & Credit Rating Agency Limited (IICRA)).

Infrastructure Partnerships Australia. (2007). *Performance of PPPs and traditional procurement in Australia: Report to infrastructure partnerships*. Allen Consulting Group and the University of Melbourne.

Kaur, J. (2014). *Case study 19: Public-private partnership: Delhi-Gurgaon Expressway, India*.

Mangu, S., Annamalai, T. R., & Deep, A. (2021). Comparison of toll and annuity PPPs: A case study of highway projects in India. *Built Environment Project and Asset Management*, *11*(1), 103–120.

Meduri, S. S., & Annamalai, T. R. (2013). Unit costs of public and PPP road projects: Evidence from India. *Journal of Construction Engineering and Management*, *139*(1), 35–43.

Ministry of Road Transport and Highways (MoRTH). (2008). *Public-private partnership in national highways: Model concession agreement*. Government of India.

Miyazaki, K. (2006). *The national highway—5 improvement projects (I) (II)*. OPMAC Corporation. https://www.jica.go.jp/english/our_work/evaluation/oda_loan/post/2007/pdf/project31_full.pdf

MoRTH. (2012). *Engineering procurement and construction agreement*. National Highway Authority of India.

MoRTH. (2019). *Road projects under TOT Model*. Ministry of Road Transport and Highways, Government of India.

MoRTH. (2021a). *Annual report 2020–2021*. Ministry of Road Transport and Highways, Government of India.

MoRTH. (2021b). *Estimates and functioning of national highway projects including Bharatmala Projects*. Ministry of Road Transport and Highways.

National Highway Authority of India (NHAI). (2000). *4/6 Laning of Tuni - Anakapalli Section of NH-5*. Ministry of Surface Transport, Government of India.

Peri, R., Chen, C., & Dey, D. (2019). *Hybrid annuity contracts for road projects in India*. Asian Development Bank.

Petersen, O. H. (2019). Evaluating the costs, quality, and value for money of infrastructure public-private partnerships: A systematic literature review. *Annals of Public and Cooperative Economics*, *90*(2), 227–44.

Planning Commission. (2013). *Twelfth Five-Year Plan (2012–2017): Faster, more inclusive and sustainable growth*. Government of India.

Planning Commission. (2014). *Second report of the High-Level Committee on Financing Infrastructure*. Government of India.

PPP Cell. (2022). *Public-private partnership in India*. Ministry of Finance, Government of India.

Projects Today. (2016). *NHAI terminates agreement with Essel Walajahpet Poonamallee Toll Road*. Projects Today. https://www.projectstoday.com/News/NHAI-terminates-agreement-with-Essel-Walajahpet-Poonamallee-Toll-Road

Rajan, T. A., Gopinath, G., & Behera, M. (2014). PPPs and project overruns: Evidence from road projects in India. *Journal of Construction Engineering and Management*, *140*(5).

Singh, R. (2019). Public-private partnerships vs. traditional contracts for highways: Comparison of cost and quality of roads. *Indian Economic Review*, *53*, 29–63.

Times of India (ToI). (2019, January 29). NHAI relays part of NH 4 after protest by truck owners. *Times of India*.

ToI. (2020, December 17). NHAI collects half the toll fee, but only after cops intervene. *Times of India*.

Verweij, S., & Van Meerkerk, I. F. (2021). Do public-private partnerships achieve better time and cost performance than regular contracts? *Public Money & Management*, *41*(4), 286–95.

Verweij, S., Van Meerkerk, I. F., & Leendertse, W. (2020). Het prestatievoordeel van publiek-private samenwerking: Een analyse van transportinfrastructuurprojecten in Nederland [The performance advantage of public-private partnerships: An analysis of transport infrastructure projects in the Netherlands]. *Beleid en Maatschappij*, *47*(3), 269–89.

Vilventhan, A., & Kalidindi, S. N. (2012). *Approval risks in transportation infrastructure projects in India*. Construction Research Congress 2012.

Whittington, J. (2012). When to partner for public infrastructure? Transaction cost evaluation of design–build delivery. *Journal of the American Planning Association*, *78*(3), 269–85.

8. Evaluation of the safety performance of PPPs versus publicly funded and managed motorways in Spain

Daniel Albalate, Germà Bel, and Paula Bel-Piñana

INTRODUCTION

The use of Public-Private Partnerships (PPPs) to build and manage motorways has a long-lasting tradition is Spain, given that it was the preferred model for the launch of the Spanish motorway network in the 1960s. Except for the period 1984–91, during which time new motorways could only be publicly managed and funded by the public budget, PPPs have always been present in the development and renovation of high-capacity roads in Spain. After this period, PPPs began to return in the early 1990s and regained momentum in the second half of the decade with the renegotiation and extension of concession contracts and, in the 2000s, with the award of several new greenfield and brownfield PPP motorways. The result of this historical development of the motorway network in Spain has been an unusual mixed model of funding and managing that provides a variety of formats with different degrees of private participation (Albalate, 2014):

- Build–Operate–Transfer (BOT) concession-type PPP motorways: privately constructed and managed with tolls.
- Operation and Management PPPs: publicly constructed but privately managed with budgetary funding.
- Traditional publicly funded and managed motorways, with neither private participation nor user charges.

In contrast to most comparable countries, in Spain these models coexist throughout the territory. In the Spanish motorway industry, we find various forms of production and financing models, also within the PPP model, with weakly or strongly vertical PPP integrations (Albalate et al., 2017). The first model above (BOT) represents strong vertical PPP integration, indicating that the concession comprises both the construction and operation of the motorway. The second model represents weak vertical PPP integration.

Reforms aiming to achieve a greater homogenization of this mixed model are currently being debated in Spain. In June 2018, the Spanish government announced that the tolled motorways in the network under central government regulation would remove user charges when the respective concessions finished. Very recently, in April 2021, the government publicly announced a proposal to toll all motorways (both currently tolled and non-tolled) by 2024. If implemented, this will entail a dramatic change in the model of financing the maintenance and renovation of the motorway network under central government control. We return to this issue in the discussion section, as our research has relevant implications in this regard.

Pending the decisions to be taken regarding the future of the financing model, here we focus on the unusual mixed model of funding and management currently in force, which offers an excellent scenario for evaluating the effects of this variability on the performance of PPPs. With this aim in mind, we investigate a relatively unexplored area of PPPs: their contribution to road safety. In this way, our chapter fits inside the broad category of service quality performance (see Chapter 1). To do so, we compare the performance of PPP-managed and publicly managed motorways.

We analyze the relative performance of PPPs regarding road safety by means of panel data econometric methods. Our database contains observations for the 50 Spanish provinces during the period 2003–2019 (850 observations). We consider all levels of government with responsibilities for the management of motorways, both central and subcentral. This allows us to empirically test whether PPPs present better, worse, or similar performance outcomes with regard to publicly funded and managed motorways. Our dependent variables will be the number of deaths and the number of accidents with victims (injuries) per million inhabitants in road crashes occurring in interurban roads. Our key independent variable will be the proportion of the whole that each form of management represents in each province (i.e., the higher or lower exposure to PPP within the whole network in the province). This empirical strategy allows us to capture the net safety effects of the PPP model, considering both its direct safety effects on the roads managed privately, as well as any offsetting indirect effects on secondary roads. As we will see below, the literature has identified potential negative safety externalities when PPPs imply user fees in the form of tolls.

Our results suggest that PPP motorways deliver better road safety outcomes than publicly managed motorways. This advantage is associated with both types of PPP considered (BOT concession-type PPPs and PPPs operating and managing publicly funded motorways). However, we do not find a statistically significant difference between the two PPP models. When we analyze the severity of accidents, measured as fatality rates, our results indicate that only tolled PPP (BOT concession-type PPPs) models perform better than publicly managed and funded motorways.

The remainder of the chapter is organized as follows. First, we present a revision and analysis of the evolution of the Spanish model of the motorway network financing and management, which provides the historical and institutional context for our country study. Next, we review the relevant literature (with special emphasis on multivariate empirical evidence) on the relationship between accident rates and the management and funding-related characteristics of the road networks. After this we present our data, empirical modeling, and implementation, based on which we obtain evidence on the relationship between management, funding, and accident rates in Spain. Finally, we discuss our results and draw policy implications.

MOTORWAY NETWORK DEVELOPMENT IN SPAIN: A HISTORY OF MIXED MANAGEMENT AND FINANCING MODELS

The earliest attempt to build motorways in Spain dates to the late 1920s, under the dictatorship of Miguel Primo de Rivera (1923–30), whose economic policy was inspired by the models introduced by Mussolini in Italy. The Spanish government probably took its lead from the private concessions for tolled motorways awarded in Italy by Mussolini's first government (Bel, 2011). In July 1928, the Spanish Ministry of Public Works was authorized by royal decree to award private concessions for the construction and operation of the Madrid-Valencia, Madrid-Irún, and Oviedo-Gijón motorways, which were to be financed with user tolls (Navas, 2002). Subsidies were to be allocated to complete the financing obtained with tolls. However, none of these projects was implemented, for two reasons: first, it was impossible to introduce motorways in a country that still had many gaps in its ordinary conventional road network; and second, the volume of traffic outside urban settings was too low to be able to bear the costs, even if subsidies were granted (Bel, 2012).

First Phase: BOT Concession-Type PPPs

The construction of motorways in Spain had to wait until well into the second half of the 20th century. An influential report by the World Bank published in 1962 on the country's economic development suggested that a new motorway was immediately needed along the Mediterranean coast, from the French border to the city of Murcia (Banco Mundial, 1962). This motorway would cross the areas with highest traffic intensity in Spain, both for freight transportation in a period of intense economic growth and for passenger transportation in a densely populated corridor connecting the country's most important tourist areas. Five years after the World Bank report, the 1967 Spanish National Motorway Program (*Programa de Autopistas Nacionales Españolas*, or PANE) was drawn up. This program envisaged the construction of 3160 km of motorways, which were to be awarded by means of concessions to private investors and would be financed with tolls, even though major public subsidies were also made available.

Later, in 1972, the PANE was updated with a project to build 6430 km of toll motorways. In the 1960s, both France and Italy had developed their toll motorways by means of government-owned firms, while other western European countries chose budget financing and public management for their motorways. The choice of toll funding and private concessions in Spain was due to two relevant factors. The first was the influence of those early (even if unfulfilled) projects for private concessions of tolled motorways in the 1920s (Bel, 2012), which followed the path of the first-ever interurban tolled motorways developed under Mussolini in Italy; and the second was the extremely low level of government revenue in Spain under the Francoist dictatorship (Bel, 1999).

The tolled PPP model was not as effective as had been hoped for the expansion of the network. There were two main reasons for this: first, the economic crisis unleashed in the mid-1970s, which profoundly affected not only economic growth but also fuel prices, thus reducing traffic volume; and second, the fact that several of the routes initially planned did not have enough demand (not even in the pre-recession forecasts) to recoup costs and had been included in the planning for political reasons. By the mid-1980s, only 1807 km of tolled networks had entered service (i.e., just 28 percent of the planned network). In addition to the limited expansion of the system, the subsidies and public guarantees included in the early concession contracts that had been awarded (for details, see Albalate et al., 2015a) imposed a heavy mid-term burden on the Treasury (for details, see Bel, 1999).

Second Phase: Traditional Budgetary Funding For Motorways

In 1982, five years after the first democratic legislative election after the Francoist dictatorship, the social-democratic *Partido Socialista Obrero Español* obtained an absolute majority in parliament. In 1984, the new government created a state-owned firm (the National Motorways Company – *Empresa Nacional de Autopistas*, ENAUSA), which took over several concessions that had failed, and a new model of budget funding and government management was adopted for the new motorways included in the General Plan of Highways (*Plan General de Carreteras*, PGC, 1984–91).

Besides the disappointment with the delivery of the PPP model, two additional drivers were key for this change. First, the modernization of the fiscal system in Spain provided the Treasury with a notable increase in revenues, so budgetary funding of motorways became more feasible. Second, Spain's entry into the European Economic Community (EEC, later European Union) in 1986 provided access to EEC regional policy funds that could be used to build motorways. The new policy aimed to transform existing conventional highways by de-coupling and doubling the number of lanes (called *autovías*, an equivalent of toll-free motorways).

This change of model implied a significant reduction of costs (also of quality standards, an issue that will become relevant later in this study), and accelerated the extension of the network: whereas the former PPP model took almost two decades to deliver 1807 km of tolled motorways, in only four years (1986–90) the budgetary financing model created almost the same number of kilometers of toll-free motorways: 1707 km (Bel, 2012). Thus, by the end of the 1980s, the Spanish motorway network had reached a balance between tolled PPPs and toll-free motorways. The construction of toll-free motorways maintained its rapid pace throughout the 1990s, and by the end of the decade, the length of free motorways was triple that of toll motorways under the PPP regime. By 1996, the toll-free state network had extended to 4123 km (i.e., 70 percent of the total state-controlled motorway network). Furthermore, between the mid-1980s and the mid-1990s, almost 1000 km more toll-free motorways had been created by the regional governments established in Spain since the early 1980s, but only 200 km of regional tolled motorways with PPPs were promoted in that period.

Third Phase: Hybrid Model Mixing Budgetary Funding and Concessions to PPPs

In 1996, the new government of the Partido Popular (conservative) introduced a new partial change in the motorway model. While construction of new toll-free motorways was maintained, albeit at a slower pace, private companies were awarded contracts to build a new set of tolled motorways. These new PPPs were mostly new access routes to Madrid, which were built in parallel to the six toll-free motorways that converged on the capital. Also, in 2003 the government privatized the government-owned motorway company (ENAUSA), a measure designed to return to the private sector a business that had only been taken over by the public sector because of the bankruptcy of private concessions (Albalate, 2014).

In the following years, more kilometers of both toll-free and tolled motorways were built under this mixed network. This hybrid model was maintained and extended by the Socialist Party on its return to power in 2004.

Additionally, a new type of PPP was introduced: shadow toll concessions, to improve and renovate the first generation of free motorways constructed during the 1980s. This form of PPP was initially introduced in Spain in 1998 by the regional governments of Madrid and Murcia, and later became popular in many regions from 2002 onward (see Vassallo & Pérez de Villar, 2010). The central government was attracted by this model, and the 2005 Transport Infrastructure Strategic Plan (2005–2020) considered a new wave of PPPs in the form of Design–Build–Finance–Operate–Maintain (DBFOM) contracts without toll charges but including a series of payments based on the volume of traffic received (Albalate, 2014). This wave of PPPs was awarded in 2007 and was applied to more than 900 km of free motorways.

As a result, both main principal political parties subscribed to a road infrastructure policy based on a continuous increase in capacity that bore no relation to the real growth in traffic (Albalate, 2014). Spain established itself as the leader in kilometers of motorway per capita in Europe,[1] and in transport infrastructure overcapacity (Albalate et al., 2015b). At the end of the 2000s, the financial crisis and the subsequent recession hit the promotion of new motorways as well as the implementation of the recent concessions awarded up until the middle of the decade (Albalate, 2014; Albalate et al., 2015a).

Figure 8.1 displays the evolution of the Spanish motorway network, distinguishing between toll-free under government management, toll-free under PPP management, and tolled motorways (the last all PPPs). In Figure 8.1, state and

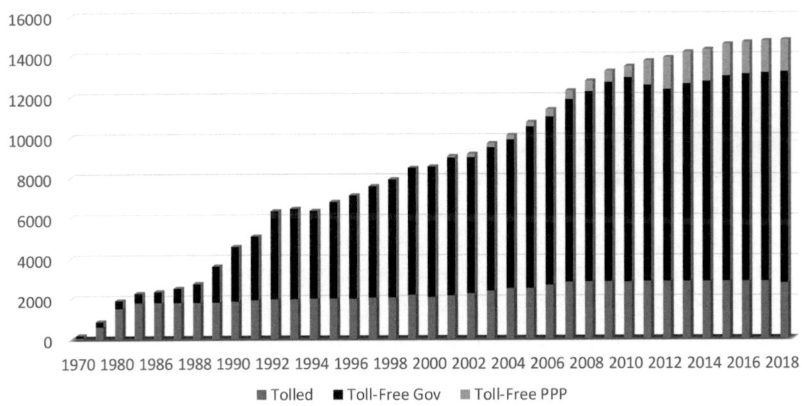

Note: There exist 1645 additional kilometers of dual-carriage ways that do not meet the technical characteristics of motorways. The total is state plus regional roads.
Source: The authors, based on statistics from the Spanish Ministry of Transportation, Mobility, and Urban Agenda.

Figure 8.1 *Evolution (km) of the tolled, toll-free government, and toll-free PPP motorway networks*

regional networks are added up. Data were obtained from the official statistics of the Spanish Ministry of Transportation, Mobility, and Urban Agenda.[2]

In June 2018, the Spanish government announced that the tolled motorways in the state-controlled network (hereafter, state network) would remove tolls as each concession came to an end, as mentioned above. The state toll-motorway network, which had reached a length of 2539 km in 2017 (22 percent of the total state network), will be left with less than 1500 km by 2022 (12 percent of the total state network), as 1097 km were freed of tolls between 2018 and 2021 and placed under government management.

A REVIEW OF THE LITERATURE ON MOTORWAY FUNDING, MANAGEMENT, AND SAFETY

Reducing accidents is one of the most important objectives for any public authority in the transportation sector in both developed and developing countries. According to the World Health Organization (2018), the number of road traffic accidents continues to rise, and road traffic injuries still represent the eighth most important cause of death for people of all ages. Data from the International Transport Forum (2019) show that even though road safety had improved in most countries in the International Traffic Safety Data and Analysis Group (IRTAD) in 2017,[3] the average annual reduction was far greater between 2010 and 2013 than between 2013 and 2017. Apart from the pain and suffering that road accidents cause to the victims and their nearest and dearest, there are also economic reasons that make road safety an important concern. A recent study of road injuries by Chen et al. (2019) estimates the economic costs related to healthcare expenditure and employment losses in 166 countries worldwide. Their data predict that between 2015 and 2030 road injuries will cost the world economy US$1.8 trillion.

Improved road design and maintenance would reduce accidents and provide users with more efficient mobility, comfort, and lower vehicle operating costs (Burningham & Stankevich, 2005). Therefore, the provision of better infrastructure is one of the strategies most commonly proposed by policy makers to improve road safety. Proposals for attracting private participation to infrastructure production and management have allowed governments to provide better infrastructure without compromising their budgets. Quite often, to finance and recover investment and maintenance costs, roads operated by a private company have an access price, and publicly operated roads may also charge tolls to users. This was the case in countries such as France and Italy before the privatization of their networks in the late 1990s and the 2000s, respectively, and it is still the case in the United States.

The Safety Externalities of Road Pricing

The economic rationale for road pricing (besides the financing of the infrastructure) is that tolling may reduce negative traffic externalities, such as congestion costs and noise (particularly important in urban areas), pollution, and accidents. However, rerouting literature analyzing the effects of tolling on adjacent free roads has shown a negative effect of tolling on accidents because charging encourages users to use alternative free roads, which are generally of lower quality and are not prepared to receive such a large amount of daily traffic. This shift is expected to be positively related to the price elasticity of the demand but negatively related to the quality of the adjacent road (Verhoef et al., 1996).

One of the earliest rerouting analyses in Europe was conducted by Broughton and Gower (1998). This study analyzed the effects of tolling on the number of accidents for two motorways: the Kent corridor in the United Kingdom and the Aalborg network area in Denmark. The most significant results were that a 10 percent diversion of traffic from the motorways would increase the number of road injury accidents in the entire county of Kent by approximately 3.5 percent. The estimates for the Danish case were lower: a 10 percent diversion of motorway traffic from Aalborg would have about one-third of the effect predicted for Kent. The article suggests that the difference between the two sites is partly explained by the lower flows registered in Aalborg.

Similarly, a more recent full-country study for Spain (Albalate, 2011) tested whether charging users on tolled motorways diminishes road safety in the adjacent freeway alternatives. The data used came from a cross-sectional database from the Spanish Traffic Map 2006, containing information on the number of accidents involving victims, speeds, and traffic composition. Applying a count data negative-binomial model, the results obtained show that roads that compete with tolled motorways have more accidents than those that compete with toll-free motorways. The article also estimated the magnitude of the rerouting effect by calculating the toll elasticity of the number of accidents; it found that a 1 percent increase in tolls produced a 0.5 percent increase in the number of accidents.

At a wider European scale, Albalate and Bel (2012) used panel data from 15 European countries for 1991 to 2002. The authors investigated, first, whether a greater presence of motorways provides better results for road safety outputs overall, and second, whether different pricing policies on motorways have any effect on road safety. The empirical strategy used to test the two hypotheses was a one-way fixed-effects semi-log model in which the dependent variable was the fatality rate per million inhabitants in each country. The results show that a larger presence of motorways reduces the fatality rates. However, results distinguishing between free or tolled motorways show that only free motorways promote road safety. Therefore, motorways improve road safety, but tolling increases traffic risk in the adjacent free roads as a consequence of the rerouting effect.

For the United States, a similar study was conducted by Swan and Belzer (2013), who estimated the crash cost for trucks that diverted from the Ohio Turnpike to avoid paying tolls. To do so, the authors used a traffic dataset from 2002 to 2006 that included interstate highways, US routes, and Ohio numbered routes. In the analysis, truck diversion from the Ohio Turnpike to other roads was estimated from price elasticity calculated in the same study. Swan and Belzer (2013) found that the estimated annual crash cost for diverted trucks was US$51 million. However, if these same diverted trucks had traveled an equal distance on the Ohio Turnpike, the annual crash costs would have been US$11 million. The results show that crash costs were 346 percent higher for the roads to which truck traffic diverted.

In the same line of research, Baumgarten and Middelkamp (2015) estimated the road safety impact of implementing a heavy good vehicle toll on traffic diversion in Germany. To compute the impact of tolling, the study used an aggregate dataset at NUTS-1 level covering 16 German regions between 2000 and 2010. The dependent variable used in the analysis to estimate the impact of tolling on traffic diversion was the number of accidents with damage to persons. By applying a panel data negative-binomial model, the study found that a toll applied in 2005 caused traffic diversion, which negatively impacted Germany's road safety outcomes.

The most recent analysis of rerouting can be found in Pereira et al. (2021), a study of the change in the number and severity of accidents after tolling the Portuguese Scut highways at the municipal level. The authors used panel data from 2008 to 2014, which included information on the number of accidents and number of victims broken down by the type of roads (Scut highways, national roads, and other roads). To test the impact of tolling on road safety, the difference-in-differences approach was applied. The results show harmful effects on road safety of the introduction of tolls. In the municipalities with Scut highways, the number of accidents and the number of victims both rose significantly after the introduction of tolls.

The accumulated research in the rerouting literature thus provides significant evidence that road accidents are more frequent on free roads that have an alternative parallel toll road. Therefore, we formulate our first hypothesis as follows:

H1. BOT concession-type PPP motorways have lower safety performance than Operation and Management PPPs and traditional publicly funded and managed motorways.

Is Private Management Safer?

While there is wide-ranging evidence of the effect on road safety of rerouting due to tolls, evidence on the effects of motorway management (public or private) on road safety outcomes is much scarcer. Some analysts suggest that roads managed by private operators are safer than roads managed by the government (Samuel & Poole, 2000; Sisiopiku et al., 2006; Block, 2009), while others hold that private procurement can endanger quality and safety (Kusnet, 2007). These suggestions from professional analysts and practitioners have encouraged researchers to look for empirical evidence of the influence of the type of management on road safety.

The first empirical study on the topic was conducted by Albalate and Bel-Piñana (2019). Using panel data from 846 Spanish motorway control stations between 2008 and 2012, the article analyzed the effects of PPPs on road safety outcomes. The dependent variables used as road safety indicators were the annual number of accidents with victims and the annual number of victims; the main variable of interest in the study was management. Given the highly heterogeneous design of the composition of the motorway network in Spain, the variable management was categorized by the quality of private and public roads in order to assess its true effect. The methodology used was the conditional two-way fixed-effects negative-binomial model. The results showed that the number of victims on roads with either high-quality or low-quality design is lower under private management, but in terms of accidents, a significant difference was found only for roads with high-quality design.

A recent study of a similar nature was conducted for Brazil by Alves et al. (2021). The authors aimed to establish whether the implementation of private road management in certain Brazilian states might improve road safety outcomes. Using panel data on road crashes in federal highways between 2007 and 2017 and applying a difference-in-differences approach, they examined whether road concessions contributed to reducing the number of road accidents, the number of people and vehicles involved, and mortality. Their results show that road segments managed under private road concessions had a small but significant impact on the reduction of road crashes. Based on the existing evidence, our second hypothesis is as follows:

H2. BOT concession-type PPP and Operation and Management PPP motorways have better safety performance than traditional publicly funded and managed motorways.

Contracts, Incentives, and Safety Outcomes

Another strand of the literature examines the role of incentives within the PPP contracts and their impact in terms of safety outcomes. For instance, studies of road safety and performance-based incentives assess whether the introduction of bonuses and penalties for contractors based on explicit road safety indicators promotes better road safety. Evidence in this field is scarce and, to our knowledge, is only available for motorways in Spain.

The first empirical analysis is Rangel et al. (2012), which used cross-sectional data on high-capacity highways in Spain since the year 2006, differentiated by road operator. The endogenous variables used in the analysis are the number of fatalities, injuries, and accidents; the main variable of interest is the dummy variable "incentives." The results show the numbers of injuries and accidents to be significantly lower on road stretches with incentives than on stretches without incentives. The authors conclude that road safety incentives in PPPs are an effective way of achieving better road safety outcomes. With regard to road operation, their results show that roads operated by a private company (toll highways) are safer than free highways operated by the public sector, which is also in line with the findings of other studies cited above.

More recently, using data only on Spanish private highways from 2007 to 2009, Rangel et al. (2013) confirmed the results found in their previous paper (i.e., that road stretches with incentives are safer than road stretches without incentives). The variable "incentives" was statistically significant for accidents and injuries, but not for fatalities. In Rangel and Vassallo (2015), the authors expanded the data used in Rangel et al. (2013), including all Spanish highways (both publicly and privately operated) between 2007 to 2009, and confirmed their results (i.e., more accidents on road stretches without incentives than on road stretches with incentives). Regarding road operation, the conclusions were in line with Rangel et al. (2012).

Overall, the studies reviewed above illustrate the interest in the effects of PPPs on road safety and the advances made in their research. On the one hand, there is very incipient evidence of a certain advantage of private management models, which could well be explained by the role played by incentives and regulation. However, the financing modalities and the use of tolls may offset these effects due to the externalities that their imposition seems to produce on the safety of the rest of the roads, as indicated by the literature on the effects of rerouting. Therefore, we formulate our third hypothesis as follows:

H3. Operation and Management PPPs have the best safety performance of the three models.

The next section delves further into this issue and contributes to the literature by providing new empirical evidence at the regional level (rare in the literature), taking as a reference the variety of management and financing models for highways in Spain (described in the previous section), to assess the net effects on the road safety of a greater or lesser exposure to these models.

EMPIRICAL STRATEGY

In this section, we describe the data, variables, and methods used to test our hypotheses. To evaluate the road safety performance of different motorway management models, we constructed a database containing the number of interurban accidents with victims and the number of road fatalities (also those occurring in interurban roads) for all Spanish provinces between 2003 and 2019, with the exception of the two African autonomous cities of Ceuta and Melilla. These two variables become the dependent variables in our empirical road safety production models and are recorded from the General Traffic Directorate of the Spanish Homeland Affairs Ministry. We have a total of 850 observations (i.e., 50 provinces followed for 17 years). This allows us to construct a panel and consider standard regression models for road safety outcomes in a panel setting.

Regressing these dependent variables on the percentage of motorways over the total road network in the Spanish provinces shows a clear decreasing relationship due to the safety effect expected from these high-capacity and high-quality roads. Figures 8.2 and 8.3 show the scatter plot and the linear fit for both the number of accidents with victims and the number of road fatalities per million population. Spanish provinces with higher percentages of motorways over the total road network are associated with lower rates of accidents and fatalities in interurban roads. This is consistent with expectations based on prior analyses (e.g., Albalate & Bel, 2012; Albalate & Bel-Piñana, 2019) that suggested a safety advantage for high-capacity roads in terms of producing better road safety outcomes than conventional roads.

As our objective is to evaluate the effects on road safety of different motorway management models, considering net effects (i.e., not only on the specific motorways), we examine four explanatory variables in our empirical strategy. The first variable is the percentage of motorways over the total length of roads in the province that are managed directly by the government (*Government Motorways*). Because of Spain's institutional structure, we consider all levels of government with responsibilities in the management of motorways (i.e., central and subcentral governments).[4]

The second variable, *PPP Motorways*, is the percentage of motorways over the total length of roads in the province that are managed under a PPP scheme. Since this includes both tolled and shadow tolled PPPs (the latter

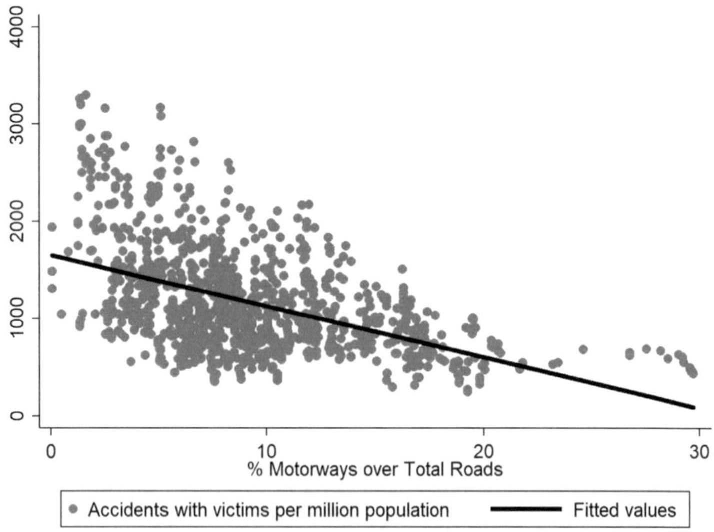

Note: Scatter plot and linear prediction fitted values for the Spanish provinces (2003–2019).

Figure 8.2 *Accidents with victims per million population on percentage of motorways over total roads*

being Operation and Management PPPs), we created two additional variables to distinguish them and to evaluate their possible differences in terms of road safety advantages. Thus, the percentage of tolled motorways with respect to the total road network in the province is denoted as *Tolled PPP*, whereas the percentage of shadow tolled PPP motorways over the total network is denoted as *Shadow Tolled*. Data on these four variables are obtained from the yearbook of the Ministry of Transportation.

To avoid omitting relevant variables, we also consider controls: the provincial population, the share of the elderly in the province (percentage of inhabitants older than 65 years in the total provincial population), the unemployment rate in the province and its square (since in some models this non-linear approach obtains a better fit), and a binary variable that takes the value of 1 for the years in which the points system has been in place (since 2006) and 0 otherwise. This measure had a notable effect on road safety in Spain, as shown in Castillo-Manzano et al. (2010).

Because of the availability of the panel dataset and the count nature of our dependent variables, together with the degree of overdispersion in the data, we use a negative-binomial fixed-effects regression model. Note that due to

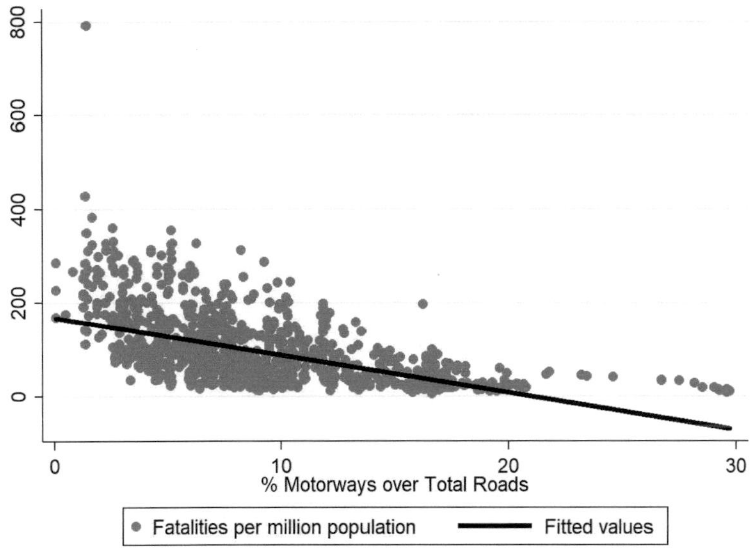

Note: Scatter plot and linear prediction fitted values for the Spanish provinces (2003–2019).

Figure 8.3 *Road fatalities per million population on percentage of motorways over total roads*

the fixed effects, we control for the main time-invariant differences across provinces and account for the heterogeneity of our data. The negative-binomial model deals better with overdispersion than the standard Poisson distribution model. In road safety models, it is common to account for the level of exposure. For this reason, we use the total number of inhabitants in the province as the exposure variable. This is equivalent to considering the dependent variable as a rate over the population. This means that our dependent variables become, in practice, the province accident rate and the province fatality rate over the population, respectively. Also, to account for the different common year-specific effects, we include fixed time effects.

Our specifications are detailed below. We consider the same two specifications for both dependent variables: one including all types of PPPs and the other splitting this variable into *Tolled PPP* and *Shadow Tolled*:

$$Accident\_Rate_{it} = PPP\ Motorways_{it} + Population_{it} + Elderly_{it} + Unemployment_{it} + Unemployment\_squared_{it} + Points\ License_{it} + \mu_i + t_t + \varepsilon_{it} \tag{8.1}$$

$$Accident\_Rate_{it} = Tolled\ PPP\ Motorways_{it} + \\ Shadow\ Tolled\ PPPMotorways_{it} + Government\ Motorways_{it} + \\ Population_{it} + Elderly_{it} + Unemployment_{it} + \\ Unemployment\_squared_{it} + Points\ License_{it} + \mu_i + t_t + \varepsilon_{it} \quad (8.2)$$

$$Fatality\_Rate_{it} = PPPMotorways_{it} + Government\ Motorways_{it} + \\ Population_{it} + Elderly_{it} + Unemployment_{it} + \\ Unemployment\_squared_{it} + Points\ License_{it} + \mu_i + t_t + \varepsilon_{it} \quad (8.3)$$

$$Fatality\_Rate_{it} = Tolled\ PPPMotorways_{it} + \\ Shadow\ Tolled\ PPPMotorways_{it} + Government\ Motorways_{it} + \\ Population_{it} + Elderly_{it} + Unemployment_{it} + Unemployment\_squared_{it} + \\ Points\ License_{it} + \mu_i + t_t + \varepsilon_{it} \quad (8.4)$$

The dependent variables are the accidents with victims and the fatality rates over the population in province *i* in year *t*, μ_i and t_t are the province and the year-specific fixed effects, respectively, and ε_{it} is the error term. Our analysis is focused on the motorway management variables, which should be interpreted with respect to the base category, namely, the rest of the conventional roads in the province. This approach reflects their absolute impact as better roads, but assessing the relative advantage between different motorway management models requires the comparison and testing of their coefficients.

RESULTS

Table 8.1 displays our main results. Models 1 and 2 test the impacts of different management schemes on the interurban road accidents with victims. The first considers the main distinction between government-managed and PPP-managed motorways, whereas the latter splits the PPP category into two groups: *Tolled PPP* and *Shadow Tolled* PPP motorways. Models 3 and 4 replicate the analysis by considering the interurban road fatality rate as the dependent variable.

Our first results indicate that among motorways, only PPP motorways seem to present statistically significant effects on the accident rate (see

Table 8.1 Conditional FE negative-binomial regressions for rates of accidents with victims and fatalities per million population

	Accidents Rate (1)	Accidents Rate (2)	Fatality Rate (3)	Fatality Rate (4)
Management Models				
PPP motorways	−0.0703*** (0.0108)	—	−0.0332*** (0.0102)	—
Tolled PPP	—	−0.0563*** (0.0148)	—	−0.0626*** (0.0137)
Shadow tolled PPP	—	−0.0816*** (0.0137)	—	−0.0022 (0.0141)
Government motorways	0.0007 (0.0068)	−0.0022 (0.0071)	−0.0270*** (0.0071)	−0.0163** (0.0078)
Controls				
Population	−0.7399*** (−0.7399)	−0.7600*** (0.0538)	−0.0952 (0.0986)	−0.0526 (0.0939)
Elderly	0.0105*** (0.0031)	0.0101*** (0.0031)	−0.0040 (0.0036)	−0.0034 (0.0035)
Unemployment	0.0115** (0.0057)	0.0124** (0.0057)	−0.0159*** (0.0025)	−0.0150*** (0.0025)
Unemployment_squared	−0.0002** (0.0001)	−0.0003** (0.0001)	—	—
Points license	−0.3928*** (0.0432)	−0.3829*** (0.0438)	−1.1921*** (0.0446)	−1.231*** (0.0463)
Province fixed effects	Yes	Yes	Yes	Yes
Year fixed effects	Yes	Yes	Yes	Yes
N	850	850	850	850
Log likelihood	−4865.92	−4865.00	−2590.48	−2585.54
Wald Chi-square	1106.95	1120.16	7127.53	7271.58

Notes: Standard errors in parentheses.
Exposure variable (province population).
*** p < .01
** p < .05
* p < .10

Model 1). The coefficient attached to the variable *PPP Motorways* is negative and statistically significant ($p < .01$), which suggests that the accident rate is lower in this type of motorway than in the conventional road network. Government-managed motorways do not seem to produce any differential effect with respect to the rest of the interurban conventional road network. This result supports the hypothesis that PPP management might offer road safety advantages over publicly managed models.

An interesting question is whether any type of PPP can provide this safety advantage. To explore this point, Model 2 distinguishes between tolled PPPs and shadow tolled PPPs, while keeping the rest of the specification as in Model 1. The results indicate that both types of PPPs achieve this lower accident rate. If we compare the coefficients of these two PPP subtypes to those of PPP models in general, we cannot reject the possibility that these two coefficients are equal (Prob > Chi-square = 0.17569). Thus, we do not find any statistical difference according to the kind of PPP model.

The same analysis applied to the fatality rate shows slightly different outcomes. Model 3, which considers all PPPs together, shows that both government-managed and PPP motorways are associated with lower fatality rates than the ones found on average in conventional roads. Although both models provide road safety benefits in terms of fatality rates, the sizes of both coefficients suggest that PPP may enjoy a relative advantage. However, after testing the difference of coefficients, we were unable to reject the null hypothesis of equal coefficients (Prob > Chi-square = 0.5379). Thus, we conclude that both types of motorway provide similar road safety benefits in terms of fatality rates.

In Model 4, we split the PPP models to assess whether the result associated with PPPs can be attributed to both tolled and shadow tolled schemes. In contrast to our findings for the accident rate, now we identify a difference between tolled and shadow tolled schemes, in so far as only tolled PPPs are associated with a lower fatality rate. Shadow tolled schemes do not seem to deliver any road safety advantage with respect to conventional roads and seem to perform worse than publicly managed motorways. However, a test of equal coefficients does not allow rejection of the null hypothesis, so we cannot argue on statistical grounds that they really perform worse (Prob > Chi-square = 0.2336).[5]

Again, we find that the coefficient associated with tolled PPPs is greater than that of the government-managed motorways. If we test the difference of coefficients between tolled PPPs and publicly managed roads, this time we find a statistically significant difference: the null hypothesis of equal coefficients is rejected and, therefore, a relative advantage of tolled PPPs with respect to publicly managed motorways emerges.

To sum up, our results suggest that PPP motorways deliver better road safety outcomes than publicly managed motorways in terms of accident rates. This advantage is found in both types of PPPs considered, and there is no significant difference between PPP models. When measured as fatality rates (i.e., accounting for the severity of accidents), we find that only tolled PPPs perform better than publicly managed toll motorways.

DISCUSSION AND POLICY IMPLICATIONS

Our empirical exercise contributes to the literature in several ways. Unlike other recent papers, such as Albalate and Bel-Piñana (2019) and Alves et al. (2021), we do not focus here on the specific motorways to examine the relative safety performance of different models in motorways, which generally point to the relative advantage of PPPs. The evidence provided by those authors is highly informative with regard to the role of management, but it obviously neglects any indirect effect or the externalities produced to the rest of the network. Any rerouting effect produced by tolls (e.g., if they damage road safety in adjacent roads) can offset this benefit and even reverse the effect in net terms.

For this reason, and because our objective was to obtain a broad overview, we followed a similar approach to that in Albalate and Bel (2012). We considered geographical units of analysis (provinces), including different roads, and examined how different degrees of exposure to specific models (accounting for the fraction of those models over the total interurban network of the province) affect the aggregate safety outcome.[6] In contrast, Albalate and Bel (2012) examined European countries as the units of analysis, taking a highly aggregate perspective. Unlike that study, here we opted for a narrower geographical area that can achieve a better identification of the regional effects using a large panel data setting of Spanish provinces and the estimation of count models. Note that by taking this aggregate approach, any rerouting effect on road safety within the interurban province network would be captured easily, although we can neither confirm nor refute that this effect exists in Spanish provinces. Previous research, however, had already provided evidence on rerouting effects (see Albalate, 2011).

Our results provide some interesting insights. On the one hand, our study supports the existence of a certain advantage of public-private collaboration models in road safety, confirming the results of some recent papers, but this time using an empirical strategy that considers potential network effects (rerouting). On the other hand, our results suggest some differences in performance within the PPP models, a novel finding in the literature. We report that tolled PPPs might perform better than shadow tolled PPPs in some safety respects, such as the fatality rate. This result is at odds with other data published in the rerouting literature.

Although this is an interesting finding, we should be cautious before deriving strong conclusions, given that this result might be partially explained by the fact that a large part of the shadow tolled network is composed by the first generation of free motorways built in the 1980s. The design of these roads was hampered by the imposed obligation of widening or doubling the existing conventional roads, as opposed to the usual new greenfield construction of tolled PPPs in Spain. This led to notable differences in quality standards, as explained in Albalate and Bel-Piñana (2019). Future research should check this result in other experiences to determine whether this is a specific trait of shadow toll motorways in Spain or can be more generalized.

Our results suggesting the superiority of PPPs regarding safety have important implications that can be generalized to other international experiences. Although motorways may seem a homogeneous product, there exist important heterogeneities in terms of design, quality standards, operation tasks, and incentives—that all can be influenced by the role of regulation.[7] The privatization of motorways is usually associated with strict and increasingly sophisticated regulations, which may involve quality measurement, firm's transparency, implementation of policies to reduce accident or congestion rates, treatment of winter viability, availability of real-time information, and so on. Conversely, if the owner is the public sector, there is less need for regulation given that the state has more leeway for arbitrariness (Albalate et al., 2009).

PPPs may also enjoy regulatory frameworks allowing for incentives to improve private returns depending on the road safety manager's performance (e.g., contract extensions). Hence, deepening the regulatory framework and the generation of incentives based on risk transfer seems a good strategy to improve road safety anywhere, and this seems more feasible to do within a PPP collaboration. In any case, public managers of motorways should also try to narrow this gap to improve their relative outcomes. Because our empirical strategy is easily extrapolated to the context of other countries with both models, future research can easily check whether our results hold in other geographical and jurisdictional contexts.

Our findings are of particular interest in the light of the current discussions on the reform of the financing and management model in Spain. As mentioned above, a proposal to toll all motorways by 2024 will be discussed in the near future. Since managing the tolling system does not involve complex operational processes thanks to the technologies available, the choice between public or private management is not expected to be a primary issue in this reform. For instance, previous research has not identified any differences in cost efficiency between privately and publicly managed tolled motorways in Spain (see Albalate & Rosell, 2019). However, the government might turn to the private sector to manage the operation and collect tolls under PPP schemes such as availability payments or operation and maintenance contracts.

In this context, our results, combined with those in the literature, can be used to discuss the future safety implications of this reform. As the motorway network in Spain is basically completed and no large-scale greenfield projects are expected soon, tolls could be set to finance the maintenance and renovation of the existing motorways. This would mean much lower tolls in already tolled motorways when their concessions finalize, but higher costs per kilometer in motorways that are currently free of charge, even if public management is maintained. Incentives for rerouting would be lowered in the already tolled motorways—which, according to our results and to those in Albalate and Bel-Piñana (2019) would mean more traffic driving on safer roads—but would rise in the currently free-of-charge motorways, with possible consequences in terms of rerouting. Our results in this chapter suggest that this should not necessarily be a source of concern; however, more research on network effects is needed. In any case, and especially if the government opts for PPP schemes, it is vitally important that the contracts include appropriate incentives for upholding standards of quality regarding motorway maintenance and renovation and thus minimize the safety risks for motorway users.

NOTES

1. See https://ec.europa.eu/eurostat/databrowser/view/road_if_motorwa/default/table?lang=en (accessed 24 May 2021).
2. See https://www.mitma.gob.es/carreteras/catalogo-y-evolucion-de-la-red-de-carreteras/evolucion-desde-1970 (accessed 18 May 2021).
3. See for the member countries: https://www.itf-oecd.org/irtad-members.
4. This includes the Ministry of Transport, regional governments, and county/province councils.
5. The test of equal coefficients also rejects the null hypothesis of equal coefficients between tolled PPP motorways and shadow tolled PPP motorways in Model 4 (Prob > chi-square = 0.001).
6. We do not have data on the specific location of accidents or the road where they happened. The official data only distinguishes whether they happened on motorways or elsewhere in the road network.
7. See Albalate and Bel-Piñana (2019) for an extensive and detailed discussion on the role and effects of regulation on the differences between PPPs and government-managed motorways.

REFERENCES

Albalate, D. (2011). Shifting death to their alternatives: The case of toll motorways. *Journal of Transport Economics and Policy*, *45*(3), 453–79.

Albalate, D. (2014). *The privatization and nationalization of European roads: Success and failure in public-private partnerships*. Edward Elgar.

Albalate, D., & Bel, G. (2012). Motorways, tolls and road safety: Evidence from Europe. *SERIEs: Journal of the Spanish Economic Association*, *3*(4), 457–73.

Albalate, D., Bel, G., & Bel-Piñana, P. (2015a). Tropezando dos veces con la misma piedra: Quiebra de autopistas de peaje y costes para contribuyentes y usuario [Tripping over the same stone twice: Bankruptcy of toll roads and costs for taxpayers and users]. *Revista de Economía Aplicada*, *23*(67), 131–52.

Albalate, D., Bel, G., & Fageda, X. (2009). Privatization and regulatory reform of toll motorways in Europe. *Governance*, *22*(2), 285–318.
Albalate, D., Bel, G., & Fageda, X. (2015b). When supply travels far beyond demand: Causes of oversupply in Spain's transport infrastructure. *Transport Policy*, *41*, 80–89.
Albalate, D., Bel, G., & Geddes, R. R. (2017). How much vertical integration? Contractual choice and public-private partnerships in the United States. *Review of Industrial Organization*, *51*(1), 25–42.
Albalate, D., & Bel-Piñana, P. (2019). The effects of public-private partnerships on road safety outcomes. *Accident Analysis and Prevention*, *128*, 53–64.
Albalate, D., & Rosell, J. (2019). On the efficiency of toll motorway companies in Spain. *Research in Transportation Economics*, *76*, 100747.
Alves, P. J., Emanuel, L., & Pereira, R. H. M. (2021). Highway concessions and road safety: Evidence from Brazil. *Research in Transportation Economics*, *90*, 101118.
Banco Mundial. (1962). *Informe del banco mundial: El desarrollo económico de España.* BIRF.
Baumgarten, P., & Middelkamp, J. (2015). On interurban road pricing schemes and the impacts of traffic diversion on road safety in Germany: Empirical findings and implications. *European Journal of Transport and Infrastructure Research*, *15*(2), 147–62.
Bel, G. (1999). Financiación de infraestructuras viarias: La economía política de los peajes. *Papeles de Economía Española*, *82*, 123–39.
Bel, G. (2011). The first privatization: Selling SOEs and privatizing public monopolies in fascist Italy (1922–1925). *Cambridge Journal of Economics*, *35*(3), 937–56.
Bel, G. (2012). *Infrastructure and the political economy of nation building in Spain, 1720–2010.* Sussex Academic Press.
Block, W. (2009). *The privatization of roads and highways: Human and economic factors.* Ludwig von Mises Institute.
Broughton, J., & Gower, P. (1998). *The likely effects of motorways tolling on accident risk: Phase 2.* Transport Research Laboratory.
Burningham, S., & Stankevich, N. (2005). *Why road maintenance is important and how to get it done.* The World Bank.
Castillo-Manzano, J. I., Castro-Nuño, M., & Pedregal, D. J. (2010). An econometric analysis of the effects of the penalty points system driver's license in Spain. *Accident Analysis and Prevention*, *42*(4), 1310–9.
Chen, S., Kuhn, M., Prettner, K., & Bloom, D. E. (2019). The global macroeconomic burden of road injuries: Estimates and projections for 166 countries. *Lancet Planetary Health*, *3*(9), e390–8.
International Transport Forum. (2019). *Road safety annual report 2019.* International Traffic Safety Data and Analysis Group.
Kusnet, D. (2007). *Highway robbery II: The many problems with outsourcing design, engineering, inspection & supervision of federally funded transportation projects: Increased costs, reduced quality & safety, and little accountability to the public.* National Association of State Highway and Transportation Unions.
Navas, T. (2002). Il riflesso della modernità: Le autostrade spagnole, 1920–1960 [The reflection of modernity: The Spanish motorways]. *Storia Urbana*, *26*(100), 27–54.
Pereira, A. M., Pereira, R. M., & Dos Santos, J. P. (2021). For whom the bell tolls: Road safety effects of tolls on uncongested SCUT highways in Portugal. *Journal of Infrastructure, Policy and Development*, *4*(2), 287–305.

Rangel, T., & Vassallo, J. M. (2015). Modeling the effect of contractual incentives on road safety performance. *Transport Policy*, *40*, 17–23.

Rangel, T., Vassallo, J. M., & Arenas, B. (2012). Effectiveness of safety-based incentives in public-private partnerships: Evidence from the case of Spain. *Transportation Research Part A: Policy and Practice*, *46*(8), 1166–76.

Rangel, T., Vassallo, J. M., & Herraiz, I. (2013). The influence of economic incentives linked to road safety indicators on accidents: The case of toll concessions in Spain. *Accident Analysis and Prevention*, *59*, 529–36.

Samuel, P., & Poole, R. (2000). *Putting customers in the driver's seat: The case for tolls*. Reason Public Policy Institute.

Sisiopiku, V. P., Waid, J. C., Rizk, T., McLeod, R., & Robbins, W. (2006). *Alternate financing sources for Alabama highways*. University Transportation Center for Alabama.

Swan, P. F., & Belzer, M. H. (2013). Tolling and economic efficiency: Do the pecuniary benefits exceed the safety costs? *Public Works Management & Policy*, *18*(2), 167–84.

Vassallo, J. M., & Pérez de Villar, P. (2010). Diez años de peaje sombra en España. *Revista de Obras Públicas*, *157*, 19–30.

Verhoef, E., Nijkamp, P., & Rietveld, P. (1996). Second-best congestion pricing: The case of an untolled alternative. *Journal of Urban Economics*, *40*(3), 279–302.

World Health Organization. (2018). *Global status report on road safety 2018*. World Health Organization.

9. Conclusions about the performance advantage of PPPs

Carter B. Casady, Stefan Verweij, and Ingmar van Meerkerk

INTRODUCTION

At the outset of this book, we observed that little was known about whether the Public-Private Partnership (PPP) performance advantage exists or not. In the opening chapter, we identified three reasons for this: the dominance of single case studies in the PPP literature (Hueskes et al., 2019; Osei-Kyei & Chan, 2015; Tang et al., 2010; Zhang et al., 2016), the performance benchmark that PPPs are compared to is often vague and underspecified and/or it involves ex-ante expectations of performance (e.g., public sector comparators) that may be biased in favor of PPPs (Boardman & Hellowell, 2017; Boers et al., 2013; Hodge, 2010), and PPP project data are often hard to obtain (Chen et al., 2016). From there, we set out to achieve two aims: (1) to critically assess and empirically explore the existence of a PPP performance advantage, and (2) to explore explanations for why the performance advantage of PPPs may exist or not. To make a meaningful contribution to the first aim, we asked the contributors to this book to comparatively analyze *actual* project data—instead of estimations or prognoses of performance found in public-sector comparators or business cases (Petersen, 2019)—that represent *materialized* performance. We also asked them to adopt a research design that focuses on the comparison of PPPs with traditionally procured projects (i.e., non-PPPs) within a single country, within a single infrastructure sector, and within a relatively short time frame. In this way, we sought to adopt a quasi-experimental design that allowed us to assess with more confidence the effects of the PPP model on project performance (see Chapter 2).

This approach increased the comparability of PPPs with the benchmark of the traditional alternative (i.e., it improved the suitability of the counterfactual situation; see Chapter 1) because it decreased the effects of project risks, complexity, institutional frameworks, and legal systems (that may differ considerably across countries, sectors, and over time) on any performance differences between PPPs and their traditional alternative. Doing so also helped the contributors to this book adopt a clearer evaluation philosophy, set specific performance criteria and measurement, ground their analyses in appropriate theoretical foundations, and select viable methodologies for the comparisons (see Chapter 2). For the secondary aim, we also asked the contributors to develop or test theoretical expectations as to why a performance difference between PPPs and traditional project delivery may exist, embedded in the specific contexts analyzed in their chapters.

In the first chapter, we made a distinction between three broad dimensions of performance that are commonly used to assess PPP project success: cost performance, time performance, and service quality performance (cf. Hodge, 2010; Hodge & Greve, 2017; Petersen, 2019). Generally, cost performance encompasses operational costs, capital costs, total (whole-life) project costs including design and construction costs, and on-budget delivery (Hodge, 2010; Petersen, 2019). Time performance refers to on-time delivery—according to the initially planned or agreed-upon schedule—of projects and services (Hodge, 2010). Service quality performance reflects the relationship between costs and quality (i.e., Value for Money [VfM]; cf. Petersen, 2019), but also the quality of the service delivery itself, independent of costs, such as functional use and perceived quality by users (Petersen, 2019), or innovative products and services or sustainability (Hodge, 2010; Weihe, 2008).

In this final chapter, we collect and discuss the evidence from our discussion of the current literature and the empirical chapters in this book to draw conclusions about the existence of any performance advantages exhibited by PPPs, as well as reasons for them. We begin by reviewing the evidence on the cost performance, time performance, and the service quality performance of PPPs compared to the counterfactual situation of traditional public procurement. We integrate the findings from our review in the introductory chapter with the findings from Chapters 3 through 8. We then build on the explanations for a PPP performance advantage provided in the chapters and highlight two in particular: bundling and private financing. Next, we discuss directions for future research and implications for policymakers and PPP practitioners.

COST PERFORMANCE

Studies on the cost performance advantage of PPPs feature mixed evidence (see also Petersen, 2019). Some studies found that PPPs outperformed traditionally procured projects (Archambeault & Deis, 1997; Cabral & De Azevedo, 2008; Meduri & Annamalai, 2013; Dos Reis & Cabral, 2017; Verweij & Van Meerkerk, 2020, 2021; Yaya, 2017). Others concluded that PPPs performed worse or that the differences were insignificant (Atmo et al., 2017; Daito & Gifford, 2014; Froud & Shaoul, 2001; Hong, 2016; Massoud et al., 2003;

Pollock et al., 2002; Reeves & Ryan, 2007). The empirical chapters in this book reaffirm these mixed findings for the most part, but also reveal specific mechanisms producing these results when comparing PPP projects with traditionally procured projects and how managers experience these different governance structures. We shortly discuss the evidence on cost performance below.

Cian O'Shea, Dónal Palcic, and Eoin Reeves in Chapter 3 compared ex-ante as well as ex-post performance of Ireland's first PPP school bundle using the Design–Build–Finance–Maintain (DBFM) model with a comparable set of traditionally procured schools with Design and Construct (D&C) contracts. Focusing here on the analysis of ex-post capital costs of the DBFM and D&C schools, they were able to compare two schools: Ballincollig Community School (DBFM) and Colaiste Chraobh Abhainn school in Kilcoole (D&C). They found that the total capital costs for the PPP school in Ballincollig were 24 percent higher than the costs of the traditionally procured school in Kilcoole. Regarding operations and maintenance (O&M), they found that over the 13-year period examined, the costs for funding O&M activities in the PPP schools were 29 percent–42 percent higher than that of the traditionally procured schools on a per-pupil basis. Their discussion revealed that this difference in costs for O&M is best interpreted as an inequality in funding received, with consequences for quality. The Irish PPP schools received more funding to cover operations, maintenance, and life-cycle costs than the traditional schools, thereby improving their service quality (see "Service Quality Performance"). As O'Shea and colleagues pointed out, it might very well be the case that the annual costs of PPP schools are more representative of the true maintenance requirements for a school building; they found that while the funding allocated to the traditional schools was lower, it was inadequate to meet the schools' O&M requirements. This might create future costs—financial and otherwise—for these schools due to insufficient maintenance. Hence, it can be argued that public schools are underfunded in this case, stressing the added value of comparing these different governance structures—PPP versus traditional procurement—in relation to different dimensions of performance (i.e., costs versus quality).

In Chapter 4, Diogo Cunha Ferreira, Rui Cunha Marques, Maria Isabel Pedro, and Gonçalo Santos compared PPP hospitals using Design–Build–Finance–Operate–Transfer (DBFOT) models with publicly managed hospitals in Portugal. Their analysis made use of multiple performance indicators (see "Service Quality Performance"), including cost efficiency which consisted of three aspects: service availability, productivity, and operational costs per patient. Taking a sample of 24 public hospitals and four PPP hospitals, they constructed monthly performance data over a period of 57 months, producing a dataset with 1368 observations for public hospitals and 228 observations for

PPP hospitals. The comparison of the two groups of observations provided clear evidence that the PPP hospitals performed better than the publicly managed hospitals.

In Chapter 5, Claudio José Oliveira dos Reis and Sandro Cabral comparatively analyzed the performance of five PPP stadiums, four public stadiums delivered under traditional public procurement, and three purely private stadiums, all of which were delivered for the 2014 FIFA World Cup in Brazil. They found evidence that the PPP stadiums performed better in terms of meeting their initial forecasted costs and also had lower costs per seat when compared to the traditionally procured stadiums. Whereas the total costs for the PPP stadiums amounted to 100 percent of the expected costs (i.e., no cost overrun) for the best-performing PPP stadium and up to 140 percent (i.e., 40 percent cost overrun) for the worst-performing PPP stadium, this was 130 percent for the best-performing public stadium and 207 percent for the worst-performing public stadium. The private stadiums had better performance than the public ones, but not as good as the PPP stadiums.

Ingmar van Meerkerk, Mike Duijn, Rianne Warsen, Stefan Verweij, Erik-Hans Klijn, Joop Koppenjan, and Samantha Metselaar, in Chapter 6, reported on their evaluation study on the performance and use of DBFM contracts in Dutch transport infrastructure projects. They compared transport projects with DBFM contracts against transport projects with D&C contracts using various data sources. One dimension of cost performance they analyzed was additional work costs, which concerns the amount of additional project costs for the public client that arises during the D&C phases of the projects, on top of what was agreed between the public and private partners when the contract was signed. The 12 DBFM projects had, on average, additional work costs of 13.59 percent of the initial contract value. This was 27.78 percent for the 18 D&C projects. This difference was statistically significant, confirming earlier analyses of different segments of the dataset they used (Verweij & Van Meerkerk, 2020). Using interview data collected in semi-structured interviews with public and private managers involved in the projects, they also observed that although the DBFM contracts lead to fewer contractual changes and therefore fewer extra costs, this comes at a price of less flexibility for both public and private partners to make changes to deal with unforeseen events or stakeholder demands (cf. Demirel et al., 2017).

Lastly, in Chapter 7, Akash Deep, Mojahedul Islam Nayyer, and Thillai Rajan A. compared publicly procured road infrastructure projects with road projects using different PPP contract types in India: Build–Operate–Transfer (BOT) with annuity payments and BOT with tolls. Their study included various analyses of actual unit costs per lane-kilometer and cost overrun. Comparing the PPP projects with the publicly procured projects using matched-pair analyses, they observed that the PPPs had higher cost overruns on average, but that the difference was statistically nonsignificant. When analyzing the cost overruns of BOT-Annuity and BOT-Toll projects separately, they found that BOT-Toll projects had significantly higher cost overruns than the publicly procured projects.

The findings from the chapters on cost performance are summarized in Table 9.1. The table shows that the evidence for a PPP cost performance

Table 9.1 Cost performance advantage

Study	Period	Country	Sector	Performance Category	Findings	Performance Advantage
Chapter 3	2001–2004	Ireland	Schools	Capital costs, operation and management costs, life-cycle costs	Capital costs for the PPP school were 24% higher; PPP schools received more funding to cover operation, management, and life-cycle costs (i.e., higher costs)	Negative
Chapter 4	2015–2019	Portugal	Hospitals	Cost efficiency	PPPs have superior performance regarding, inter alia, efficiency	Positive
Chapter 5	2010–2014	Brazil	Sport Stadiums	Provision costs: compliance with initial cost forecast and costs per seat	PPP stadiums had better performance than public stadiums on both indicators	Positive
Chapter 6	2003–2020[a]	Netherlands	Roads	Additional work costs during D&C phase, perceptions of cost performance, experiences with project costs	DBFM projects have significantly lower additional work costs for the public sector	Positive
Chapter 7	1996–2017	India	Roads	Actual cost incurred for construction per lane-km, percentage of cost overrun	Actual costs for the PPP projects are higher and cost overruns are significantly higher for BOT-Toll projects	Negative

Note: [a] See Koppenjan et al. (2020).

advantage over traditionally procured projects is mixed. This confirms our observations from Chapter 1, which we based on earlier reviews by Graeme Hodge and Carsten Greve (see also Chapter 2), Petersen's (2019) systematic literature review, and other studies we found and compared. The chapters' focus on actual, materialized costs presents an important contribution to the literature on PPP cost performance that to date remains dominated by discussions and analyses of estimated, ex-ante costs. The chapters in this book reaffirm the status quo on the matter of cost performance and also expand it. They have further unraveled some of the trade-offs and mechanisms at work. For instance, the Irish schools' case shows that higher costs for PPP schools cannot be seen as separate from the governance of the O&M of the schools and its service quality; the Dutch infrastructure case shows that the better cost performance in terms of additional work costs for PPPs has consequences for the flexibility and adaptability of the contract.

As a next step, it now also becomes important to look ahead and start paying more attention to the analysis of O&M costs and life-cycle costs. However, given the difficulties involved in the data collection and measurement of life-cycle costs, as discussed in Chapter 2, this will be a monumental challenge. Studies focusing on small numbers of cases, which are then analyzed in-depth and over time, may present more feasible research strategies. Chapter 3 can be considered an illustrative example of such an approach.

TIME PERFORMANCE

Our discussion of time performance in Chapter 1 indicated that PPPs have a time performance advantage over the counterfactual of traditionally procured projects (Atmo et al., 2015, 2017; Dos Reis & Cabral, 2017; O'Shea et al., 2019; Rodrigues & Zucco, 2018; Verweij et al., 2020; Verweij & Van Meerkerk, 2021; Whittington, 2012). This adds credence to the conclusion recently drawn by Lewis (2021), that PPP projects have a "solid record of on-time delivery" which "is largely a result of the financial incentives incorporated into the terms of PPP contracts" (p. 70). This observation is further supported by the empirical chapters in this book which examined this performance dimension in their comparative analyses.

In Chapter 5, Dos Reis and Cabral concluded that PPP stadium projects in Brazil performed better in terms of implementation time than both the stadiums delivered under public and private provision (see also Dos Reis & Cabral, 2017). Two PPP stadiums were finished ahead of schedule, two stadiums were delivered on time, and one stadium was delivered after 39 months instead of the 36 months that were planned for implementation. In contrast, the delivery times of the four public stadiums were delayed by 10 percent (best performer) up to 53 percent (worst performer). For the three private stadiums, this was 5 percent and 43 percent, respectively. They also noted that almost all PPPs had a shorter bid execution time or tendering period than traditionally public procured projects. This adds credence to claims made by some scholars regarding the efficiency of PPP procurement (e.g., Casady et al., 2019).

Ingmar van Meerkerk and colleagues reached similar conclusions in Chapter 6. Their comparative analysis of the Dutch transport infrastructure projects showed that the DBFM contracts performed significantly better regarding time performance than their traditionally procured comparators using D&C contracts. Whereas the seven DBFM projects had an average acceleration of 18.89 percent of the planned implementation phase, the 12 D&C projects had an average delay of 6.84 percent. This difference is statistically significant and strengthens earlier analyses performed on previous versions of their dataset (Verweij & Van Meerkerk, 2021). The conclusion is supported by their qualitative interview data, from which it became clear that respondents agreed that the DBFM contract provides strong incentives to reach set milestones and to deliver on time.

The findings from Chapters 5 and 6 are similar to the results from the matched-pair analyses presented by Deep and colleagues in Chapter 7. Their analyses of the construction phase, which starts at financial close, focused on the percentage of time overrun (similar to Chapters 5 and 6), but also on the actual time taken for construction per lane-kilometer. The analyses clearly showed that, across the board, highway PPPs in India have a better time performance when compared to publicly procured projects, on both indicators.

For the analyses in Chapters 5, 6, and 7, the findings of which are summarized in Table 9.2, the researchers took the signing of the contract between the partners (Chapter 5), the contract award moment (Chapter 6), or financial close (Chapter 7) as the events that marked the beginning of the implementation phase. Taking these events as the starting points of implementation for these projects, and then taking the implementation phase as the focus for evaluating the time performance of PPPs, makes sense because the financial incentives for PPP projects mentioned by Lewis (2021) and the authors of Chapter 6 (see also Verweij & Van Meerkerk, 2021) are only present from the moment the contract is enacted. We therefore argue that a focus on project implementation (i.e., project design and construction) is a good proxy for evaluating the time performance of PPPs.

At the same time, Hodge and Greve warn us in Chapter 2 that there are other proxies, too—proxies that take into account the "messier history" of projects. We are reminded here of the seminal work by Bent Flyvbjerg and colleagues (Flyvbjerg, 2011; Flyvbjerg et al., 2003), who documented the lingering history of project cost overruns and also the relationship with time: as projects are delayed or stretch out over time—often as a consequence of messy political decision-making and changing ambitions and, hence, project

Table 9.2 Time performance advantage

Study	Period	Country	Sector	Performance Category	Findings	Performance Advantage
Chapter 5	2010–2014	Brazil	Sport Stadiums	Delivery time	PPP stadiums had better delivery times (with one exception) than public and private stadiums	Positive
Chapter 6	2003–2020[a]	Netherlands	Roads	On-time delivery of the project regarding commissioning milestone, perceptions of time performance	DBFM projects have significantly better time performance; DBFM incentivizes on-time delivery	Positive
Chapter 7	1996–2017	India	Roads	Time overrun, time taken for construction per lane-kilometer	The PPPs are implemented significantly faster in terms of both indicators	Positive

Note: [a] See Koppenjan et al. (2020).

scopes—costs increase. From a governance or policymaking perspective, that complete time frame matters, and one may ask how private involvement may contribute to good and realistic solutions early on (cf. Lenferink, 2013) and speed up the development of infrastructure. However, there is also the risk of sidelining politics and diminishing policymakers' influence on project development if private actors become involved too early. A widely shared critique on PPPs concerns the risk that democratic control and political steering by elected politicians are diminished (Willems & Van Dooren, 2011). Involving private-sector actors early in the development may lead to a dominating focus on private-sector values and solutions. In addition, it may lead to a dynamic of depoliticization early in the process, again shifting decision-making away from elected politicians and democratic arenas (Willems & Van Dooren, 2016).

Considering that PPPs have been studied in this book in the narrow meaning of "projects" or "organizational project delivery forms" (Hodge & Greve, 2017), a focus on the implementation time for the evaluation of time performance is perhaps the "most valid" or "best defensible" option we have (cf. Chapter 2). A direction for further research could be, though, to explore the relationship between time performance in tendering and time performance in implementation. Some studies have found that PPPs have faster construction times but longer tendering processes (O'Shea et al., 2019), a point also suggested in Chapter 7. Other studies, including Chapter 5, found that procurement is not any longer for PPPs. This brings forth the question as to whether spending more time on tendering translates into shorter implementation time, and if not, whether at least that extra time spent in tendering increases the quality of the service delivery during and after implementation.

SERVICE QUALITY PERFORMANCE

Studies on quality performance discussed in Chapter 1 offered an initial justification that PPPs have a service quality performance advantage over traditional alternatives. With some exceptions where no significant quality performance differences were found between public and public-private facilities (Ferreira & Marques, 2021), or where PPPs outperformed private but not public alternatives (Shet et al., 2011), the clear majority of studies concluded that PPPs outperformed the traditional alternatives (Archambeault & Deis, 1997; Atmo et al., 2015, 2017; Barrera-Osorio, 2007; Cabral et al., 2010, 2013; Cabral & De Azevedo, 2008; Cercone et al., 2005; Gauri et al., 2004; Hafeez et al., 2016; Massoud et al., 2003; Rodrigues & Zucco, 2018; Yaya, 2017). The empirical chapters of this book lend further credence to this conclusion.

O'Shea, Palcic, and Reeves's evaluation of Irish schools in Chapter 3 showed that satisfaction with facility management and the quality of school buildings was higher in PPP schools. These differences in quality stem from the additional costs spent on PPP schools (see "Cost Performance")—in other words, higher capital costs improved school building quality, and these facilities received more funding to cover their operations, maintenance, and life-cycle costs. It also meant that school principals had to devote less time to facility management and could spend more time on education-related tasks. This confirms other studies of PPP schools (Rodrigues & Zucco, 2018). The analysis in Chapter 3 specifically showed that the higher service quality in PPP schools can be explained by proactive management and more extensive governance structures coordinating stakeholders and managing risks. The private partner was incentivized to meet contract obligations and to ensure that quality did not drop below a certain level (proactive). In contrast, because tasks for O&M were retained by school management in the traditionally procured schools, these facilities were characterized by reactive management and less formalized and developed governance structures. Action was taken after something had broken down (reactive). The analysis in Chapter 3 shows that PPP schools in Ireland are better able to plan and steer on maintenance and operations, leading to a higher quality of services. This higher service level comes with a price (i.e., higher costs). Whether that is acceptable—or how much this higher quality is worth—is a matter of political decision-making and of perspective; it is a question that may be answered differently from a financial perspective or an educational perspective (see Chapter 2).

In Chapter 4, Ferreira, Marques, Pedro, and Santos point to similar service quality advantages in Portugal's PPP hospitals. According to their analysis, PPP hospitals performed better in every year than their publicly managed (corporatized) counterparts on a number of indicators, such as access to care, care appropriateness, and clinical safety. The study is a unique contribution to the literature on PPPs in healthcare in that it adopted a broader than usual perspective on performance, including many different performance indicators. It also speaks to policymakers and may inform their decision-making on whether to use PPPs for the provision of public services. Currently in Portugal, as the authors describe, governments are about to stop using PPP arrangements in spite of evidence showing their benefits. This is a situation we also recognize in the Netherlands, where considerations to abandon (certain types of) PPPs seem to be informed by unfavorable imagery of some major projects developed using PPP contracts (Verweij et al., 2021). We are not advocating here that policymakers should adopt or continue with PPPs at the expense of public alternatives. Instead, we are saying that evidence should be considered—comparative evidence, that is, which goes beyond single studies of good or bad examples of projects—and included in decision-making on public service delivery. Depending on the goals the project is set to achieve and on the relevance given to certain performance indicators over others (see Chapter 2), procuring public services through PPPs can make a lot of sense.

In Chapter 7, Deep, Nayyer, and Rajan A. also suggest that the service quality of PPP roads across a number of dimensions (e.g., speed of travel, number of accidents, quality and smoothness of the road, and roadside support for vehicle repair and breakdowns) is superior to that of public roads. They reached this conclusion by examining empirical evidence documented by other researchers, as well as findings from public audit reports scrutinizing the Indian road sector. The authors provided additional illustrations of these performance differences using prominent case examples from the Indian road sector.

Lastly, Daniel Albalate, Germà Bel, and Paula Bel-Piñana, in Chapter 8, analyzed the road safety of motorways in Spain. Their chapter offers compelling analyses and results. They collected safety data on the 50 provinces in Spain over a period of 17 years, amounting to 850 observations. Road safety was measured by two indicators: traffic accidents with and without fatality. The numbers of accidents were set relative to the percentage of motorways in a province—as a percentage of all roads in a province—and then broken down by three types of highways: PPP motorways with Design–Build–Finance–Operate–Maintain (DBFOM) contracts, PPP motorways with concessions for maintenance that were publicly financed using shadow tolls, and traditional public motorways. Their analysis showed that PPP motorways deliver better road safety outcomes (i.e., lower accident rates) than publicly funded and managed motorways. The study included possible negative externalities due to rerouting effects because of tolls. This performance advantage was associated with both types of PPPs considered. When it comes to the severity of accidents, measured by fatality rates, the results indicated that only the tolled PPP model performed better than publicly managed and funded motorways, a dif-

Table 9.3 Service quality performance advantage

Study	Period	Country	Sector	Performance Category	Findings	Performance Advantage
Chapter 3	2001–2004	Ireland	Schools	School building quality, school maintenance (facilities management)	Higher capital costs improved school building quality; level of satisfaction with facilities management was high in PPP schools (proactive management) and lower in traditional schools (reactive management)	Positive
Chapter 4	2015–2019	Portugal	Hospitals	Productivity, access to health care, care appropriateness, clinical safety	PPP hospitals generally perform better on all indicators (access, care appropriateness, and clinical safety), in all years examined	Positive
Chapter 7	1996–2017	India	Roads	Travel speeds, accident rates, International Roughness Index, roadside assistance	Service quality of PPP roads across a number of dimensions is superior to that of public roads	Positive
Chapter 8	2003–2019	Spain	Roads	Road safety: accident rates and fatality rates	PPP motorways have better performance regarding accident rates than publicly funded and managed motorways; for fatality rates, only the tolled PPP motorways performed better than the publicly funded and managed motorways	Positive

ference which needs further examination. For road authorities, the research approach taken by Albalate and colleagues is very promising for evaluating the contribution that DBFM can make to road safety, which to date has remained a rather underexplored question.

The chapters' findings on service quality performance are summarized in Table 9.3 and contribute to the evidence base that PPPs maintain a service quality performance advantage. Combining our discussion of previous studies in Chapter 1 with the results of the comparative studies in this book, we can conclude that PPPs appear to have a clear performance advantage when it comes to service quality.

CONTRACT INCENTIVES

What explains performance differences between PPPs and traditional procurement? In the empirical chapters, different theoretical arguments were used to answer this secondary question of the book. As emphasized by Hodge and Greve in Chapter 2, the different ways in which performance is defined and measured, the different types of PPPs and non-PPP alternatives that are analyzed, as well as the particular theoretical perspective that is adopted and the academic discipline that is the point of departure (e.g., Bovaird, 2010)—which also influence the definition and measurement of performance and the PPP phenomenon itself—naturally lead to a variety of explanations for performance differences. Added to this, different empirical contexts—among other things: different countries and different policy sectors—may be affected by different factors or by similar factors in different ways; it does not require much imagination to see that this question cannot be answered in any single way. We do, however, observe from the empirical chapters in this book that most explanations for a performance advantage reference the features of the PPP contract in one way or another.

One feature is bundling. By integrating project design and construction with maintenance and operation, efficiency gains can be achieved because private actors are incentivized to design and build better infrastructure (i.e., fewer maintenance costs produce higher profits), leading to higher service quality (Casady & Geddes, 2016, 2019). In Chapter 5, for instance, Dos Reis and Cabral suggested that the transfer of asset property rights to the private sector gave private partners greater autonomy and managerial flexibility to make investments and deal with potential contingencies and risks. Because the private partner now has a responsibility for the entire project life-cycle, this encourages investments in the infrastructure. Bundling incentivizes the private partner to invest in high-quality infrastructure designs so that they will receive maximum payments for performance after the construction period. In this way, bundling can lead to economies of scope (Bovaird, 2004; Lewis, 2021;

Moore et al., 2017), resulting in increased efficiency of the construction and maintenance of the infrastructure as well as increased quality. As mentioned in Chapter 3 by O'Shea, Palcic, and Reeves, bundling may also lead to economies of scale, when a private contractor is responsible for a bundle of projects under a single contract. As Chapter 3 also showed, bundling also implies trade-offs at the project and policy levels when considering PPPs. Their findings specifically emphasize that the transfer of risks for the entire life-cycle comes at a price. Irish PPP schools were designed for a 25-year life-cycle, and maintenance was priced into the estimated capital costs under the PPP model. This means that the higher construction costs associated with PPP schools were linked to lower operations costs over the project life-cycle. Thus, although PPP schools cost significantly more on an annual basis per pupil relative to traditionally procured schools, their traditional counterparts were more poorly constructed and had significantly higher deferred maintenance. Hence, the PPP school's operational performance benefited from project bundling, but at a higher cost. That bundling is a central feature of PPPs and a core motivation to develop infrastructure through PPPs should not come as a surprise. Some chapters in this book have now provided empirical evidence that bundling actually leads to better performance.

Another feature associated with the PPP performance advantage is private financing in combination with performance-dependent payments. In Chapter 6, Van Meerkerk and colleagues stress that private financing and the "shadow of the banks," the availability criterion to deliver on time (performance-dependent payments), and the transfer of risks to the private partner together play an important role in explaining the differences in performance between the PPP projects and the traditionally procured projects (see also Verweij & Van Meerkerk, 2020, 2021). The effect of performance-dependent payment on performance is also featured in Chapter 8 by Albalate, Bel, and Bel-Piñana, where they assert that the PPP contracts introduce bonuses and penalties for contractors based on explicit road safety indicators. In fact, when roads are publicly owned, less-strict regulations may apply, giving the state more "leeway for arbitrariness" and therefore the adoption of more relaxed road safety measures and less motorway maintenance and renovation. Improved risk allocation was also mentioned in Chapter 5 as a crucial reason for the performance advantages observed in Brazil's PPP stadium projects. These explanations are in line with arguments from principal–agent theory and transaction cost economics, at least from the public principal's point of view. Private financing in combination with performance-dependent payment also creates strong incentives for the private consortium to deliver on-time and according to agreed quality levels. In relation to cost performance (see Chapter 6), the strong incentives for the public and—in particular—the private partners to not make any contract changes due to transaction costs and the role of the financiers lead to better risk management and lower additional work costs. At the same time, however, this creates less flexibility to deal with unforeseen events or stakeholder demands, as noted in Chapter 6. In addition, as also noted there, the rather negative perceptions of private partners regarding cost performance (i.e., profits and margins) raises some questions as to the long-term sustainability of DBFM contracts. Furthermore, as Van Meerkerk and colleagues conclude in Chapter 6, it is also important to take the learning history into account (see also Casady & Parra, 2021). Both public- and private-sector partners have over the years learned how to collaborate better than in the early years of PPP projects. This brings us to the issue of collaboration in PPPs.

COLLABORATION

Relational governance mechanisms play an important role, in addition to contractual governance mechanisms, in explaining the performance of PPPs (e.g., Verweij, 2018; Warsen, 2021). We can safely say that there is consensus in the literature that well-designed and well-managed collaboration positively impacts PPP performance. Through good collaboration, in which trust and commitment are built, public and private partners are more likely to jointly address problems and unexpected events or developments, leading, for instance, to lower additional work costs and higher satisfaction (e.g., Edelenbos & Klijn, 2009; Hueskes et al., 2019; Koppenjan et al., 2022; Kort & Klijn, 2011; Reeves, 2008; Smyth & Edkins, 2007; Verweij, 2015; Warsen et al., 2018; Zheng et al., 2018). That much is clear. What is much less clear, however, and what has received remarkably little attention, is whether or not—or the extent to which—collaboration also explains performance *differences* between PPPs and the counterfactual situation of traditional public procurement. A particular theory that is sometimes referenced or alluded to in the PPP literature is the theory of collaborative advantage (Bovaird, 2004, 2010; Huxham & Vangen, 2000; Roberts & Siemiatycki, 2015; Weihe, 2008), which is said to be one of the "meta-theories rationalizing the role of PPPs" (Bovaird, 2010, p. 45). A core argument of this theory is that collaboration leads to better outcomes or better performance. The question remains if this is also the case for the performance advantage of PPPs. Can a performance advantage of PPPs over the counterfactual situation of traditional public procurement be attributed to collaboration? For that to be the case, increased performance in PPPs needs to be caused by increased collaboration in PPPs, when compared to the performance and collaboration present in alternative projects (Verweij, 2023). Bovaird (2010) noted over a decade ago that the theory's "empirical evidence base has been relatively weak, consisting largely of (often contested) case studies of specific collaborations and partnerships. Key parts of the theoretical foundations have been tested only sporadically and weakly"

(p. 59). To date, this status has not changed much. The notion of collaboration occupies a central position in much of the discussions about PPP, especially in Rhineland contexts (Koppenjan & De Jong, 2018), and it seems important in explaining performance; however, whether it also leads to improved performance in PPPs over non-PPPs still demands investigation (Verweij, 2023).

Here, the potential role of boundary spanners should also be mentioned (Noble & Jones, 2006; Jones & Noble, 2008). PPPs are cross-sectoral organizations, and much of their success may depend on the ability of the partners to collaborate effectively. As said, contractual governance mechanisms present one important dimension. Collaborative mechanisms present another. Collaboration, however, does not come naturally in cross-organizational settings where the stakes are high, value orientations differ, and where interests conflict. Boundary spanners are people who “employ activities to cross organizational or institutional boundaries…and coordinate between their ‘home’ organization…and its environment, and connect processes and actors across these boundaries” (Van Meerkerk & Edelenbos, 2018, p. 3). They can play an important role in improving the relational quality and effectiveness of cross-organizational partnerships (Van Meerkerk & Edelenbos, 2018), particularly so because many types of PPPs are characterized less by collaboration and risk sharing and more by the division of risks and responsibilities. Contracts and the incentives they include are part and parcel of PPPs—how we define them and how they work—but they are also only one part of the story. The quality of the script also depends on the actors at play.

WHAT’S NEXT?

In this book, we brought together research on the performance advantage of PPPs in an attempt to critically assess and empirically explore the existence of PPP performance advantages, focusing on actual, materialized performance instead of ex-ante estimations of performance. The scant research into actual, materialized performance differences between PPPs and non-PPPs has so far remained scattered across the literature. It was only recently that Petersen (2019) made the effort to synthesize the extant literature on the matter. This book can be considered a continuation of that effort. So, apart from a call for continued empirical research into the performance advantage of PPPs (Lewis, 2021), where do we go from here?

To begin, more systematic reviews on the performance advantage of PPPs are needed. We agree with the reflection of Hodge and Greve in Chapter 2 that systematic literature reviews are necessary. We also want to stress that secondary data analyses and meta-reviews, where possible, would be of specific added value. These analyses and reviews may include grey literature as well. These reviews, we propose, should focus on specific dimensions of performance and on specific policy sectors (e.g., road safety in transport infrastructure development or the quality of education in school infrastructure) so that it becomes possible, as a next step or perhaps already as part of those reviews, to identify specific explanations for performance that apply to specific sectors (after all, what explains performance in one policy sector may not explain performance in another). At the same time, this will open up the possibility of policy transfer and learning across countries (e.g., Van Assche et al., 2020; Casady & Parra, 2021). Policy transfer and cross-country learning would require appropriate systematic methodologies that account for context-specific variations. One promising method already discussed in Chapter 2 is Qualitative Comparative Analysis (Gerrits & Verweij, 2018). The method could be applied to the aim of identifying those parts of explanations for performance—or performance advantages—that apply to countries specifically and those parts that are transferable across countries.

Our discussion of the extant literature in Chapter 1, and the findings presented in Chapters 3 through 8, suggest that a PPP performance advantage exists for time and quality, but that it remains more nuanced when it comes to costs. In fact, time and, in particular, quality performance may come at the price of increased costs. One message to public policymakers and PPP practitioners is to consider developing infrastructure through PPPs, not so much for their financial benefits (cf. European PPP Expertise Centre, 2011), but more so for their ability to increase public service delivery in terms of policy outcomes such as improved road safety, healthcare, and education—as demonstrated in this book. Much of the attention goes to the costs and cost performance of PPPs (Petersen, 2019). In many countries, especially countries that are faced with budget deficits and deteriorating infrastructure—economic or social infrastructure alike (Grimsey & Lewis, 2004)—inviting private financing into the development of infrastructure indeed makes a lot of sense. Improved cost performance of infrastructure delivery through PPPs then becomes a core rationale. However, in many developed countries where budgets are not the problem, per se, it seems to us that the core rationale should be improved service quality and—ultimately—increased public value.

This brings us to the dimensions of performance compared in this book and suggestions for next steps. The focus of this book was on the performance dimensions of cost, time, and service quality. Although these dimensions cover a broad spectrum, we see additional areas of performance that need more future comparative research. A first area concerns democratic control, transparency, and accountability in PPPs compared to traditionally procured projects (cf. Hueskes et al., 2019). A common claim is that PPPs lead to less democratic control and public accountability (Flinders, 2005; Willems & Van Dooren, 2011). The question is whether this is true and in what ways exactly. As Willems and Van Dooren (2011) show, reduced accountability is not necessarily the case. Their explorative analysis of the policy and governance of Belgian PPPs shows that PPPs lead to a shift in the focus of accountability toward more performance-oriented accountability, partly at the expense of more traditional notions of democratic and constitutional accountability (see also Peters & Pierre, 2010). At the same time, they also note that these latter forms of accountability are not guaranteed in traditionally procured projects. It may well be that PPPs lead to shifts in accountability and risks for democratic control. As noted by other scholars, although often mentioned as a risk, democratic control, transparency, and accountability in PPPs are rarely examined empirically (e.g., Hodge, 2006; Kort & Klijn, 2013; Shaoul et al., 2012). We argue that it should be put to the test in a more explicit and systematic way, comparing traditionally procured projects with PPPs to determine whether and how PPPs might harm democratic control, transparency, and accountability and what it means for the governance of PPPs.

The second area is sustainability. Sustainability is a contemporary core topic for PPPs. PPPs have the potential to improve economic, social, and ecological dimensions of sustainability (Pinz et al., 2018; Koppenjan & Enserink, 2009; United Nations, 2002). While previous studies have assessed some contributions of PPPs to the dimensions of sustainability, a recent systematic review by Pinz et al. (2018) showed that the literature is inconclusive, and that PPP research rarely integrates the sustainability concept. Yet, it is an increasingly important performance dimension that begs future study and assessment. To what extent can and do PPPs contribute to these sustainability dimensions and how well are they able to adapt to future demands? The dominant focus in public procurement on competition based on price is increasingly under pressure in several countries, especially when it comes to issues of sustainability. This provides further motivation for integrating sustainability performance dimensions into future studies on PPP performance.

There are many PPP projects that are now coming to the end of their contracts and maintenance periods. As a result, PPP contract expiry and hand-back to the public sector are becoming a growing area of concern for the industry. It is our view that these periods of hand-back offer an important opportunity for researchers to assess the ex-post performance of PPPs across the project life-cycle and to compare them with traditionally procured and maintained projects. At the same time, contractual expiry will allow researchers to compare service quality performance between the private and public sector before and after the hand-back period under quasi-experimental conditions.

The findings of this book and directions for future research have direct implications on the decision-making and procurement of PPPs. Current tools, such as the Public Sector Comparator and the Public-Private Comparator, still compare the PPP option to a hypothetical public alternative focusing on VfM expressed in terms of costs (Grimsey & Lewis, 2005, in Lewis, 2021). We wish to call attention to the development and application of ex-ante evaluation methods for decision-making and procurement more focused on the quality of the service delivery. At the very least, more attention must be given to the value aspects embedded in VfM assessments (cf. European PPP Expertise Centre, 2018). Then, after projects are constructed or finished, evaluation should focus on the extent to which the ex-ante quality expectations have been achieved ex-post.

REFERENCES

Archambeault, W. G., & Deis, D. R. (1997). Cost effectiveness comparisons of private versus public prisons in Louisiana: A comprehensive analysis of Allen, Avoyelles, and Winn correctional centers. *Journal of the Oklahoma Criminal Justice Research Consortium*, *4,* 1–88.

Atmo, G. U., Duffield, C. F., & Wilson, D. I. (2015). Structuring procurement to improve sustainability outcomes of power plant projects. *Energy Technology & Policy*, *2*(1), 47–57.

Atmo, G. U., Duffield, C. F., Zhang, L., & Wilson, D. I. (2017). Comparative performance of PPPs and traditional procurement projects in Indonesia. *International Journal of Public Sector Management*, *30*(2), 118–36.

Barrera-Osorio, F. (2007). *The impact of private provision of public education: Empirical evidence from Bogota's concession schools*. The World Bank.

Boardman, A. E., & Hellowell, M. (2017). A comparative analysis and evaluation of specialist PPP units' methodologies for conducting value for money appraisals. *Journal of Comparative Policy Analysis: Research and Practice*, *19*(3), 191–206.

Boers, I., Hoek, F., Van Montfort, C., & Wieles, J. (2013). Public-private partnerships: International audit findings. In P. de Vries, & E. B. Yehoue (Eds.), *The Routledge companion to public-private partnerships* (pp. 451–78). Routledge.

Bovaird, T. (2004). Public-private partnerships: From contested concepts to prevalent practice. *International Review of Administrative Sciences*, *70*(2), 199–215.

Bovaird, T. (2010). A brief intellectual history of the public-private partnership movement. In G. A. Hodge, C. Greve, & A. E. Boardman (Eds.), *International handbook on public-private partnerships* (pp. 43–67). Edward Elgar.

Cabral, S., & De Azevedo, P. F. (2008). The modes of provision of prison services in a comparative perspective. *Brazilian Administration Review*, *5*(1), 53–69.

Cabral, S., Lazzarini, S. G., & De Azevedo, P. F. (2010). Private operation with public supervision: Evidence of hybrid modes of governance in prisons. *Public Choice*, *145*(1–2), 281–93.

Cabral, S., Lazzarini, S. G., & De Azevedo, P. F. (2013). Private entrepreneurs in public services: A longitudinal examination of outsourcing and statization of prisons. *Strategic Entrepreneurship Journal*, *7*(1), 6–25.

Casady, C. B., Flannery, D., Geddes, R. R., Palcic, D., & Reeves, E. (2019). Understanding PPP tendering periods in Canada: A duration analysis. *Public Performance & Management Review*, *42*(6), 1259–78.

Casady, C. B., & Geddes, R. R. (2016). *Private participation in US infrastructure: The role of PPP units*. American Enterprise Institute.

Casady, C. B., & Geddes, R. R. (2019). Private participation in US infrastructure: The role of regional PPP units. In R. E. Levitt, W. R. Scott, & M. J. Garvin (Eds.),

Public-private partnerships for infrastructure development: Finance, stakeholder alignment, governance (pp. 224–42). Edward Elgar.
Casady, C. B., & Parra, J. D. (2021). Structural impediments to policy learning: Lessons from Colombia's road concession programs. *International Journal of Public Administration*, *44*(5), 359–71.
Cercone, J., Briceño, R., & Gauri, V. (2005). Contracting primary health care services—The case of Costa Rica. In G. M. la Forgia (Ed.), *Health system innovations in Central America: Lessons and impact of new approaches* (pp. 109–33). The World Bank.
Chen, Z., Daito, N., & Gifford, J. L. (2016). Data review of transportation infrastructure public-private partnership: A meta-analysis. *Transport Reviews*, *36*(2), 228–50.
Daito, N., & Gifford, J. L. (2014). U.S. highway public-private partnerships: Are they more expensive or efficient than the traditional model? *Managerial Finance*, *40*(11), 1131–51.
Demirel, H. Ç., Leendertse, W., Volker, L., & Hertogh, M. J. C. M. (2017). Flexibility in PPP contracts—Dealing with potential change in the pre-contract phase of a construction project. *Construction Management and Economics*, *35*(4), 196–206.
Dos Reis, C. J. O., & Cabral, S. (2017). Public-private partnerships (PPP) in mega-sport events: A comparative study of the provision of sports arenas for the 2014 FIFA World Cup in Brazil. *Brazilian Journal of Public Administration*, *51*(4), 551–79.
Edelenbos, J., & Klijn, E. H. (2009). Project versus process management in public-private partnership: Relation between management style and outcomes. *International Public Management Journal*, *12*(3), 310–31.
European PPP Expertise Centre. (2011). *The non-financial benefits of PPPs: A review of concepts and methodology*. European Investment Bank.
European PPP Expertise Centre. (2018). *Ex-post assessment of PPPs and how to better demonstrate outcomes*. European Investment Bank.
Ferreira, D. C., & Marques, R. C. (2021). Public-private partnerships in health care services: Do they outperform public hospitals regarding quality and access? Evidence from Portugal. *Socio-Economic Planning Sciences*, *73*, 100798.
Flinders, M. (2005). The politics of public-private partnerships. *British Journal of Politics and International Relations*, *7*(2), 215–39.
Flyvbjerg, B. (2011). Over budget, over time, over and over again. In P. W. G. Morris, J. K. Pinto, & J. Söderlund (Eds.), *The Oxford handbook of project management* (pp. 321–44). Oxford University Press.
Flyvbjerg, B., Bruzelius, N., & Rothengatter, W. (2003). *Megaprojects and risk: An anatomy of ambition*. Cambridge University Press.
Froud, J., & Shaoul, J. (2001). Appraising and evaluating PFI for NHS hospitals. *Financial Accountability & Management*, *17*(3), 247–70.
Gauri, V., Cercone, J., & Briceño, R. (2004). Separating financing from provision: Evidence from 10 years of partnership with health cooperatives in Costa Rica. *Health Policy and Planning*, *19*(5), 292–301.
Gerrits, L. M., & Verweij, S. (2018). *The evaluation of complex infrastructure projects: A guide to qualitative comparative analysis*. Edward Elgar.
Grimsey, D., & Lewis, M. K. (2004). *Public-private partnerships: The worldwide revolution in infrastructure provision and project finance*. Edward Elgar.
Grimsey, D., & Lewis, M. K. (2005). Are public-private partnerships value for money? Evaluating alternative approaches and comparing academic and practitioner views. *Accounting Forum*, *29*(4), 345–78.

Hafeez, F., Haider, A., & Uz Zafar, N. (2016). Impact of public-private-partnership programmes on students' learning outcomes: Evidence from a quasi-experiment. *Pakistan Development Review*, *55*(4), 955–1017.

Hodge, G. A. (2006). Public-private partnerships and legitimacy. *University of New South Wales Law Journal*, *29*(3), 318–327.

Hodge, G. A. (2010). Reviewing public-private partnerships: Some thoughts on evaluation. In G. A. Hodge, C. Greve, & A. E. Boardman (Eds.), *International handbook on public-private partnerships* (pp. 81–112). Edward Elgar.

Hodge, G. A., & Greve, C. (2017). On public-private partnership performance: A contemporary review. *Public Works Management & Policy*, *22*(1), 55–78.

Hong, S. (2016). When does a public-private partnership (PPP) lead to inefficient cost management? Evidence from South Korea's urban rail system. *Public Money & Management*, *36*(6), 447–54.

Hueskes, M., Koppenjan, J. F. M., & Verweij, S. (2019). Public-private partnerships for infrastructure: Lessons learned from Dutch and Flemish PhD-theses. *European Journal of Transport and Infrastructure Research*, *19*(3), 160–76.

Huxham, C., & Vangen, S. (2000). What makes partnerships work? In S. P. Osborne (Ed.), *Public-private partnerships: Theory and practice in international perspective* (pp. 293–310). Routledge.

Jones, R., & Noble, G. (2008). Managing the implementation of public-private partnerships. *Public Money & Management*, *28*(2), 109–114.

Koppenjan, J. F. M., & De Jong, M. (2018). The introduction of public-private partnerships in the Netherlands as a case of institutional bricolage: The evolution of an Anglo-Saxon transplant in a Rhineland context. *Public Administration*, *96*(1), 171–84.

Koppenjan, J. F. M., & Enserink, B. (2009). Public-private partnerships in urban infrastructures: Reconciling private sector participation and sustainability. *Public Administration Review*, *69*(2), 284–96.

Koppenjan, J. F. M., Klijn, E. H., Duijn, M., Klaassen, H. L., Van Meerkerk, I. F., Metselaar, S. A., Warsen, R., & Verweij, S. (2020). *Leren van 15 jaar DBFM-projecten bij RWS: Eindrapport* [Learning from 15 years of DBFM projects at RWS: Final report]. Rijkswaterstaat en Bouwend Nederland.

Koppenjan, J. F. M., Klijn, E. H., Verweij, S., Van Meerkerk, I. F., Duijn, M., Warsen, M., & Metselaar, S. (2022). The performance of public-private partnerships: An evaluation of 15 years DBFM in Dutch infrastructure governance. *Public Performance & Management Review*. https://doi.org/10.1080/15309576.2022.2062399

Kort, M., & Klijn, E. H. (2011). Public-private partnerships in urban regeneration projects: Organizational form or managerial capacity? *Public Administration Review*, *71*(4), 618–26.

Kort, M., & Klijn, E. H. (2013). Public-private partnerships in urban regeneration: Democratic legitimacy and its relation with performance and trust. *Local Government Studies*, *39*(1), 89–106.

Lenferink, S. (2013). *Market involvement throughout the planning lifecycle: Public and private experiences with evolving approaches integrating the road infrastructure planning process*. University of Groningen.

Lewis, M. K. (2021). *Rethinking public-private partnerships*. Edward Elgar.

Massoud, M. A., El-Fadel, M., & Abdel Malak, A. (2003). Assessment of public vs private MSW management: A case study. *Journal of Environmental Management*, *69*(1), 15–24.

Meduri, S. S., & Annamalai, T. R. (2013). Unit costs of public and PPP road projects: Evidence from India. *Journal of Construction Engineering and Management, 139*(1), 35–43.

Moore, M. A., Boardman, A. E., & Vining, A. R. (2017). Analyzing risk in PPP provision of utility services: A social welfare perspective. *Utilities Policy, 48*(C), 210–218.

Noble, G., & Jones, R. (2006). The role of boundary-spanning managers in the establishment of public-private partnerships. *Public Administration, 84*(4), 891–917.

Osei-Kyei, R., & Chan, A. P. C. (2015). Review of studies on the critical success factors for public-private partnership (PPP) projects from 1990 to 2013. *International Journal of Project Management, 33*(6), 1335–46.

O'Shea, C., Palcic, D., & Reeves, E. (2019). Comparing PPP with traditional procurement: The case of schools procurement in Ireland. *Annals of Public and Cooperative Economics, 90*(2), 245–67.

Peters, B. G., & Pierre, J. (2010). Public-private partnerships and the democratic deficit: Is performance-based legitimacy the answer? In M. Bexell, & U. Mörth (Eds.), *Democracy and public-private partnerships in global governance* (pp.41–54). Palgrave Macmillan.

Petersen, O. H. (2019). Evaluating the costs, quality, and value for money of infrastructure public-private partnerships: A systematic literature review. *Annals of Public and Cooperative Economics, 90*(2), 227–44.

Pinz, A., Roudyani, N., & Thaler, J. (2018). Public-private partnerships as instruments to achieve sustainability-related objectives: The state of the art and a research agenda. *Public Management Review, 20*(1), 1–22.

Pollock, A. M., Shaoul, J., & Vickers, N. (2002). Private finance and "value for money" in NHS hospitals: A policy in search of a rationale? *BMJ, 324*, 1205–1209.

Reeves, E. (2008). The practice of contracting in public-private partnerships: Transaction costs and relational contracting in the Irish schools sector. *Public Administration, 86*(4), 969–86.

Reeves, E., & Ryan, J. (2007). Piloting public-private partnerships: Expensive lessons from Ireland's schools' sector. *Public Money and Management, 27*(5), 331–8.

Roberts, D. J., & Siemiatycki, M. (2015). Fostering meaningful partnerships in public-private partnerships: Innovations in partnership design and process management to create value. *Environment and Planning C: Government and Policy, 33*(4), 780–93.

Rodrigues, B., & Zucco, C. (2018). A direct comparison of the performance of public-private partnerships with that of traditional contracting. *Brazilian Journal of Public Administration, 52*(6), 1237–57.

Shaoul, J., Stafford, A., & Stapleton, P. (2012). Accountability and corporate governance of public-private partnerships. *Critical Perspectives on Accounting, 23*(3), 213–29.

Shet, A., DeCosta, A., Heylen, E., Shastri, S., Chandy, S., & Ekstrand, M. (2011). High rates of adherence and treatment success in a public and public-private HIV clinic in India: Potential benefits of standardized national care delivery systems. *BMC Health Services Research, 11*(277), 1–8.

Smyth, H., & Edkins, A. (2007). Relationship management in the management of PFI/PPP projects in the UK. *International Journal of Project Management, 25*(3), 232–40.

Tang, L., Shen, Q., & Cheng, E. W. L. (2010). A review of studies on public-private partnership projects in the construction industry. *International Journal of Project Management*, *28*(7), 683–94.

United Nations. (2002). *Report of the world summit on sustainable development.* United Nations.

Van Assche, K., Beunen, R., & Verweij, S. (2020). Comparative planning research, learning, and governance: The benefits and limitations of learning policy by comparison. *Urban Planning*, *5*(1), 11–21.

Van Meerkerk, I. F., & Edelenbos, J. (2018). *Boundary spanners in public management and governance: An interdisciplinary assessment.* Edward Elgar.

Verweij, S. (2015). *Once the shovel hits the ground: Evaluating the management of complex implementation processes of public-private partnership infrastructure projects with qualitative comparative analysis.* Erasmus University Rotterdam.

Verweij, S. (2018). Voorbij de dichotomie: Op zoek naar een succesvolle combinatie van contractuele aspecten en relationele aspecten in publiek-private samenwerking [Beyond the dichotomy: Looking for a successful combination of contractual and relational aspects in public-private partnerships]. In M. Sanders (Ed.), *Publiek-private samenwerking: Kunst van het evenwicht* [Public-private partnership: Art of balance] (pp. 91–106). Boom Bestuurskunde.

Verweij, S. (2023). *De meerwaarde van publiek-private samenwerking: Een vergelijkende analyse van Nederlandse infrastructuurprojecten* [The added value of public-private partnerships: A comparative analysis of Dutch infrastructure projects]. Boom Bestuurskunde.

Verweij, S., Koppenjan, J. F. M., Klijn, E. H., & Van Meerkerk, I. F. (2021). Evaluatie 15 jaar DBFM-projecten: Gooi de expertise niet zomaar overboard [Evaluation of 15 years of DBFM projects: Don't just throw the expertise overboard]. *Verkeerskunde*, *72*(1), 42.

Verweij, S., & Van Meerkerk, I. F. (2020). Do public-private partnerships perform better? A comparative analysis of costs for additional work and reasons for contract changes in Dutch transport infrastructure projects. *Transport Policy*, *99*, 430–8.

Verweij, S., & Van Meerkerk, I. F. (2021). Do public-private partnerships achieve better time and cost performance than regular contracts? *Public Money & Management*, *41*(4), 286–95.

Verweij, S., Van Meerkerk, I. F., & Klaassen, H. L. (2020). *De performance van DBFM bij Rijkswaterstaat: Een kwantitatieve analyse van projectendata* [The performance of DBFM at Rijkswaterstaat: A quantitative analysis of project data]. Rijksuniversiteit Groningen en Erasmus Universiteit Rotterdam.

Warsen, R. (2021). *Putting the pieces together: Combining contractual and relational governance for successful public-private partnerships.* Erasmus University Rotterdam.

Warsen, R., Nederhand, J., Klijn, E. H., Grotenbreg, S., & Koppenjan, J. F. M. (2018). What makes public-private partnerships work? Survey research into the outcomes and the quality of cooperation in PPPs. *Public Management Review*, *20*(8), 1165–85.

Weihe, G. (2008). Public-private partnerships and public-private value trade-offs. *Public Money & Management*, *28*(3), 153–8.

Whittington, J. (2012). When to partner for public infrastructure? Transaction cost evaluation of design–build delivery. *Journal of the American Planning Association*, *78*(3), 269–85.

Willems, T., & Van Dooren, W. (2011). Lost in diffusion? How collaborative arrangements lead to an accountability paradox. *International Review of Administrative Sciences*, *77*(3), 505–530.

Willems, T., & Van Dooren, W. (2016). (De)politicization dynamics in public-private partnerships (PPPs): Lessons from a comparison between UK and Flemish PPP policy. *Public Management Review*, *18*(2), 199–220.

Yaya, R. (2017). Twelve years of Scottish school public-private partnerships: Are they better value for money? *Journal of Public Procurement*, *17*(2), 187–228.

Zhang, S., Chan, A. P. C., Feng, Y., Duan, H., & Ke, Y. (2016). Critical review on PPP research—A search from the Chinese and international journals. *International Journal of Project Management*, *34*(4), 597–612.

Zheng, X., Yuan, J., Guo, J., Skibniewski, M. J., & Zhao, S. (2018). Influence of relational norms on user interests in PPP projects: Mediating effect of project performance. *Sustainability*, *10*(6), 2027.

Index